THE DUBIOUS LINK

# The Dubious Link

## Civic Engagement and Democratization

ARIEL C. ARMONY

STANFORD UNIVERSITY PRESS

STANFORD, CALIFORNIA

2004

Stanford University Press

Stanford, California

www.sup.org

Library of Congress Cataloging-in-Publication Data

Armony, Ariel C.

    The dubious link : civic engagement and democratization / Ariel C. Armony.

     p.  cm.

    Includes bibliographical references and index.

    ISBN 0-8047-4898-5 (alk. paper)

    1. Civil society.   2. Political participation.   I.  Title.

JC337.A76 2004

300'dc22                                  2004001039

Printed in the United States of America on acid-free, archival-quality paper.

Original Printing 2004

Last figure below indicates year of this printing:

13   12   11   10   09   08   07   06   05   04

Designed and typeset at Stanford University Press in 10 / 12.5 Palatino.

*To Mirna, Ian, and Alan*

# Contents

# Tables

# Figures

# Preface and Acknowledgments

Jorge Luis Borges, the great Argentine writer, once said: "I publish my work in order to stop revising it." I do not have the talent of Borges, but I deeply empathize with his feeling. The project that resulted in this book evolved over the years from a single-country study of voluntary groups to a much broader and complex undertaking. Initially, my goal was to show some of the significant limitations in the work of Robert Putnam and others on civil society. But as I became fascinated by the nuances of the link between civic engagement and democratization, the project took a different spin that led me to other cases, bodies of literature, and new questions.

This book explores the question of whether and how civil society influences democracy, showing that the link between them is neither necessary nor universal—as many others have claimed. I argue that civil society has a "dark side" (i.e., a nondemocratic face) and that the specific sociohistorical context determines the nature of civic participation and its potential effect on democracy. I claim that institutions, the law, and dominant patterns of social interaction structure the conditions in which individuals organize.

The book's three case studies (of associational life in Weimar Germany, of the antidesegregation movement in the United States, and of civil society in contemporary Argentina) use historical and ethnographic data. The Argentine analysis is based on original data that I gathered in that country. The study also examines quantitative data from twenty-eight additional nations. On occasion, I briefly introduce other cases (e.g., Rwanda) to highlight certain points of analysis. I should note that the analysis includes no more than a passing reference to the unprecedented crisis that erupted in Argentina in December 2001. The new forms of civil society mobilization that have emerged with the crisis and their implications for democracy might be the topic for another book. The case study of Argentina, however, anticipates several critical undercurrents of the recent crisis.

The main reason I chose to write on the topic of civil society is my belief in the power of organized citizens to improve democracy. Indeed, in the 1990s, I thought that emerging rights organizations in Argentina would effectively promote a civil liberties agenda, strengthen the independence, reliability, and efficiency of the judicial process, and disseminate tolerance and trust among citizens. This conviction took me to Argentina in the mid-1990s to corroborate that Putnam and others were right. But as I conducted preliminary field research, I began to uncover evidence that did not support conventional wisdom on the link between civil society and democracy. Indeed, the data revealed that civic participation had another, less hopeful face. These initial findings opened my eyes to an overlooked, alternative perspective to accepted views of democracy and society. The rest is in this book.

Many people helped me with this project. I am very grateful for their generosity. My most special thanks go to Alison Brysk, Margaret Crahan, Diego Puig, Bert Rockman, Bill Scheuerman, Mitchell Seligson, Iris Young, and Mark Ungar. They contributed in innumerable ways to improving this study. I would also like to thank Muriel Bell, Tony Hicks, Amanda Moran, and Janet Mowery of Stanford University Press; and Martín Abregú, Lucía Bertranou, Michael Cain, Alec Campbell, Lizzy Heurtematte, Andrew Konitzer, Bill Roberts, Raffael Scheck, Andrew Selee, and Robert Weisbrot. The continuous support of my wife, Mirna Kolbowski, was crucial for the completion of this study. She pushed me to set firm deadlines, listened to my (often) incoherent ideas, and put up with long hours of work that disrupted dinners, soccer games, and more events than I can remember.

Funding for this project was provided, at various stages, by the Inter-American Foundation, the Aspen Institute, the Woodrow Wilson International Center for Scholars, and Colby College's Social Science Division. A 2002–3 residential fellowship at the Woodrow Wilson Center in Washington, D.C., allowed me to complete the manuscript in the most stimulating environment a scholar could dream of. I am truly thankful for the support of all these institutions and their continuous belief in this project.

THE DUBIOUS LINK

# Introduction

If the police catch those criminals, they should execute them.
—A human rights activist, Buenos Aires, 1996

It would be no surprise to see Klansmen, vigilantes, and mafiosi display attitudes and behaviors at odds with democratic practices. No one would be surprised if the aggregation of hate groups, vigilante organizations, mafia networks, and similar organizations contributes to debilitating democracy. Thus it is relatively simple to dismiss these groups as outliers in the study of the link between civil society and democracy. Indeed, many would argue, we should be concerned with the civic engagement of average citizens. It is in their participation that we are expected to find the democratic effects of civil society. After all, we are told, civil society is positively linked to democracy across countries. But what happens when the involvement of average citizens contributes to the collapse of democracy, to the exclusion of minorities, and to the deepening of society's fragmentation? Then we have a serious conceptual and empirical problem. This book centers on this problem.

The main focus of my study is on average participants. I am particularly interested in understanding the relationship between ordinary forms of civic engagement and undemocratic dispositions, objectives, and results. To do so, I study well-established and new democracies at different historical conjunctures. I examine the "dark side" of civil society in Weimar Germany, looking at the connection between the richness and vitality of associational life and the acceptance of antisystem and Nazi ideas; the United States in the decades following Word War II, focusing on antidesegregation movements of average citizens in the North and South; and postauthoritarian Argentina in the 1990s, analyzing new patterns of civic engagement that emerged with democratic rule and their link to noncooperation, distrust of others, and political cynicism among participants.

The historical and ethnographic investigation is complemented with a quantitative cross-national study, which affirms and expands key aspects of the analysis—for instance, showing that economic equality, and not civic participation, plays an important role in strengthening the quality of democracy. The cases I investigate are not the only examples of the dark side of civil society. Indeed, several others confound what we thought we knew about civil society. One that I explore briefly is Rwanda, where civically minded health care and relief workers, human rights activists, and members of religious groups supported the genocide of 1994.

The case studies and the quantitative analysis pose a critical test of theories about the universal connection between civic engagement and democracy. They challenge conventional wisdom on this subject (Rogowski 1995: 467–70). There is nothing inherently unusual about the types of civil society activity that are the focus of my study. In fact, as I noted, these are average participants and organizations; the very ones that are expected to advance democracy. However, their civic engagement led to nondemocratic outcomes, rather than to the opposite, "expected" results. In Weimar Germany, civil society was dense and vibrant, but rather than help to strengthen democracy it contributed to its demise. In the United States, vast networks of solidarity and reciprocity among law-abiding citizens did not unite society behind the effort to end racial discrimination, but contributed to the perpetuation of social exclusion. Finally, in Argentina, an active and mobilized sector of civil society identified with human and civil rights values did not deepen democracy by creating links between state and society and constructing bridges across different sectors of society, but instead helped to intensify divisions and conflicts and to erode confidence in democratic institutions.

Employing a wide-ranging and multi-method approach, I revise the assumption that the relationship between civil society and democracy is largely or wholly a positive one (see, e.g., Putnam 1993: 89–91; 1995a: 65–67). I argue that civil society may or may not lead to democracy because what matters is the context in which people associate, not because association is inherently and universally positive for democracy.

In Weimar Germany, civil society was a destabilizing force to democracy, while in the United States after World War II some elements of civil society undermined the democratic character of the liberal state. In turn, in the 1990s, Argentina's civil society reinforced "vicious circles" of noncooperation and conflict in a democratic system. These case studies allow me to examine the civil society–democracy link in new and in well-established democracies. Argentina and Germany are both new democracies (in different waves of democratization), while the United States is a well-established but exclusionary democracy. The cross-national analysis also includes new and well-established democracies in the sample, seeking to obtain answers that are valid across a wide range of democratic systems. The different impacts and pathways of civil society identified in the study do not cover, of course, all possible links to democracy, but they are representative of a larger universe of ways in which civil society can become problematic.

In order to explain the various ways in which civil society affects democracy, I examine how different types of civic organizations and other associational forms relate to specific aspects of democracy. For example, groups and movements that encourage racial, ethnic, or religious discrimination will affect the individual rights guarantees of a democracy. Civil rights groups that promote an antisystem discourse with violent overtones will influence state decisions about the use of coercion. Organizations that engage in corrupt or clientelistic exchanges with the state will affect the legality of decision-making processes and the principles of accountability and transparency.

When considering the impact of context on association, I examine the ways in which civic engagement is directly affected by political institutions and shaped by conditions of social and economic inequality. This analysis shows that the sociohistorical context influences the nature, dispositions and orientations, and impact of civic engagement. Institutional and societal conditions establish the cost threshold and enabling conditions that determine the democratic potential of associations and movements. We should pay attention to the extent to which state institutions protect the rights of individuals and build societal expectations of respect for the law, and to the ways in which social and economic inequalities structure interactions in society (see O'Donnell 1999b: 307; Edwards and Foley 2001: 228; Lomax 1997: 60). I emphasize the role of the rule of law, which I view as an institutional and cultural construct (see Chapter 1), and which, in a democracy, state and private actors must uphold and abide by. For civil society to develop its democratic potential, it must be firmly rooted in and backed by the rule of law (Linz and Stepan 1996: 10, 14). As both the qualitative and the quantitative evidence show, social and economic inequality erode the rule of law. In brief, socioeconomic inequalities impinge on the rule of law, which affects civic engagement and, in turn, its impact on democracy.

Civil society does not necessarily promote the public interest or reforms that are beneficial for the majority (Heller 2001: 138). Indeed, the optimization of outcomes (viewed from the perspective of the majority) is not a necessary result of civic engagement. Smaller groups of participants with ample resources and privileged access to decision-making spheres can impose narrow and parochial interests on the public agenda and, as a result, impose unreasonable burdens on the broader society (Fiorina 1999: 395–403).

Civil society reinforces contextual conditions, and thus it can work as a multiplier of inequalities and tensions among political and social forces (Berman 1997a: 427). For example, associationism can exacerbate social disparities, discriminatory patterns, or "a systematically skewed overrepresentation" of dominant social sectors (Schmitter 1992: 436–37; see Schlozman, Verba, and Brady 1999).[1] This means that civil society is not an inherently consensual arena, as many have argued, but often a terrain of struggle and negotiation over the distribution of and access to public goods and political / social resources and entitlements (see Foley and Edwards 1999: 166–68). For instance, the empirical analysis shows that race, religion, and related forms of identity can prompt patterns of organizing, which in turn are likely to deepen racial, religious, and other divisions in society.

Even though my emphasis in this study is on domestic factors, international forces also shape the context in which groups operate. Political and economic changes in the international arena influence the conditions under which people organize, and international forces can play an important role in the creation of societal cleavages—as in the case of the colonial role of Belgium in Rwanda (see Chapter 6). These externally created societal segmentations can have a marked impact on the nature and orientations of civil society—sometimes leading to undemocratic, even extreme, outcomes. The international and transnational links between groups and movements are crucial too. In newly established democracies, for example, international action can help or undermine organizations of civil society by imposing certain agendas (e.g., affecting the scope of groups' goals and demands) or withdrawing or lessening support at critical junctures in the democratization process, thus affecting domestic associational capacities and relations within civil society and between civil society and the state.

## The Civil Society Boom

Whereas a generation ago the debate about the "success" of democracy was largely centered on economic, political, and institutional factors, most of the discussion in the late 1990s converged on the role of societal and cultural variables, with special emphasis on the importance of civil society and its connection to democratic politics and practices. As new democracies completed their transitions from authoritarianism and well-established democracies began to confront fundamental transformations in the fabric of their societies, scholars increasingly turned to a classic political conundrum: Does citizen participation undergird democracy?

Undoubtedly, the widespread fascination with civil society that began in the 1990s is related to the unprecedented global wave of democratic transitions that started in the mid-1970s—the so-called third wave of democratization (see Huntington 1991). Sweeping political change toward electoral forms of rule as well as market-oriented economic reforms throughout the world have generated increasing attention to the question of what makes democracy possible and successful over the long term.

The inauguration of democratic processes in Latin America, East-Central Europe, and Africa persuaded researchers that the idea of civil society could open a new framework for understanding an emerging grassroots space in which citizens organize independently from the state in order to pursue their interests and advance their demands via peaceful means. Following the earlier "civic culture" theories (e.g., Almond and Verba 1963)—which shifted the emphasis from elites and institutions to the role of mass culture in the democratic process—students of democracy increasingly pointed to civil society as a "school of virtue" for both citizens and leaders (Rosenblum 1998: 26). This emphasis led to a profusion of studies based on the premise that associative relationships and an active conception of citizenship produce norms linked to the viability of a democratic political system (see Rockman 1997). Civic participation, these studies claim, promotes democratic orientations among citizens, which in turn improve the performance of democratic governments (Schlozman, Verba, and Brady 1999: 428).

The idea that institutional patterns spring from the nature of society—that is, that there is a bottom-up approach to institutional performance—has been particularly influential in recent years. Within this approach, "neo-Tocquevillean" studies have focused on organized groups of civil society as a surrogate measure of associational life and have argued that the disposition of individuals to voluntarily form and join different types of organizations produces a more cooperative culture, which in turn results in a more effective government. This society-to-institutions effect has been articulated as a theory that proposes a positive relationship that runs from civil society to democracy.

Much of the recent effort to "bring the people back in" has been based on Putnam's study of Italian politics (1993).[2] In this study, Putnam argued that democratic institutions rest on a strong "civic community." By civic community he means dense horizontal networks of associations in which citizens pursue their self-interest defined in a framework of the broader public interest. Putnam views civil society as a sphere in which citizens participate in various types of associations, from theater groups to football clubs and bowling leagues. In his analysis, the interactions within voluntary organizations are the source of effective government. Thus he argues, "democratic government is strengthened, not weakened, when it faces a vigorous civil society" (Putnam 1993: 88, 175–76, quotation on 182).

In Putnam's version of the civil society–democracy thesis, associational life contributes to institutional performance in two ways. First, associations inculcate in their members practices of cooperation, solidarity, and public spirit. The assumption of this neo-Tocquevillean model is that face-to-face interactions among members of voluntary organizations result in "virtuous circles" of cooperation. Second, associations have external effects on the broader political system by improving the articulation and aggregation of interests, facilitating consensus, and, in general, resulting in more effective coordination to solve collective action problems (Putnam 1993: 89–90, 167, 180). Indeed, the debate on civil society has largely centered on the key notion of *social capital*—that is, broad networks of trust and reciprocity, which are said to spring from civic engagement (Putnam 2000: 19).[3] The lesson of this social-psychological perspective is simple: nations with high levels of civic engagement accumulate social capital, and a large stock of social capital is a key determinant of effective democracy.

As a policy blueprint, this approach suggests that if we manipulate the variable of civil society, we can produce democratic outcomes. In general, neo-Tocquevilleans argue that promoting citizen participation depends on strengthening the role and number of civic associations. Efforts to promote democracy through civil society seem to be based on at least one of three core assumptions about the effects of civic engagement: (1) changes at the micro-social level produce macro-political results; (2) within a given society, "dispositions and practices shaped in one association spill over to other contexts"; and (3) the same associational structures will operate in similar ways in different sociohistorical contexts (in other words, we can extrapolate the "democratic" effect of associational life from one setting to another) (quotation from Rosenblum 1998: 40). This assumption has led analysts to argue, for instance, that the more associations there are in a country (and, even better, the more groups of the "correct" type), the greater the likelihood that democratic institutions will improve there (see Barber 1998).

Proponents of civil society–building in the United States and in new democracies have argued that civic engagement can offer a solution to government's ineffectual delivery of services, weak community institutions and ties, and low levels of social cooperation, among other ills. In the 1990s, public policy analysts emphasized the vital role that civil society could play in the production of social capital in new democracies. For example, based on the assumption that structural reform in such regions as Latin America entailed a new developmental phase characterized by a rapidly increasing division of labor between state, market, and civil society, some analysts recommended that emergency aid funds be targeted to social capital formation, which they viewed as a precondition for economic growth, greater equality, and in the end, better democracy (Reilly 1996: 24). Multilateral development organizations (e.g., the World Bank and the Inter-American Development Bank) adopted the civil society–democracy assumption for their funding rationale in new democracies.

In recent years, supporters of civil society in less-developed countries have stressed at least three areas where organized community life can play a decisive role. First, they say that structural reforms have provided civic associations the opportunity to step in as the state receded in its influence, thus allowing civil society groups to become involved in areas that were previously under state responsibility, such as the provision of social services (Carothers 1999–2000: 19; see Thompson 1995; Wuthnow 1991b: 289). Second, civil society can become a key actor in controlling and limiting state power in new democracies by taking an active role in promoting the accountability of public officials and the transparency of government actions (see Smulovitz and Peruzzotti 2000). Third, association has been seen as a tool to equalize representation by providing low-income people the possibility to combine resources through association (Cohen and Rogers 1995: 43). In highly stratified societies, some scholars argue, the underprivileged can find in association a vehicle to break their dependent and subordinated situation (a result of long-term patterns of clientelism and patronage) and effectively convene around their collective interests (Diamond 1999: 244).

A common thread in these approaches is the assumption that civil society has certain roles to play regardless of the sociohistorical context. The evidence I will present, drawn from different national experiences, shows that, under certain conditions, civil society may not play any of these prodemocratic roles, and it may even undermine democracy by eroding democratic habits, practices, and institutions and intensifying social hostility. In other words, civil society can serve as an incubator and multiplier of antidemocratic forces, associations can obstruct efforts by the state and citizens to democratize society, and even groups that might at first be regarded as the ones most compatible with nurturing social trust, tolerance, and cooperation can carry the opposite tendencies.

The analysis I propose also has implications for the study of social capital, probably the most important "celebrity" of the civil society boom. My analysis of social capital departs from ahistorical approaches that link the production of social capital exclusively to associationism. I argue that social capital is not an automatic result of civic engagement. Rather, the creation of social capital is dependent on the capacity of actors to access and mobilize resources. Also, I demonstrate that social capital can be employed for different ends, including the promotion of particularistic interests, discrimination, and even coercion and violence. The evidence as a whole reveals interesting paradoxes; for instance, the cross-national analysis shows that social capital can play a positive role for democracy at the aggregate level (by promoting institutional quality), but the case studies reveal that social capital can be used for purposes and goals inimical to democratic values and practices by different groups and movements. Moreover, trust may be created within groups but not translated into broader circles of social cooperation, a process that breeds segmentation and undermines social cohesion. These findings suggest that the study of social capital needs to be attentive to critical differences in the broader political context, as well as to the specific socioeconomic conditions that shape the civic involvement of social actors.

## The Concept of Civil Society

During the recent "boom," the concept of civil society has been often employed without careful attention to its definition. Instead of diving into a detailed theoretical and historical discussion of the concept of civil society (which others have done very effectively, such as Cohen and Arato 1992; Keane 1998), I approach the question of defining civil society by pointing to two claims about association and the main criticisms advanced against them. These claims and challenges stand out as especially relevant for the issues discussed in my study and, in particular, they help me to set up a framework for my working definition of civil society, which I discuss below.

First, in their effort to correct the lack of conceptual precision, some analysts have proposed definitions of civil society that attach highly restrictive conditions for organized groups to qualify as such. This approach excludes from civil society associations and movements considered potential threats to democracy, such as "maximalist, uncompromising interest groups or groups with antidemocratic goals and methods" (Diamond 1994: 11; see also Diamond 1999: 221–33). It sets standards that associations must meet in order to be considered part of civil society: "Groups must be 'moderate' and restrained in their demands; they should be democratic themselves or at least support democracy; they should be institutionalized and have a stake in the system; they should not reinforce social cleavages, but cut across them; and so on" (Foley and Edwards 1996: 52 n. 21).

As critics of this "restrictive" approach have argued, defining civil society in a way that excludes, impugns, or delegitimizes certain groups or actors prevents analysts from understanding how societal interests are actually identified, defined, and disputed. As Bruce Rutherford (1993) has argued, groups often viewed as "dogmatic and rigid, and therefore incapable of any constructive contribution to democratization"—Islamic groups such as the Muslim Brotherhood in Egypt, for instance—may advance "democratization by strengthening the institutions and practices of democratic politics, while also gradually modifying [their] ideology in a democratic direction" (p. 315). Therefore, excluding associations because of such features as their "nondemocratic" internal organization or objectives prevents us from considering the ways in which different civil society organizations influence democracy.

Second, a large number of studies, especially those that examine the question of social capital, measure civil society exclusively as membership in formal associations. This is true for most quantitative research on associational life. Critics of the operationalization of civil society as group membership have argued that this approach reduces the concept of civil society to only one of its multiple dimensions, ignoring the various forms of civic engagement (particularly those *not* channeled through formal groups) that constitute the phenomenon of association (Cohen 1999: 56–59; see Newton 1997; Foley and Edwards 1997a; 1997b). In other words, critics have posed the following question: if the vitality of civil society is viewed as a function of the presence or absence of voluntary associations and the size of their membership, what is the role of social movements, informal networks, and other social forms of interaction that do not fit the mold of formal organizations? (Cohen 1999: 61–62).

In reaction to a "reductionist" approach to the study of civil society, some authors have argued that counting the number of members in voluntary groups (or even the number of associations) does not provide enough evidence to argue that civil society is healthy or vital or that it contributes to the public interest.[4] As Morris Fiorina (1999) has noted, in a community with many joiners but a small group of intense activists who "push extreme or narrow causes, framing an overall public debate only tangentially relevant to the values and concerns of most citizens," we may find that it is only those few participants who drive the procedure of agenda-setting, sometimes even hijacking the democratic process (pp. 395–403; quotation from Skocpol and Fiorina 1999b: 2). In brief, numbers can tell us that civic participation is widespread in a given setting, but these numbers do not necessarily show that civil society plays a prodemocratic role. Historical and ethnographic evidence tell a story very different from that told by crude numbers.

I am convinced of the legitimacy of the positions against restrictive and reductionist approaches to civil society, mainly for two reasons. First, if we decide which associations should be part of civil society on the basis of their features, we introduce a high degree of selection bias into the analysis (see King, Keohane, and Verba 1994: 128–37). In other words, the presence of "democratic" features in groups cannot be used as a decision rule for determining what civil society is and what it is not. Second, conceptually speaking, the notion of civil society should not be limited to a single dimension (such as group membership) because of a methodological decision. In fact, it should be the other way around. As Gary King and colleagues (1994) have argued, empirical methods of research should be driven by theoretical considerations. If we want to examine whether and how civil society influences democracy, we should employ a broad definition of civil society together with methods and data that allow us to examine different dimensions of civic engagement. As Theda Skocpol and Fiorina (1999b) have argued, a combination of methods "affords a more nuanced picture" of civil society "than any one methodology deployed in isolation could generate" (p. 9).

Considering the factors just mentioned, I have chosen a broad definition of civil society. I abstain, though, from suggesting my own definition. I use the one proposed by Skocpol and Fiorina (1999a) in their volume on civic engagement in the United States—a definition that has been widely accepted in the political science community. They conceive of civil society as "the network of *ties and groups* through which people connect to one another and get drawn into community and political affairs" (1999b: 2, italics added). This definition emphasizes that, in addition to formal groups (which are, for the most part, the most evident expression of associational life), there are multiple other ways in which people link themselves to each other. The notion of "ties" effectively conveys the idea of this variety of social links, which range from social movements to various "publics" that engage in debates in the public sphere (see Chapter 1 for a detailed discussion). In my writing, civil society, civic engagement or civic participation, and associational life are used interchangeably to denote the idea of people connecting to each other as expressed in Skocpol and Fiorina's definition.[5]

As this definition implies, civil society excludes the family. It also connotes the idea that civil society results from the uncoerced action of individuals. It understands civil society as different from political society, which is the arena in which political actors compete for the "right to exercise control over public power and the state apparatus" (Linz and Stepan 1996: 8). Finally, this working definition does not make any references to "for-profit" objectives. However, as a type of activity, I consider that civil society is, in principle, different from involvement in the marketplace in the sense that it is not dominated by "the objectives of making profit and enlarging market shares" (Young 1999: 143–48, quotation on 144; see Fish 1994; Cohen and Arato 1992: 1–26). This distinction does not mean that organizations in civil society cannot promote a group-specific economic agenda, as in chambers of commerce and economic policy think tanks.

## Defining Democracy

Many civil society studies have been characterized by a restricted emphasis on membership in formal groups, and the conception of democracy employed in most of these studies has been equally restrictive. As Sidney Tarrow (1996) and others have argued, the operational conception of democracy in several of the most influential studies of civil society has a major flaw: it does not discriminate between democratic and undemocratic politics and practices. I seek to remedy this problem in my analysis.

The conception of democracy that I employ departs from the Schumpeterian emphasis on elections, an approach that dominated the study of democracy in the last half of the twentieth century.[6] My conception also departs from equally restrictive approaches that homologize democracy with policy performance, as Putnam (1993) does: his idea of "making democracy work" is primarily centered on the creation of efficient administration and rational public policies (see Chapter 5) (Walker 1966: 293). In contrast, I conceive of democracy, first, as a system that concerns not only political institutions but society as well, and second, as a system in which significant segments of the population are de facto excluded from the full benefits of democratic citizenship (Holston and Caldeira 1998: 263–64; O'Donnell 1999b: 305). This calls our attention to a central dimension of democracy: the various and continuous ways in which the rights of citizens expand and contract in democratic systems. Accordingly, if we want to assess the strength or quality of democracy, we need to consider not only policy performance but also such issues as the effectiveness of civil rights for different social sectors and limits on the coercive power of the state (Varas 1998: 147).

Let me situate this alternative approach to democracy in the context of recent debates. The expansion of democratic forms of government throughout the world means that a refined concept of democracy is needed to understand the wide variation brought about by this multiplicity of cases. As Guillermo O'Donnell (1999b) has noted, the expansion in the number of countries claiming to be democratic has required "democratic theory to become more broadly comparative than it used to be when its empirical referent was almost exclusively limited to countries in the northwestern quadrant of the world" (pp. 303–4). However, the need for a more comprehensive conceptualization of democracy is desirable not only because of the increase in the number of cases to be accounted for, but also because in the North American and Western European cases traditional notions of democracy have been increasingly questioned (see, e.g., Fraser 1993). One challenge of a broadly comparative democratic theory is to identify what is inherently democratic about this system without posing a hierarchical model that establishes stages to be followed by "less democratic" nations.

If democracy is understood as a bipolar phenomenon, then complex and fluid political and social processes—particularly at the subnational level—cannot be properly understood. This bipolar perspective views democracy and authoritarianism as separate, distinct, and opposite re-alities—often defined by the presence or absence of electoral competi-tion (von Mettenheim and Malloy 1998b: 175). In contrast, as Teresa Caldeira and James Holston (1999) have argued, political and social processes in democracies tend to be "uneven, unbalanced, irregular, heterogeneous, arrhythmic, and indeed contradictory"—thus involving both democratic and authoritarian features (p. 717). In addition, polar categories tend to focus exclusively on institutional questions, leading to a belief that the construction and deepening of democracy is a matter of creating rational and modern administrations without paying atten-tion, for instance, to democratic practices in the social sphere (Ospina 1999: 2–3; see Yashar 1999: 97–103). In contrast, I argue that the democ-ratization of state institutions is reciprocal to the democratization of so-cial relations (Caldeira and Holston 1999: 719).

The broader approach to democracy that I propose is crucial to un-derstanding how civil society and democracy are related. Indeed, the characterizations of democracy that I criticize and, particularly, the ho-mologation of democracy with elections—the "electoralist fallacy," as Juan Linz and Alfred Stepan (1996) put it (see also Karl 1986)—yield a reductionist approach that limits our understanding of democratization processes and citizen participation. This is particularly relevant in con-texts marked by conditions inimical to democratic citizenship for vast sectors of the population (Holston and Caldeira 1998: 264). These con-ditions (which I describe in Chapter 1) affect the democratic impulses and potentials of civil society. In other words, without this crucial angle we miss some of the most important aspects of the relationship between civil society and democracy, which are not captured in analyses of policy performance or democratic stability. Civil society's paradox is that the "disjunctions" of democracy shape the character of civic engagement and, in turn, influence its prodemocratic impact (see Walzer 1992; Holston and Appadurai 1999).

## The Plan of the Book

The book starts with a discussion of key conceptual issues in the study of the civil society–democracy link and then moves to the empirical analysis, which includes three case studies (of Germany, the United States, and Argentina) and a quantitative study of twenty-eight nations. The concluding chapter summarizes the book's arguments and findings and suggests lessons, questions, and new ideas for future research.

Chapter 1 introduces key theoretical ideas that frame the discussion of civil society and sets up the conceptual background for the empirical analysis. The first half of the chapter describes the sources, functions, and structures of civil society as well as the mechanisms expected to connect civic engagement with democracy. This section discusses three major analytical perspectives on civil society, namely, social capital, the "third sector," and the public sphere. Three main questions orient the discussion: What are the different forms of civil society activity? What functions is civil society expected to perform? What are the mechanisms through which these functions are effected? The discussion shows that the phenomenon of civil society covers a wide range of associational forms; therefore only by taking into account this heterogeneity can we fully examine the link between association and democracy.

The second half of the chapter addresses the relationship between civic engagement and context. My analysis unfolds from the assumption that all democracies are characterized by a skewed distribution of the rights of citizenship across socioeconomic and territorial cleavages. This uneven distribution is expressed, for instance, in various forms of discrimination and unlawful relations between citizens and the state, and among citizens themselves (Holston and Caldeira 1998: 288; O'-Donnell 1999b: 305, 308). I argue that cross-national and within-country variations in the degree of democratization of both political and social spheres lead to critical differences in the nature, objectives, and outcomes of civil society participation. The discussion centers on the problem of assessing variations in the effectiveness of the rule of law, approaching this problem with a delineation of levels of analysis (state institutions, state-society relations, and interactions within society) in order to understand the ways in which institutional/legal and social/cultural factors influence civic participation.

Chapters 2–5 present the empirical analysis. I draw from both the quantitative and the qualitative traditions, seeking to "make sense" of case studies and to draw inferences from the quantitative evidence (see Ragin 2002; Brady, Collier, and Seawright 2002). The use of these different methodological approaches is helpful in assessing the explanatory power of macro-level variables in combination with detailed, case-oriented analyses (see Foley and Edwards 1999: 163, 170 n. 8). I am interested in using the case studies to trace processes that explain the connection between civic participation and democracy. The statistical analysis imposes some limits on the understanding of complex causal processes, but illuminates important dimensions uncovered by the case studies.

I draw from the work of historians on Germany and the United States, reading their rich evidence in light of the theoretical questions that inform my study. I work with ethnographic and other original data, which I gathered in Argentina during field research in 1996 and 2000. Throughout the analysis, I draw connections between the cases to highlight similarities and differences in mechanisms, patterns, and processes. These are "crucial cases" for analyzing the dark side of civil society because they confound the conventional wisdom about the relationship between civil society and democracy (see Goldhagen 1996: 469). The quantitative analysis complements and generalizes some of the findings of the qualitative study. It tests models that explore the relationship of civic engagement, social trust, income inequality, and other variables with the quality of democratic institutions across nations. The cross-national study employs, among other statistics, public opinion surveys, polls of experts, and economic data.

Chapter 2 presents two examples that demonstrate the antidemocratic nature and orientations of powerful associational networks and social movements. The chapter examines the cases of Germany in the pre-Nazi years and the United States in the decades following World War II. In Weimar Germany, political and economic decay—a result of economic catastrophes, weak and ineffectual political institutions, a party system in dissolution, serious national-local tensions, and foreign pressures (e.g., war reparations imposed by the Treaty of Versailles)—

intensified tensions and conflict in society. Associational life reproduced these social strains, intensified citizen resentment toward parliamentary democracy, and communicated antisystem and Nazi ideas. Indeed, in the Germany of the 1920s and 1930s, a vital civil society contributed to intensifying confrontation in society and to citizens' alienation from the political system. Also, a wide range of local and regional associations were gradually penetrated by the Nazis, who used these social networks to their ideological advantage. This is a case of civil society's contribution to the collapse of democracy.

In the United States, a variety of factors created the conditions under which average citizens mobilized around the issue of segregation: historical patterns of social exclusion, vast urban migration, industrial transformations and their impact on the labor force, a "racialized" formulation and implementation of public policy, and political efforts at social engineering. Under these conditions, whites organized to defend the value of their homes and the identity of their schools and communities, and to affirm long-term goals of racial separation. In the South, a vast movement of "nonextremist" civic associations championed an agenda focused on preventing any disruption of the racial status quo in response to the U.S. Supreme Court's school desegregation decision. In the urban North, average civil society associations channeled a broad movement of resistance to residential integration in cities such as Detroit and Chicago and generated a strong antibusing mobilization in cities such as Boston. In other words, from the 1950s through the 1970s, both an underlying racism—part of the societal context—and a defensive attitude toward threats to middle-class status, aspirations, and identities galvanized whites over specific issues such as housing and school segregation. This trend continued into the 1980s and beyond, as the objective of safeguarding property values and the goal of spatial differentiation and separation between social groups led to the boom of gated communities in the United States.

Among other findings, these case studies reveal that the democratic or undemocratic orientations of civil society cannot be predicted. The social networks in which people participate transmit beliefs and behaviors across society, but these mechanisms do not guarantee democratic outcomes—the outcomes depend on specific contextual conditions. Indeed, the historical evidence shows that organizational patterns and their objectives are dependent on institutional and economic factors, policy-making, and underlying social and cultural conditions. These case studies portray a civil society that contrasts with neo-Tocquevillean views of civil society as an arena of consensus; civil society materializes from the analysis as a realm in which competing groups contend over resources, rights, and political influence.

Chapters 3 and 4 explore civic engagement in a "third-wave" democracy: Argentina. Chapter 3 sets up the background for the analysis of civil society. The case of Argentina illustrates the *problématique* of nations that are exploring the potential of active participation of civil society in the construction of a new democracy. Still, this case shows that issues of social exclusion, discrimination, and limited rights—which played a major role in the U.S. analysis of civic participation—are common to both new and well-established democracies. Employing Argentina as a test case, I propose a multidimensional strategy for assessing the democratizing impact of civic engagement under specific political, social, and economic conditions. The similarity of Argentina in these circumstances to many other new democracies conveys several comparative lessons.

In Argentina, weak accountability and transparency, lack of effective controls of state violence (e.g., police abuse), widespread impunity and corruption, and deepening poverty and a rapidly increasing gap between rich and poor defined the conditions under which civil society operated during the 1990s. The analysis of civil society in Chapter 4 initially focuses on a sample of organizations in the area of human and civil rights created (or radically transformed) in the late 1980s and 1990s. The study of these associations produces several counterintuitive findings. These groups did not promote tolerance, generalized trust, and belief in the legitimacy of institutions among their members; they failed to develop effective links among themselves and with the rest of civil society, or with the state apparatus; and their contribution to controlling and imposing limits on the coercive power of the state and to affirming individual rights was limited. Chapter 4 also probes the civil society–democracy link with other evidence. First, it introduces survey data that confirm and generalize some of the key patterns found in the ethnographic study. Then it analyzes whether and how civil society (civic organizations, public opinion, media, and citizen action) influenced the outcome of legal cases involving police violence as well as legislation and legislative debates on issues of police reform and law enforcement for nearly two decades. The analysis reveals a modest level of effectiveness of civil society in the legal arena and limited influence on the lawmaking sphere.[7]

Chapter 5 shifts the empirical analysis to a quantitative mode. This research uses data from various sources to test causal models in a sample of old and new democracies. The study tests a set of core hypotheses of the theories of civil society and social capital. It shows, for example, that civic participation is not a significant predictor of generalized trust or of institutional quality. Also, the chapter examines two alternative claims, namely, that social capital should be studied in connection with specific contextual conditions (in my model, income and ethnic cleavages) and that patterns of economic distribution are crucial to understanding questions of institutional quality, particularly the problem of creating a rule of law. The statistical analysis confirms the core ideas of the book.

The conclusion (Chapter 6) uses another case, that of Rwanda, to underscore the book's arguments. It presents another powerful example of civil society's dark side, where, as in Nazi Germany, societal beliefs and associationism contributed to the most extreme of outcomes. The chapter then provides a final review of the book's theoretical ideas and empirical findings, draws additional connections among the case studies, and discusses lessons for new democracies and questions for future research. Finally, it suggests a new conceptual model of democratization, envisioned as a framework for bridging "top-down" and "bottom-up" approaches to democracy in a more effective and parsimonious way than traditional conceptions based on a sharp analytical distinction between state and society.

# CHAPTER 1

# Conceptual Issues

THIS CHAPTER advances a set of theoretical considerations concerning civil society and its connection to democracy. The chapter undertakes two conceptual tasks. First, it systematizes core approaches to the analysis of civic engagement in order to establish a clear picture of the forms and effects of civil society activity. The discussion focuses on the three perspectives of social capital, voluntary organizations (the "third sector"), and the public sphere in order to look at civil society's indicators, functions, and mechanisms. The first issue concerns operationalization. Measuring civil society is a complex problem because association occurs at different levels of aggregation and in many forms. Any attempt to develop precise indicators would entail some level of reductionism. Indeed, we can operationalize civil society as membership in formal groups, the number of voluntary associations, social movement activity,[1] or in several other ways. Then, the problem of functions zeroes in on the kinds of contributions that can be expected from civil society.[2] Last, the question of mechanisms refers to the different (hypothesized) connections between civil society and democracy.

The chapter's second task is to analyze the relationship between civil society and the institutional, economic, and social context. I argue that we need to examine how institutional/legal and social/cultural factors influence civic participation. This demands attention to the ways in which the state interacts with society, the impact of socioeconomic stratification and cultural patterns on social interactions, and especially, the extent to which the rule of law (an institutional and cultural construct) permeates the political and social spheres.

## Approaches to Civic Engagement

Members of the Aryan Brotherhood, the Aryan Circle, the Texas Syndi-
cate, the Crips, the Bloods, and the Confederate Knights of America—
all prison gangs in Texas—attend meetings, elect officers, have a system
of rules and sanctions, exercise internal accountability, make the bulk of
their decisions democratically, distribute benefits according to merit,
and write their own constitutions. Members learn to trust each other
and thus discover the benefits of cooperation and reciprocity. They develop organizational skills by handling paperwork and taking responsibility for specific tasks. They also learn to exercise their rights, for example, by demanding from prison officials the inviolability of legal
documents, which are often used by the groups to conceal their internal
communications (Berryhill 1999: 21–23).

  In order to become a member of one of these voluntary associations,
a candidate is often required to pledge loyalty to the group's sacrosanct
principles. For instance, a new member of the Confederate Knights
must pledge to "bear true allegiance to the sacred principles of Aryan
Racial Supremacy and political freedom in Government upon which
our forefathers founded a new nation upon this continent" (Berryhill
1999: 21). Those who join the group receive a tattoo bearing the SS light-
ning bolts. In the hostile environment of a Texas prison, membership in
these organizations provides prestige, camaraderie, and protection
against extortion and rape. For men accustomed to being "misfits in the
small towns where they grew up," membership also carries the invalu-
able opportunity to be accepted into a community of equals (p. 21). In
other words, the experience of association renders "relief from solitude
and the mutual regard of similar men" (Rosenblum 1998: 274).

  Member John King found a nurturing space in the Knights. The
group offered him, among other things, an identity. And his membership seems to have had an impact on his values and attitudes. His
racism, for instance, became increasingly ardent with his involvement
in the group (Kane 1998: 1C; Berryhill 1999: 23). Membership in the
Knights contributed to shaping his vision of society. In prison, he wrote
to his girlfriend:

Sometimes I just feel like "fuck comeing home." I'm better off here. I have it
made in all actuality, why give it up for a world full of nothing? What do I have
to look forward too returning to Jasper? A town full of race traitoring nigger
loveing whores? Bitches that are so fuckin stupid and blind to the pride of their

race and heritage that they should be hung on the limb adjacent their nigger loveing man. (As quoted in Berryhill 1999: 23)

King's prison term and his experience in the Knights preceded his brutal murder of James Byrd, a black man, in Jasper, Texas, in June of 1998, and may have played a role in his decision to commit the crime. Indeed, King killed Byrd in association with another member of the Knights. The victim was "chained by his ankles to the bumper of a pickup truck and dragged three miles down country roads" (Berryhill 1999: 18). He was dismembered: "His head, neck and right arm were found in a ditch. His mangled torso was discovered about a mile away" (*Daily News* 1998: 42).

King's loyalty to the Confederate Knights was not, as one might think, only a response to the tough life in prison. After his release, he tried to start a Knights chapter in Jasper (Berryhill 1999: 23). Indeed, prosecutors said in the trial that King killed Byrd "to gain credibility for a racist group he was organizing" (Associated Press 1999: A22).[3] This example illustrates that prison gangs do not play a democratic role in society. Their fostering of racism and fanaticism are obviously not conducive to the development of democratic attitudes and practices. They do not foster "generalized" trust—that is, trust in "those whom we don't know and who are different from us"—but rather "particularized" trust, a type of trust that strengthens in-group relations while discouraging members to trust beyond their kin (Uslaner 1999: 124–25; Yamagishi and Yamagishi 1994).

One may argue, though, that prison gangs do promote democracy in other ways. Let me mention four possibilities. First, they offer members an environment in which to develop and practice civic skills (see Verba, Schlozman, and Brady 1995: chap. 11). Second, even if organizations exhibit violent or authoritarian dispositions, their existence may serve as a "safety valve" for their members, especially when they are publicly condemned, and thus isolated, by large sectors of society (Chalmers 1997). Third, this type of association (gangs, hate groups, militias) offers individuals membership, that is, "an occasion not only to belong but also to exclude others." Such associations may not develop social practices congruent with liberal democracy, but they can, theoretically, contribute to political pluralism by limiting "exhibitions of hate and hostile outbreaks of envy" as well as by offering individuals "some place where their contributions are affirmed and where the likelihood of failure is reduced" (Rosenblum 1998: 13, 17, 26, 46, quotations on 22, 349).

Fourth, prison gangs can offer marginalized individuals the opportunity to empower themselves. Through participation, they learn about their rights and experience the benefits of organization as a means of promoting common interests (Diamond 1999: 244).

These contrasting dispositions of prison gangs raise a fundamental question about civil society: What is it about associational activity that contributes to democracy? The recent study of civic engagement has revolved around analytical approaches focused on individuals, associations, and the public sphere. If we want to test the civil society–democracy link in its various dimensions, we need to take into account that the study of civil society entails more than an examination of individual experiences of participation or features of particular associations. For instance, a certain form of participation in civil society (such as associations) can have varied and *parallel* effects at different levels of aggregation.[4] This means that civic engagement may simultaneously shape the attitudes of individuals while influencing debates in the public sphere. These effects may carry positive and negative implications for democracy at the same time.

Testing the civil society–democracy relationship requires that we examine this link at three different but interrelated levels. First, we need to study how the experience of association influences individual group members. What are the formative effects of civic engagement on individuals? This question is often the focus of quantitative studies of social capital. Irrespective of how the causality runs, many of these studies assess the relationship between civic engagement and values such as social trust, taking the individual participant as their unit of analysis (see, e.g., Uslaner 1997; 1998; 1999).[5] This level of analysis is important to test, for instance, whether certain groups breed generalized or particularized trust among their members.

Second, if we want to map the varied roles of groups in the associational field and their impact on society and the state, we need to work at the level of the associations themselves. Thus, the question is, what is the role of civil society groups in a democracy? According to this approach, some associations will serve as safety valves, others as government watchdogs, and so on. Ideally, a prodemocratic civil society would display a balanced combination of different associations. This aggregate of associational "niches and specializations"—what has been called a "democratic ecology of associations"—would in theory provide an "optimal mix of democratic effects" (Warren 2001: 12–13).

However, as the empirical analysis will show, a democratic ecology of groups does not necessarily lead to democratic outcomes.

Finally, we need to study the melange of social movements, informal networks, associations, and gatherings in which citizens build discourses and public action (Ryan 2001: 233–34, 237, 242; Clemens 2001: 248–49). For groups such as the Knights, for example, we might assess their broader appeal in society and their role in the legitimation of violence in the public sphere (Warren 2001: 207). This means that we need to consider, beyond individual participants and organizations, the ways in which different forms of association (formal and informal) shape the public space and the political arena. In this framework, we would examine the interaction among formal associations, social movements, informal interpersonal networks, and social practices, and how they structure cultural spaces, shape public discourse, and influence state action (Greene 2001: 153; Clemens 2001: 248–50).

As noted, I will structure the discussion on the basis of three theoretical and empirical approaches to civic engagement: social capital, the so-called third sector of voluntary organizations, and the public sphere. Each of these approaches, which represent generic trends in recent studies of civil society, focuses on a different level of analysis: individual persons, associations, and broader social networks and practices. Table 1.1 summarizes the most important elements of these perspectives: (1) the indicators that each approach selects for examination; (2) the functions that each perspective assigns to civil society; and (3) the mechanisms through which civil society is expected to fulfill these functions.

## Social Capital

The debate on civil society has largely centered on the potential of associational life to generate changes at the level of the individual—that is, changes in participants themselves, which may be aggregated into broader societal patterns. In general, these studies focus on the effect of participation on the values, beliefs, and attitudes of individual persons. In this respect, civil society may function as a "school of democracy" or, in other words, as an incubator of civic culture. As Nancy Rosenblum (1998) said, this approach is essentially moral; that is, "civil society is seen as a school of virtue where men and women develop the dispositions essential to liberal democracy" (p. 26). Accordingly, ordi-

TABLE 1.1

Civic Engagement: Analytical Perspectives

|  | Social Capital | Third Sector | Public Sphere |
|---|---|---|---|
| Unit of analysis | Participants in voluntary organizations (group membership) | Civic associations and NGOs (number, goals, makeup, structures, links, distribution) | Informal networks, social movements, public forums, associations, media, publishing |
| Expected functions | Associational life socializes individuals into cooperative behavior | Primarily, associations serve as government watchdogs, channel demands, and provide services to citizens | "Publics" exercise informal control and influence over policy-makers, legislatures, and courts |
| Mechanisms | Production of social trust | Monitoring, public exposure, advocacy, interest articulation, and administration | Grassroots mobilization and social protest, identity-building, creation and circulation of critical discourses |

SOURCES: Habermas 1989; Fraser 1993; Putnam 1993; 1995a; 1995b; 2000; Cohen and Arato 1992: chap. 10; Tarrow 1994: chap. 1; Salamon and Anheier 1996: chap. 1; 1997: chaps. 3 and 18; Brehm and Rahn 1997; Chalmers 1997; Cohen 1999; Diamond 1999; Foley and Edwards 1999; Skocpol and Fiorina 1999b; Young 1999; Smulovitz and Peruzzotti 2000.

nary citizens who join associations are expected to trust widely and learn practices and dispositions conducive to pluralist democracy, such as bargaining, tolerance, and compromise (p. 13). According to this social-psychological approach, associations in democracies have "developmental effects" on individuals because they bolster the "capacities of democratic citizens," particularly their capacity "to develop *autonomous* judgements that reflect their considered wants and beliefs" (Warren 2001: 70–77, quotations on 61).

As noted in the Introduction, the theory of social capital has played a central role in the recent debate on civil society. The concept of social capital was popularized by Putnam's (1993) study of Italian politics.[6] In his study, social capital entails "features of social organization, such as trust, norms, and networks, that can improve the efficiency of society by facilitating coordinated actions" (p. 167). Social capital, in other words, "refers to connections among individuals—social networks and the norms of reciprocity and trustworthiness that arise from them" (Putnam 2000: 19). Putnam (1993) argued that trust in others, civic engagement, and reciprocity are "mutually reinforcing" (p. 180). How do we recognize social capital when we see it? From this perspective, social capital is manifested in "familiarity, tolerance, solidarity, trust, habits of cooperation, and mutual respect" (Putnam 2000: 362).[7]

According to neo-Tocquevilleans, social capital is a result of civic engagement because associational activity generates social interaction that facilitates and promotes cooperative behavior. However, whether associational life is a source of social capital or its outcome has been a matter of intense debate (Foley and Edwards 1999: 148). Most studies have assessed this causal relationship by exploring the role of membership in voluntary associations in the production of social trust, or conversely, the effects of social trust on membership in voluntary associations (cf. Newton 1997: 579; see also Uslaner 1997).[8] Conceptually, this decision tends to be based on a preference for either the capacity of social connectedness to influence individual-level behavior or the role of more-or-less stable values in society (Uslaner 1997: 3).

Studies of social capital often measure participation in civil society as membership in voluntary organizations (see, e.g., Putnam 1995a; 1995b; Fukuyama 1995; Inglehart 1997; Howard 2002).[9] Surveys ask people if they are members of different types of voluntary organizations, such as religious organizations, human rights groups, or professional associations. These data can provide the basis for an overall measure of civic engagement that totals the number of different organizations to which a respondent belongs or for which he does volunteer work (see Chapter 3). As Table 1.1 shows, associational life is considered vital for democracy because it socializes citizens into cooperative behavior. The key mechanism through which civic participation is expected to promote democracy is the production of social trust.

Face-to-face interactions in voluntary groups are expected to have an aggregate effect on the broader political system and the economy. This approach assumes a teleological process in which social interactions result in positive political and economic developments (McIntosh 2001:

141; see also Gamm and Putnam 2001). The premise is "that associations facilitate economic growth or democratic performance through their impact on individual norms and attitudes, which in turn have an impact on society through individual behavior" (Foley and Edwards 1999: 154). A dense civil society, neo-Tocquevilleans say, improves the articulation and aggregation of interests, facilitating cooperation, leading to a more efficient use of resources, and lowering transaction costs (Putnam 1993: 89–90; Fukuyama 1999: 3; Walzer 1992: 99). Therefore, a large stock of social capital is viewed as a key asset for development. One of the benefits of social capital is that its growth is positively related to its consumption: the stock of social capital is not depleted by its utilization; on the contrary, it is increased when put to work.

The problem of transporting social capital (particularly, radii of trust and reciprocity) from the micro to the macro level of society is an important question that most studies of social capital do not address directly. As Elisabeth Clemens (2001) has argued, the concept of social capital advanced by neo-Tocquevilleans "embodies a seeming paradox—a deeply embedded capacity for social action that is transposable from one setting to another, from one domain to other diverse projects" (p. 247). Therefore, social capital may not be endowed with "the same portability or fungibility that makes financial capital such a powerful motor of economic growth and transformation" (pp. 247, 250; see also McIntosh 2001: 150–51). In other words, it is not clear what guarantees the transfer of social capital from social ties at the micro level into social networks at a broader level.

As a way to understand how to maximize the positive effects of social capital, Putnam introduces the distinction between "bonding" and "bridging" forms of social capital. "Bonding" refers to "exclusive" connections that reinforce "our narrower selves," whereas "bridging" points to "inclusive" networks that "can generate broader identities and reciprocity" (Putnam 2000: 22–23).[10] In Putnam's view, "bonding and bridging are not 'either-or' categories into which social networks can be neatly divided, but 'more or less' dimensions along which we can compare different forms of social capital" (p. 23). According to this perspective, a form of social capital that is broadly inclusive lies at the foundation of successful societies.

*The Question of Trust.*   Many have viewed social trust as the "celebrity" of societies that are able to cooperate to resolve collective problems (e.g., Inglehart 1999; Uslaner 1998; 1999). Trust is considered a precondition for both thriving democratic institutions and a successful market economy.[11] There appears to be a consensus that trust is at the core of social capital (Uslaner 1997: 3). Researchers have devoted considerable effort to identifying the payoffs of having high levels of social trust in a society. Among the studies that have posited a direct link between social trust and political / economic outcomes at the macro level, several have argued that social trust is a critical condition for an effective democracy. Ronald Inglehart (1999), for example, has found a strong positive association between trust and democratic quality across nations (pp. 88, 103).[12]

Recent investigations into the phenomenon of trust in society have posited the idea of two types of trust: generalized and particularized trust (Yamagishi and Yamagishi 1994). The first one refers to confidence in all kinds of people (particularly those we do not know); the second one, as noted in the example of the Confederate Knights, refers to confidence in one's narrow circle of family, friends, or group members (Uslaner 1997: 2–3). According to students of trust, the distinction between generalized and particularized trust emphasizes the role of widespread cooperation in the ability of societies to solve collective problems: "Societies that are marked by more particularized trust than generalized confidence in others will not generate enough social capital to prosper" (p. 9).[13]

Particularized trust, some argue, hinders the emergence of *broad* networks of cooperation and reciprocity in society and may lead to various degrees of prejudice and intolerance. In contrast, generalized trust is associated with predictability in interactions beyond our immediate social circles. Predictability involves "having an expectation that stability or manageable change exists in society and our interpersonal relationships" (Janoski 1998: 87). The question is whether generalized trust is the source of predictability or, as some argue, the state and the legal system generate predictability, which, in turn, promotes broader networks of trust (O'Donnell 1999b: 317).

*The Production and Uses of Social Capital.* How is social capital created? If one considers trust to be the essential component of social capital, then the question is how to produce trust. This has been a matter of intense debate. For Putnam (1993; 1995a), civic engagement leads to interpersonal trust. If we want to create social capital, we should get people to participate. For Eric Uslaner (1997), the causal relationship runs the other way around: "Trust in others has powerful effects on membership in voluntary associations, but membership in voluntary associations does *not* shape trust" (p. 3). Uslaner (1999) has argued that the causal chain begins—and ends—in optimism: "Optimism leads to generalized trust, which promotes civic activism, which creates a prosperous community, leading to increasing optimism" (p. 138).[14] He proposes the idea that if people work on common projects, namely, "superordinate tasks," social capital will emerge as a by-product (pp. 145–46).

Recent studies have argued that the real question is not the relationship between civic engagement and social capital but the ways in which contextual conditions affect this link. Those who challenge social capital theory's disregard for context argue that the production and uses of social capital vary across social cleavages (Uvin 1999: 50; Foley and Edwards 1999: 146).[15] "Winners" trust widely and "losers" do not because the structural and cultural conditions that sustain the lives of the former offer them positive life chances, while the latter suffer not only from a lack of socioeconomic resources but also from social exclusion, discrimination, and prejudice (what Peter Uvin calls "assaults on people's dignity") (Newton 1999: 80–85; Uvin 1999: 50). The idea is that variations in social capital are "the result of a social, economic or political system that works well for some, if not others" (Foley and Edwards 1999: 162). The qualitative and quantitative findings in my study support this claim.

Challenging neo-Tocquevillean claims, these authors argue that the use value of social capital is not necessarily tied to prodemocratic objectives (Foley and Edwards 1999: 168). Groups may employ social capital for intolerant and aggressive purposes as they confront other, competing social networks (Clemens 2001: 251).[16] Whether social capital is employed for good or ill depends on the particular contexts within which social capital is produced. Thus the question is not just how broadly people trust, but under what conditions they trust and what they do with that trust (Foley and Edwards 1999: 161).[17]

Social capital is dependent on institutional and socioeconomic factors. Economic inequality, selective enforcement of the law on the part of the state, and social patterns of domination and subordination are some of the factors that affect the capacity of groups to produce social capital. The potential of groups to create and mobilize social capital depends not only on the capacity of individual actors to access resources in a given social network, but more important, on the location of a network within the broader socioeconomic and political context (Foley and Edwards 1999: 165–68; Tarrow 1994: 10, 13–18; see also Eastis 1998). Individuals and groups "appropriate" various types of resources and transform them into social capital (Foley and Edwards 1999: 155, 166). Given that civil society is a terrain of social contestation, privileged groups may use their social capital to preserve and even increase their position of power in society (Cohen 1999: 57). As we shall see, some organized actors may employ their stock of social capital to oppose the expansion of rights to other groups (see the case of U.S. segregation in Chapter 2).

## The "Third Sector"

Four decades ago, Gabriel Almond and Sidney Verba (1963) argued that voluntary associations play a critical role in democracy because they are "the prime means by which the function of mediating between the individual and the state is performed" (p. 300). Voluntary associations are expected to connect citizens to the political sphere while serving as a vehicle to prevent "the retreat of individuals into their private lives" (Wuthnow 1991b: 304).[18]

By engaging citizens in the public sphere, voluntary associations are expected, on one hand, to avert the emergence of arbitrary rule, and on the other hand, to prevent only a small sector of society from defining the public agenda, excluding others from effective participation (Wuthnow 1991b: 304–5). This approach, also advanced by Putnam's work on the importance of civic engagement for democracy, follows the path of earlier theorists who sought to explain the rise of totalitarianism in Europe by updating some of the ideas of Alexis de Tocqueville on the role of associational life in the nineteenth-century United States. These theorists, who also drew on the work of Marx and Durkheim (focusing on the questions of "alienation" and "anomie"), argued that intermediary associations worked as a stabilizing and protective device against mass society and the emergence of totalitarian movements (Hagtvet 1980: 68–71). William Kornhauser (1959), for instance, argued that a variety of independent associational forms is a precondition of democracy, because these independent groups prevent social atomization and guarantee adequate autonomy for citizens. Associations, he argued, protect citizens from the rulers' arbitrary power and provide a foundation for pluralism (p. 32; see also Berman 1997a: 404).[19]

What is the place of associational activity in the framework of the "third sector"? This conceptual perspective posits a "three-sector" model, which consists of the state, the market, and the "third" sector of voluntary, nonprofit associations (Wuthnow 1991a: 5–7). Often, the third sector (also known as the "nonprofit" sector) is defined as a residual category, that is, as the realm characterized by "those activities in which neither formal coercion nor the profit-oriented exchange of goods and services is the dominant principle" (p. 7). This model of society is based on the assumption that each sector operates according to a principle that distinguishes its activities, namely, coercion in the state, profitability in the market, and voluntarism in the third sector. According to this scheme, the third sector pursues "activities that are indeed voluntary in the dual sense of being free of coercion and being free of the economic constraints of profitability and the distribution of profits" (pp. 7–8). The voluntary sector is often described as "the antithesis of impersonality, bureaucracy, materialism, [and] utilitarianism"—ideas often associated with governmental action and crude market practices (Wuthnow 1991b: 302). Nonprofit associations are viewed as synonymous with notions of community, responsibility, civility, values, and morality.[20]

*The Makeup of the Third Sector.* The third sector consists of voluntary associations such as civic groups (e.g., sports clubs, singing societies), service providers (e.g., hospitals, universities), and nongovernmental organizations (NGOs) (e.g., grassroots development organizations, advocacy groups). These are defined as "organizations that are private in form but public in purpose" (Salamon and Anheier 1996: 2). According to Lester Salamon and Helmut Anheier (1997), the associations that make up the third sector should meet, in at least rough terms, the following set of standards: These entities should be (1) "*Organized,* i.e., institutionalized to some extent," (2) "*Private,* i.e., institutionally separate from government," (3) "*Non-profit-distributing,* i.e., not returning any profits generated to their owners or directors," (4) "*Self-governing,* i.e., equipped to control their own activities," and (5) "*Voluntary,* i.e., involving some meaningful degree of voluntary participation, either in the actual conduct of the agency's activities or in the management of its affairs" (pp. 33–34). These standards have been used to map the third sector in various countries.[21]

Following the idea that formal associations are the cornerstone of civic participation, early 1990s studies talked about an "organizational explosion" in regions such as Latin America. They often meant considerable growth in the number of NGOs (see, e.g., Fisher 1992; 1993;

Thompson 1992). Analysts have tried to measure the growth of the NGO sector—particularly since the onset of democracy in the 1980s—by examining the expansion in the number of foundations, cooperatives, single-issue organizations, private research centers, and nongovernmental development organizations (see Thompson 1995a; 1995b; González Bombal 1995; Landim 1997). Data on the number of organizations come from such sources as government registries, NGO directories, and surveys.[22]

Indeed, one common feature of studies focused on surveying voluntary groups is that they place a great deal of attention on the *number* of organizations. The emphasis on the quantity of voluntary associations often assumes that the impact of civil society on democracy can be evaluated by counting the existing number of organizations in a given country. The enthusiasm propelled by the rise of voluntary associations in the 1990s prompted many scholars and think tanks to equate a large number of formal associations with a healthy and vital civil society. In general, they claim that the growth in the number of voluntary groups has a positive impact on democracy in different social and political settings because, among other effects, large numbers of organizations contribute to the dispersal of power away from government and toward citizens, thus improving government responsiveness to citizen demands (Fisher 1993: 17; 1992: 71; Thompson 1992: 389; Marks 1993; 1996). But this is not what happens when, for instance, we consider the effectiveness of smaller numbers of groups on issues of high political saliency, especially during critical historical phases. Even on less important decisions, as already noted, few intense activists can push their extreme or narrow agenda to the forefront, imposing undue costs, both monetary and emotional, on the community—as Fiorina (1999) demonstrated in his ethnographic study of Concord, Massachusetts (pp. 395–403).

When operationalizing civil society, the third-sector perspective does not focus on the psychological and cultural aspects of individual participants but on the features of voluntary associations. As Table 1.1 shows, studies of the third sector have examined the number of voluntary associations, their goals, the makeup of their membership, their internal organizational structures and external links (vertical relations with the state and donors, as well as horizontal links among voluntary associations), and their patterns of distribution in civil society (see Esman and Uphoff 1984; Rutherford 1993; Hadenius and Uggla 1996; Salamon and Anheier 1996; Stolle and Rochon 1998). Some studies have emphasized one or more of these features—such as the internal deci-sion-making structure of associations and their relationship with the state; others try to incorporate all these aspects into a universalistic model that can help explain what kinds of organizations play a prode-mocratic role in society (Chalmers 1997: 2). For example, some studies have focused on the action of groups in order to establish whether they operate according to the rules of the democratic game, as an indication of their contribution to institutionalizing democratic practices in state and society (Rutherford 1993). Others have argued that heterogeneity in the makeup of an organization is a condition that helps lead to gen-eralized trust (Hadenius and Uggla 1996: 1625; Chazan 1992: 291).[23]

Associations are expected to serve a number of democratic functions. Some studies have emphasized the role of watchdog over state institu-tions and its agents, the transmission of citizen demands, and the pro-vision of services to citizens. Some argue that civil society associa-tions—particularly NGOs—may play a fundamental role in advancing the accountability of public officials and transparency of government acts. The mechanisms through which they play this role include advo-cacy (in such areas as individual rights), the monitoring of state behav-ior, and the public exposure of wrongdoing by politicians and bureau-crats (Smulovitz and Peruzzotti 2000: 149).[24] In this respect, associations are seen as an important check on authoritarian/arbitrary governance (in addition to traditional electoral and constitutional mechanisms) be-cause of their potential role in controlling abuses of state power, partic-ularly in contexts characterized by corrupt and weak institutions oper-ating in an environment of systemic crisis (Chazan 1992: 281–82, 287; Hershberg 2000: 294–96, 304; Mainwaring 1995: 151). This approach stresses associations' "call for accountability," but does not explain the specific means by which this pressure can result in actual accountabil-ity in the administrative and political realms of the state (Avritzer 2002a: 133).

Some authors emphasize the role of voluntary associations as effec-tive means of channeling citizens' demands, with the capacity to influ-ence legislation, budgeting, and policy-making. This perspective gives attention to the mechanism of interest articulation. A key idea is that voluntary organizations (especially nonpolitical groups) are important for democratization because of their potential to represent diverse con-stituencies more effectively than political parties. Accordingly, this ap-proach argues that one of civil society's central functions is to help marginalized groups incorporate their voice into public debates and shape the public agenda through institutional channels (Diamond 1999: 244). Often there is no clear account of how this happens when, for example, the state employs repression and hostility to respond to popular demands or simply ignores those demands.

Another function assigned to associations is the provision of services the state is considered ineffective in delivering. The premise is that voluntary, nonprofit associations have the knowledge, direct connections to society, flexibility, horizontal structures of decision-making, and expertise that the state lacks (Hadenius and Uggla 1996: 1624). Associations' capacity for transparent and accountable administration is viewed as a mechanism that promotes democratic practices in society. According to this perspective, nonprofit organizations hold the promise to "provide alternative modes of governance" while relieving the state of its welfare burden (Warren 2001: 83). The role of associations as service providers (in collaboration with or as an alternative to the state) include health (hospitals, clinics), social services (child care, drug treatment, domestic violence), culture and recreation (sports clubs, orchestras, art galleries), and education and research (elementary and secondary schools, universities) (Salamon and Anheier 1996: 46–49).

In many new democracies, the emphasis on nonprofits as service providers coincided with the implementation of neoliberal programs of economic reform, which greatly reduced the welfarist role of the state. One of the key questions raised by the increased reliance on voluntary associations for the provision of public services is whether this trend can erode the "positive" traits of associations, mainly their flexibility, horizontal decision-making capacities, and volunteerism (see the reference to Norway in Chapter 6).

## *The Public Sphere*

The sphere of social movements, different types of public forums (in which people debate about collective problems), the media, publishing, informal social networks, and manifold instances of socialization is another crucial arena of civil society, which is generally overlooked in studies focused solely on membership in formal associations (Ryan 2001: 237; Cohen 1999: 58; Young 1999: 150–53).[25] The public sphere, as Margaret Somers (1993) argues, is the public space where individuals "engage in negotiations and contestations over political and social life" (p. 589). The notion of the public sphere also alludes to the multiple structures connecting "the myriad mini-publics that emerge within and across associations, movements, religious organizations, clubs, local organizations of concerned citizens, and simple socializing" (Cohen 1999: 58). This sphere, it is argued, has the potential to create spaces for debate over power, claims to authority and policy-making, and norms and practices in society (Ryan 2001: 242; Warren 2001: 162–81; Cohen 1999: 58–59; Young 1999: 157).

A key function assigned to civil society as public sphere is the exercise of control and influence over legislatures, courts, and the arenas of policy-making. The mechanisms associated with the public sphere include social protest and grassroots mobilization, identity-building, and the production and circulation of information and critical discourse (Fraser 1993; Cohen and Arato 1992: 558, 560–63; Warren 2001: 77–82). The role of civil society in the creation and dissemination of "counter-discourses" has been seen as fundamental to expose arbitrary power, express dissent and innovative social practices, and advance new ideas for public deliberation (Young 1999: 151–53).

One of the main tasks of studies on civil society, some argue, is to examine the processes of communication in civil society and how debates in the public sphere enter the sphere of the state (Cohen 1999: 71). For instance, as some studies have shown, the connection between civil society and parliaments played a fundamental role in the development of prodemocratic civil societies in nineteenth-century Europe (Bermeo 2000: 244–46). Associational life may contribute to "public opinion and public judgement," as Mark Warren (2001) said, "especially by providing the social infrastructure of public spheres that develop agendas, test ideas, embody deliberations, and provide voice" (p. 61). This function, which he refers to as "*public sphere* effects," has the potential to "generate the 'force' of persuasion, as distinct from the forces of coercion and money" (pp. 34, 61, 77–82).

As explained, the public sphere is a fundamental locus for deliberation over political and social issues. However, it is important to qualify the idea of the public sphere as an arena of discursive debate among *peers* (Habermas 1989: 36). Indeed, given the unequal distribution of social resources in all societies, the public sphere cannot stand as an arena where people produce a consensus about an all-encompassing "common good" (Fraser 1993: 4; Cohen 1999: 58). Societal actors in the public sphere cannot "deliberate as if they were social peers" because the "discursive arenas" in which they interact are placed "in a larger societal context that is pervaded by structural relations of dominance and subordination" (Fraser 1993: 12).

Understanding the implications of this idea requires attention to two issues. First, we cannot ignore the role of inequality, social exclusion, and attacks on people's dignity (discrimination, racism, and so on) in the analysis of the processes of interaction in civil society (Uvin 1999: 50–54. See the section "Civil Society and Context," below). The structural position of individual and collective actors in society is a fundamental element of relations within civil society. Second, any analysis of the public sphere should examine how organized actors in society establish alliances with sectors of the state in order to ensure that their interests "emerge on top and that the requirements rooted in these special interests get taken as society's requirements" (Ollman 1992: 1015). Indeed, certain groups may exert a dominant influence within civil society (and the public sphere in particular), which they may utilize to legitimize a monopoly of authority in the broader society (Lomax 1997: 61; Sparrow 1992: 1013).

Another approach, resource mobilization theory, focuses on social movements and argues that the success of these movements is dependent upon their access to resources (e.g., financial support, prior organization, leadership skills, and links to centers of power); this theory does not support any major emphasis on beliefs, values, and ideas to explain social movement activity (McCarthy and Zald 1977; Jenkins 1983). The contribution of resource mobilization theory to explaining the connection between structural factors and organization is important for the analysis of association. However, an exclusive emphasis on material conditions neglects "the way a given structural situation is defined and experienced and the meanings that will be attached to actions" as well as the various expressions of stratification in society other than economic inequality (Oliver, Cadena-Roa, and Strawn 2003: 226, quotation on 227). Without attention to these elements, especially societal beliefs and practices, the analysis proposed by resource mobilization theory conveys the sense of a socially neutral multiplier effect of organizational activity.

*Widening the Public Sphere.* The role of the public sphere in democracy raises the following question: How can the public sphere be made more inclusive? Nancy Fraser (1993) has argued that the broadening of the public sphere is linked to the opportunities available for underprivileged groups to constitute what she calls "subaltern counterpublics"— by which she means "parallel discursive arenas where members of subordinated social groups invent and circulate counterdiscourses, so as to formulate oppositional interpretations of their identities, interests, and needs" (pp. 14–15). These groups may expand the arenas for delibera- tion if they contribute to creating a "plurality of competing publics," which have the potential to promote the interests and agendas of the underprivileged by presenting new issues as "a matter of common con- cern" (pp. 14, 20).[26] These issues may include the cultural rights of in- digenous groups, access to retributive justice, and demands for distrib- utional economic policies.

The result of this widening is not always a democratic one because some subaltern counterpublics are antiegalitarian, extremist, or favor the exclusion and marginalization of others (see Richard and Booth 2000; Pásara et al. 1991). Civil publics may generate public opinion with the power to destabilize democracy. In Weimar Germany, for example, an "antisystem" discourse attained widespread public appeal, became an attribute of the public sphere (regardless of political orientations), and produced a decisive antagonism toward the republic across society (Lieberman 1998: 369–75). The Nazis eventually succeeded in control- ling the meaning of this discourse and used it to their political advan- tage.

Sometimes the multiplication of counterpublics may result in a dem- ocratic broadening of *discursive* formulations, but this process needs certain institutional channels to actually influence policy decisions (Fraser 1993: 15). In fact, the broadening of debate may contribute to the remaking of public agendas if certain contextual conditions, such as broad access to legislatures empowered to make authoritative deci- sions, are present (Bermeo 2000: 244). The emergence of new publics is important for one of the central functions ascribed to the public sphere: the capacity to "penetrate" the state through parliament, which medi- ates between civil society and the state (Cohen and Arato 1992: 162–63; Habermas 1995: 110; Avritzer 2002a: 49–50, 105).[27]

The production of discourses—and the transformation of these dis- courses into action oriented to influence political decisions—often trig- gers responses from adversary segments of society, who consider that the expansion of the rights of subordinated social groups may infringe upon their own rights. This reaction could be dealt with as public de- liberation, or it could escalate into aggressive and sometimes violent ac- tion against those groups seeking access to the rights of citizenship (po- litical, civil, and social rights). Indeed, the negotiation of "the terms of citizenship" in civil society constitutes an important aspect of understanding democratization processes (Hagopian 2000: 904; quotation from Brysk 2000a: 285).

Under certain conditions, associational activity may figure prominently in obstructing the expansion of rights to excluded sectors and in supporting the coercive power of the state to discipline those who challenge the existing distribution of rights. Struggles for rights, then, are not just "struggles against the state" but also conflicts between competing forces within civil society (Foweraker and Landman 1997: 17; Alvarez, Dagnino, and Escobar 1998: 12, 18). As I will show, these struggles may lead to heightened conflict in society, delegitimization of democratic institutions, and increased tolerance for authoritarian practices, as they did in Weimar Germany, the United States, and Argentina.

## Civil Society and Context

If we argue that civil society is context-dependent, then it is necessary to establish a conceptual framework to explain how contextual factors shape civic engagement. To do so, I refer to the role of the state, the question of individual rights, and the effectiveness of the rule of law as an institutional and cultural construct. The underlying rationale of my analysis is that the conditions that shape civic engagement are to be found in both the institutional and social spheres, and that broader political and economic factors are as important as the specific conditions (micro-contexts) under which social actors interact.

Recent studies have argued that we need to look at the state to understand why civil society is linked to both democratic and undemocratic outcomes. For example, drawing on the work of Samuel Huntington (1968) on political instability in developing countries, Sheri Berman has focused on political institutionalization as a fundamental variable in the analysis of civil society activity. In two cogent articles she has argued that the difference between democratic and undemocratic civil societies is a function of a nation's level of political institutionalization (see Berman 1997a; 1997b). Thus, in her view, the answer to the variation in civil society's orientations is not to be found in civil society itself but in the nature of political institutions. Civil society participation is supported, according to Berman (1997a), by "strong political institutions capable of overcoming the diverse and often competing interests of individual citizens and focusing on the achievement of long-term rather than short-term goals—of representing and implementing, in other words, the public rather than merely private interests" (p. 568). She emphasizes the level of responsiveness and legitimacy of state institutions as a key explanatory variable in the analysis of civil society's democratic potential (Berman 1997b: 427). As she explains,

If a country's political institutions are capable of channeling and redressing grievances, then associationism will probably buttress political stability and democracy by placing its resources and beneficial effects in the service of the status quo. . . . If, on the other hand, political institutions are weak and / or the existing political regime is perceived to be ineffectual and illegitimate, then civil society activity may become an alternative to politics for dissatisfied citizens. (Berman 1997b: 569–70)

The importance of a favorable institutional environment for a prodemocratic civil society has received increasing attention in other studies too. In a study of civil society in postwar El Salvador, Michael Foley (1996) has argued that the outcome of civic engagement is dependent upon the response of the state to citizen demands and the nature of political society (the party system mainly) (pp. 89, 91). Also, attention has been given to the degree of state coercive activity, as in regime repression in Central America, and the types of official controls over associational life, as in several African countries (Booth and Richard 1998; Richard and Booth 2000; Chazan 1992).

Students of civil society in well-established democracies have also stressed the role played by democratic institutions as a framework for prodemocratic civic engagement. As Rosenblum (1998) has argued in her study of associational life in the United States, the potential uses of pluralism in civil society depend on a context of strong democratic institutions. She observes that voluntary associations and democratic outcomes can be positively linked when institutions and the law protect individual rights (pp. 16, 154, 362). Bo Rothstein (1998b) has argued that in Sweden social capital originates in institutions, particularly those responsible for law and order (pp. 48–49). In turn, historical research has shown that the likelihood of creating prodemocratic civil societies in nineteenth-century Europe was influenced by the availability of channels to influence the policy-making arena and the state's decision to incorporate the demands and debates originating in the sphere of associations (Bermeo 2000; Bermeo and Nord 2000). Other historical analyses have produced similar findings, showing, for example, that state behavior shaped the nature of civic engagement and the production of social capital in the nineteenth-century United States (Ryan 2001).

Conceptually, the emphasis on institutions points to the importance of restoring the role of the state in the creation of associational capacity. Tarrow (1996), for instance, has questioned the "bottom-up" causal model advanced by advocates of the civil society–democracy thesis, arguing instead that the state plays a fundamental role in shaping civic capacity (pp. 394–96). According to this approach, the character of the state accounts, to a great extent, for the quality of civic participation. For example, in order to assess the capacity of organized sectors of society to influence the democratic decision-making process, we need to ask if the state effectively sustains the legal capacity of citizens that allows them to exercise their individual rights (Hagopian 2000: 904; see Walzer 1992; Hadenius 2001).

Where the state is unresponsive, its institutions are undemocratic, or its democracy is ill designed to recognize and respond to citizen demands, the character of collective action will be decidedly different than under a strong and democratic system. Citizens will find their efforts to organize for civil ends frustrated by state policy—at some times actively repressed, at others simply ignored. Increasingly aggressive forms of civil associations will spring up, and more and more ordinary citizens will be driven into either active militancy against the state or self-protective apathy. (Foley and Edwards 1996: 48)

I agree with the position that the state plays a fundamental role in shaping civil society. However, I argue that we need a more refined approach that can account not only for the role of the state and the political sphere but also for the impact of societal features on civic engagement. As noted in the Introduction, the approach that I take here emphasizes the "disjunctive" nature of contemporary democracies, both old and new, which is expressed in the irregular distribution of rights across social, economic, and cultural lines (Holston and Caldeira 1998; Chalmers, Martin, and Piester 1997: 576). These disjunctures are not the same in all democracies (Caldeira and Holston 1999: 727). Indeed, rights—which are "those licenses and empowerments that citizens must have in order to preserve their freedom and to protect themselves against abuse"—vary according to a number of factors (Shklar 1989: 37). These factors include the extent to which agents in the state hierarchy exercise their power illegally or arbitrarily, the tendency of state institutions to use repression and confrontation, the degree of impunity in state-society interaction, and the level of violence and discriminatory practices exercised by social actors (Holston and Caldeira 1998; Pinheiro 1999; O'Donnell 1999a).

This approach emphasizes two ideas. First, formal membership in the nation-state does not automatically confer the bundle of rights (political, civil, and social rights) to all citizens; usually the poor, minorities, and other underprivileged sectors enjoy only a few of these rights (Holston and Appadurai 1999: 4).[28] Second, the constitution of individuals as legal subjects needs to be complemented by conditions that guarantee that these individuals will be able to exercise their legal rights and thus be responsible for their decisions (O'Donnell 1999c: 18–19; del Cid Avalos 2001: 4).

This analytical perspective brings us to the question of the rule of law. Indeed, there is a direct relationship between the distribution of rights in a given society and the effectiveness of the rule of law (Foweraker and Landman 1997: 21). Therefore, if we want to understand the full range of factors that shape the nature and dispositions of civil society, we need to pay attention to the multiple ways in which the state influences society, and the micro-contexts in which social interactions characterized by cooperation, discrimination, subordination, or other forms of interaction are defined (O'Donnell 1999a: 59, 90; von Mettenheim and Malloy 1998a: 6). Table 1.2 provides a summary of the levels and dimensions that, in my view, need to be incorporated into the analysis. They are discussed in the next section.

Before moving along in the analysis, let me note that the emphasis I place here on domestic factors does not mean that we should neglect the role of international forces. Indeed, the international impact on national contexts in general and civil society in particular is important for understanding differences in civic engagement across nations. As I explain later, we need to account for the impact of international and global forces on the domestic political and economic conditions that shape civic engagement. In addition, we need to acknowledge that changes in international support for and attention to civil society organizations in newly established democracies have a large impact on these groups, particularly in their relationship with the state.

## The Rule of Law

The rule of law is a necessary but not sufficient condition for democracy. My approach to the rule of law is broad and encompasses both institutional and societal perspectives. From a traditional perspective, the centerpiece of the modern rule of law is "the idea that governmental action must be rendered calculable and restrained" (Scheuerman 1994:

TABLE 1.2

The Context of Interactions in Civil Society: Levels of Analysis

| | Dimensions of Interaction |
|---|---|
| State and legal system | • Responsiveness and legitimacy<br>• Moral standards<br>• Constitutionalism<br>• Accountability and transparency<br>• Positive predictability |
| State–society | • Formal rules<br>• Procedures and policies<br>• Obedience and voluntary compliance<br>• Public access and evaluation |
| Citizen–citizen | • Socioeconomic stratification<br>• Culture of legality<br>• Strategies of social navigation<br>• Social violence and exclusion<br>• Domination and subordination |

68–69). "In a democratic legal system," O'Donnell (1999c) has argued, "all powers are subject to the legal authority of other powers—this legal system 'closes,' in the sense that nobody is above or beyond its rules" (p. 25). The idea of predictable and restrained governmental action entails two conditions: first, "a division between executive and legislative power as well as an independent judiciary" and, second, "the deceptively simple demand for cogent, general (or formal) law" (Scheuerman 1994: 70; see also Bobbio 1987: 143–46).[29] The latter condition stresses the idea that "the law defines the basic structure within which the pursuit of all other activities takes place" (Rawls 1971: 236). I argue that it is fundamental not only to consider the rule of law at the level of the institutional separation of power, but also to explore how the law textures the interaction between state and society and relations among citizens. In a democracy, as already argued, civil society requires the support of the rule of law (Linz and Stepan 1996: 14–15). As we shall see, this support should go beyond the provision of basic legal guarantees for organizing (e.g., freedom of association)—for example, there should be clearly defined limits on state power and effective protection of individual rights.

As said, the rule of law involves the legal / institutional sphere of the state and the sphere of social life as well (Örkény and Scheppele 1999: 74). This particular lens allows us to capture, first, a broad range of institutional features that play a vital role in shaping civic engagement and, second, the systems of meanings that guide the action of citizens and their attitudes toward the law (which are as significant as formal institutions for the overall effectiveness of the rule of law) (O'Donnell 1999a: 59, 90, 138–42; von Mettenheim and Malloy 1998a: 6; Caldeira and Holston 1999: 719). This means that it is important to understand how questions of justice, equality before the law, and rights, among others, are dealt within the social sphere (Caldeira 1996).

If we focus on the rule of law as a "variable achievement" that can be traced at different levels of aggregation and in different types of interactions, we will observe how the incompleteness of the rule of law affects democratic practices in the institutional realm, in relations between citizens and the state, and in interactions within society (O'Donnell 1999a: 55; Örkény and Scheppele 1999: 57, 73). Cooperation in society cannot be built when state mechanisms to monitor, regulate, and ensure the effectiveness of the law are inoperative or seriously biased toward certain social groups and when formal rules and the culture of legality in society are weak. Therefore, by helping to sustain the rule of law, both state institutions and society provide the conditions under which "behaviors and expectations of rule adhesion and reciprocity" can emerge among state and private actors (Edwards and Foley 2001: 228).[30] These conditions are critical for understanding the uncertain link between civic engagement and democratization.

Although I differentiate among levels of analysis in the discussion that follows, these levels are interrelated, and the state and society are not completely separate entities. The boundaries between state and society are elusive and fluid (Mitchell 1991: 89–91, 93; Nugent 1999). I address this issue later, in the empirical analysis, showing its implications for the study of civil society.

*State Institutions and the Legal System.*   As noted, the state plays an important role in shaping the activities of civil society (Tarrow 1996: 394–96). Responsive and legitimate political institutions protect individual rights and create a favorable environment for the development of a prodemocratic civil society. In addition to emphasizing political institutionalization, particularly the capacity of institutions to incorporate and process the diverse and usually opposing interests of citizens, the perspective of the rule of law points to other factors that are important for determining the nature of the institutional and legal realm (see Table 1.2). For the purposes of this discussion, the state can contribute to positive conditions for civic engagement in three central respects.

First, institutions should set norms of legality in the political and social arenas. Institutional decision-making can influence "not only what future actors will regard as rational action" (i.e., from the perspective of their self-interest), but *"what they will regard as morally correct action as well"* (Rothstein 1998a: 139). This is illustrated *a contrario* in Latin America, where political institutions in most of the region have failed to establish moral standards mainly because of the predominance of government corruption and "delegative" styles of rule (i.e., executive "insulation" from the constitution, the legislature, and the judiciary) (O'Donnell 1999a: chap. 8). Also, governments in the region have frequently responded with constitutional reforms to citizens' demands focused on the rights of minorities or underprivileged groups (e.g., indigenous peoples), but often these rights have hardly permeated the administrative structure of the state (Yashar 1999: 90; Ospina 1999: 9–10; Dandler 1999: 133–35).[31]

Respect for the law depends not only on enforcement but also on voluntary compliance. Accordingly, the disposition of state officials toward citizens is a fundamental variable in the creation of voluntary acceptance of rules (Tyler 1998: 290; Peel 1998: 316).[32] The law cannot be considered "a sort of abstract, formal framework, superimposed above social practice," but, to be effectively implemented, it must be incorporated into the fabric of society (Mitchell 1991: 94; Krygier 1997: 56). The effectiveness of the law can only be built, as Jean Cohen (1999) has argued, upon the "law as sanction *and* law as institutionalized cultural values, norms, rules, and rights" (p. 66). In brief, top-down norms create opportunities for the development of a culture of legality in society (see below for an analysis of bottom-up patterns).[33]

Second, institutions should guarantee the principles of constitutionalism, accountability, and transparency. According to the first principle, no state institution should be above the law of the constitution, which enumerates the powers of the different institutions of government and regulates disputes between institutions (Lane 1996: 19; Örkény and Scheppele 1999: 58).[34] Accountability results from the interconnected action of state agencies—networks of organizations at all levels of the state apparatus—that sustain formal rules. This is akin to what O'Donnell calls *horizontal accountability*. An effective system of horizontal accountability, he argues, is based on "state agencies that are authorized and willing to oversee, control, redress, and if need be sanction unlawful actions by other state agencies" (O'Donnell 1998: 119). In turn, the principle of transparency entails that the acts of government have to be open to public evaluation (Bobbio 1987: 33–34, 79–93). It is thus expected that democratic systems will have in place adequate mechanisms of scrutiny of government acts. These mechanisms should be open to state agencies and the public in general (Schedler 1999: 16).

When horizontal accountability and transparency are effective, institutions are likely to set norms that define acceptable behaviors by agents of the state and private actors. In turn, they help sustain the principle of sanction by implementing proportionate punishment when state officials fail to abide by formal rules. The principle of accountability is not satisfied if, for instance, a human rights commissioner advises that a police officer, who killed an innocent citizen, be detained. There is no accountability without "some punishment for demonstrated abuses of authority" (Schedler 1999: 14–17).[35]

Ineffectual constitutionalism, weak horizontal accountability, and insufficient transparency of governmental acts create hostile conditions for the development of civic capacity and seriously limit the potential of civil society to influence the democratic decision-making process. In this context, individuals are likely to find their civic efforts hindered by state structures and policy. Unresponsive, polarizing, or repressive states foster hostility in civil society and often drive average citizens to reject the political regime or to disengage in self-defense (Foley and Edwards 1996: 48; Berman 1997b: 569–70).

Third, the legal system—which is defined by the nature of the law and its implementation—should establish a framework in which social interactions can attain a basic level of predictability—that is, a minimum level of stability or "manageable change" (O'Donnell 1999b: 317, quoting Finnis 1980: 268). Only when and if the law conforms to certain standards, can the rule of law be effective and thus uphold individual rights (O'Donnell 1999b: 316–17). The law should guide people's actions by providing them with security against the actions of others, by eliminating "the grounds for thinking that others are not complying with the rules," and by setting the boundaries within which people are expected to act (Raz 1979: 218; Krygier 1997: 47; quotation from Rawls 1971: 240). The ability to estimate possible sanctions for our and others' actions facilitates cooperative interpersonal relations and improves the interaction between citizens and the state. This "positive" predictability helps create social (horizontal) and institutional (vertical) trust (Rothstein 1998b: 48–49; Brehm and Rahn 1997: 1018). In contrast, when certain social attributes such as class or race are strongly associated with discrimination in the exercise of power by state and private actors or when the state cannot be held accountable for offenses committed by its agents, positive predictability tends to vanish, eroding horizontal and vertical trust and contributing to fragmentation in civil society.[36]

Whereas the law defines individuals as citizens in terms of their legal capacity—and, by doing so, makes them equals—the law by itself "does not necessarily guarantee that those who possess the status of citizen will be able to exercise their legal rights or legal capacities" (quotation from del Cid Avalos 2001: 4; Stavenhagen 1996: 151; Janoski 1998: 9). Among the core features required for effective *implementation* of the law are unrestricted access to the courts, an independent judicial system, and legal processes that are open, fair, and impartial (Raz 1979: 216–19). However, the question of implementation does not pertain only to courts because, in addition, "the whole state apparatus and its agents are supposed to submit to the rule of law" (O'Donnell 1999b: 318). As the problem of police abuse in Argentina will illustrate, the organization and deployment of violence by the state must be subject to the law (which includes effective supervision by other state agencies and public organizations) (Dahl 1989: 244–45; Pinheiro 1996: 18; Linz and Stepan 1996: 10; Becker 1997: 11).

One should note that the different categories of the law (e.g., criminal, civil, commercial) relate to individual rights and shape their effectiveness in a different manner. For Argentina I examine how changes in criminal law affected individual rights—sometimes positively; other times, negatively—as they established, for example, precise rules about police detention procedures, gave new rights to victims and their relatives in criminal proceedings, but arbitrarily introduced harsher punishments for crimes deemed politically sensitive at a critical juncture for the government.

When considering the problem of implementation, it is important to note that the state's enforcement of the law is often marked by a high degree of territorial and functional heterogeneity (Migdal 1994: 11–18; O'Donnell 1999a: 137–38). As Atul Kohli (1994) has argued, "What the national leaders do, or do not do, cannot be discovered without traveling down the political and social hierarchies, where at the 'periphery' the social and political forces provide the context that conditions the nature of central rule" (p. 106). Accordingly, we should note that states do not "pull in single directions" (Migdal 1994: 8). Occasionally, responses by state agents at one level collide with policies, guidelines, or behaviors crafted at other levels of the state (pp. 9, 23–26). This means that the state's impact should be assessed not only at the "commanding heights" (e.g., at the level of the executive), but also in the "trenches," where state agents have the "mandate to apply state rules and regulations directly" (pp. 4, 16).

This approach calls for attention to the interaction between street-level officials (such as policemen and low-ranking bureaucrats) and citizens. A research strategy must distinguish among the state's different bureaucratic levels in order to examine its capacity to generate, sanction, and back a system of legality, and to investigate its interaction with social actors (Migdal, Kohli, and Shue 1994: 3; O'Donnell 1999a: 136–37; Holston and Caldeira 1998: 289). For example, while a "delegative" style of rule injects authoritarianism into the policy-making process, its broader impact—including violations of civil rights (e.g., restrictions on press freedom), curtailment of social rights (e.g., drastic erosion of labor entitlements), and infringement of policy agreements—travels down state and social hierarchies in an uneven way, thus working "in a different fashion and to a different extent with regard to different actors" (quotation from Vilas 1997: 29; see also O'Donnell 1999a: 138; Vacs 1998).

*State-Society Interaction.*   In democratic systems, citizens can learn that they have rights and understand the appropriate ways to exercise them (Jelin 1996: 101, 112, 114). But even if citizens learn their rights and how to practice them, they need state institutions that guarantee the legal conditions to exercise those rights as well as an institutional framework they perceive to be legitimate enough to warrant playing by the rules. "Educating people in their civic rights and responsibilities will seem incongruous when governments simultaneously undermine those same rights and responsibilities," Mark Peel (1998) has argued; "Insisting that government listens will seem ludicrous when experience and common sense tell people that it rarely does. And urging more informed participation when participation leads nowhere may well create more apathy and more disillusionment" (p. 338).

This tells us that the legitimacy of the decision-making process, which is built on people's judgment about rules and authorities, is

strengthened when rules are perceived as "procedurally fair" and authorities are considered knowledgeable and trustworthy, thus "entitled
to be obeyed" (Levi 1996: 51; Tyler 1998: 272–73). Indeed, the decision
to obey the law is a rational gamble built upon what citizens "know
about institutions and their ability to orient action" (Cohen 1999: 82 n.
27, quoting Offe 1996: 23). Where political institutions fail to create
moral standards and formal rules are weak, civil society is likely to express and reinforce values and attitudes at odds with the law. Moreover, when democratic institutions and authorities are not perceived as
effective and legitimate, then involvement in civil society may turn into
an alternative to politics for disgruntled individuals—thus fostering
cynicism toward the political regime and even breeding antisystem
ideas (Berman 1997b: 569–70).

Learning the practices of citizenship is especially important in new
democracies, where long histories of authoritarian state-society relations have shaped the view of marginalized social groups with respect
to their own rights (Jelin 1996: 107). As Elizabeth Jelin notes with respect to Latin America, in spite of the region's intense experience with
popular mobilization and revolt, "In everyday life, subordinated social
sectors tend to consider their subordination as 'normal,' a naturalizing
view of social hierarchy predominates, and the relationship with the
state is expressed more often in terms of clientelism or paternalism than
in terms of citizenship, rights and obligations"(p. 107).[37]

Education and organizing may lead citizens to increasingly seek legal reparations for abuses committed by government actors, but this
alone does not guarantee that they will develop a culture of legality.
Seeking justice through the courts often leads to direct contacts with
various segments of the state (e.g., court officials, government bureaucracies, police officers). When those state agents exercise discriminatory
power, act corruptly, or just ignore demands, citizens seeking redress
lose confidence in political institutions and the process of participation
itself. Indeed, distrust in institutions and mechanisms of participation
is a rational response to unresponsive and arbitrary treatment and generally corrupt governance (Peel 1998: 316; Pásara et al. 1991).

More broadly, when a large portion of the population accepts that
formal rules work to their disadvantage—for instance, because the
powerful act above the law—the courts, police, and other law enforcement and criminal justice agencies lose much of their legitimacy. As
O'Donnell (1999b) has argued with regard to Latin America, there is a
widespread sense that "first, to voluntarily follow the law is something

that only idiots do and, second, that to be subject to the law is not to be the carrier of enforceable rights but rather a sure signal of social weakness" (p. 312). Eventually, this pattern feeds a vicious circle in which few demand their rights, few have confidence in the justice system, and many opt to evade the law whenever possible (Jelin 1996: 107–9).

For many new democracies, law enforcement, particularly the interaction between the police and the citizenry, shows the serious limitations of democratization at the local level. In Latin America, the abuse of deadly force by the police became a conventional practice in most of the region during the 1990s. Reports revealed, for example, that the police regularly used torture in at least thirteen countries in Latin America (Chevigny 1999: 52–53). Public opinion sometimes supported this kind of practice if it promised to reduce crime (Caldeira 1996: 197–98, 202; Chevigny 1995: 195). Most police abuse is not random but is largely directed at the poor, marginal, and vulnerable sectors of the population (e.g., blacks, shantytown dwellers) (Brinks 2002; Mitchell and Wood 1999; Fry 1999; Pinheiro 1996). Relative to the number of abuses, few police officers have stood trial and received punishment. Lack of transparency in the police's disciplinary system, tampering with forensic evidence, coercion of potential witnesses, and threats to judges, lawyers, and journalists are among the practices that have sustained a high degree of impunity (see Chevigny 1999; 1995: chaps. 5–6; Waldmann 1996; Centro de Estudios Legales y Sociales [CELS], various years).

Weak accountability of an abusive police force is also a problem in well-established democracies, though smaller. Race is a factor in U.S. police abuse: minorities (primarily blacks and Latinos) are proportionally more affected by police mistreatment and violence than whites. Police forces in several of the largest U.S. cities (e.g., Los Angeles, New York) have developed an interlocking network of mechanisms that limit accountability by other state organizations and civil society groups. These mechanisms include a "code of silence" among officers, pressures on local prosecutors who need police assistance for civilian criminal cases, the absence of effective oversight in police departments, and a biased process for handling citizen complaints (Human Rights Watch 1998).

Many other dimensions of the state-society relationship are pertinent to this discussion. Some are examined in the case studies. Conceptually speaking, it is important to note that state actors and agencies may ally themselves with sectors of civil society to defend a model of democracy that entails restricted rights for some groups, as in the United States during the 1950s and 1960s. In addition, we should pay attention to the ways in which government agencies craft policies that benefit some groups over others and the extent to which policies are distorted by social stigmas (Loury 2002: 73; Gotham 2000: 292–95). This is illustrated by the disproportionately negative impact of certain laws and policies on the African-American population in the United States, which reinforce a structural system that confers important advantages on the basis of race (Nelson 1996: 358). The existence of a "racial stigma"—according to which low-income African Americans are perceived as more likely to break the law and as carriers of a "spoiled" social identity—reinforces a vicious circle of discrimination (Loury 2002: 61). This pattern of state-society interaction (which is related to issues other than race in different contexts) breeds socialization processes that help to perpetuate prejudice and inequality by supporting assumptions about the inherent qualities of social groups (Rao and Walton 2002: 4).

*The Level of Society.* Because the law pertains to the institutional sphere and is also related to social practices, it is part of the social fabric (Mitchell 1991: 94; Krygier 1997: 56). From this perspective, laws are "free-floating forms of empowerment and cultural resources," whose significance depends on social practices and relationships (Somers 1993: 611). This is a critical dimension often overlooked in the study of the rule of law. I concentrate on several elements that influence the effective presence of the rule of law within society. After addressing the key problem of inequality, I focus the analysis on personal relations, violence within society, and patronage, clientelism, racism, and other underlying forms of social exclusion (see Table 1.2).

The uneven effectiveness of the rule of law across social divisions demands that we pay attention to the question of inequality. Economic inequality, poverty, and systematic denial of equal access to public goods and services restrict individuals' operation as legal subjects and thus the exercise of their rights (O'Donnell 1999a: 203–5; Vilas 1996: 468; 1997: 21–26).[38] It is important to note that the role of economic inequality is blunted by the *level* of the poorest in a given society. Inequality tends to have less political and social impact when the less equal sectors feel economically secure. The perceptions of the middle class about inequality are similarly important. In Latin American countries, for instance, the perception of being downwardly instead of upwardly mobile has influenced the middle class's views of democracy and its role in democratic politics. Sudden economic misfortune for the bulk of society, as in the recent experience of Venezuela and Argentina, usually affects state-society relations in wealthier countries more strongly than in countries long accustomed to widespread poverty, such as Bolivia—even if the average Venezuelan or Argentine still remains better off than the average Bolivian.[39]

The problem of inequality is not only economic, though. Other "institutionalized" forms of inequality also insult the dignity of individuals (racism, sexism, and xenophobia, for example); such discriminatory patterns are embedded not only in laws and institutions but also in social practices and structures (Uvin 1998: 103–39; 1999: 49–54, citing ILO/UNDP 1996: 11; Brysk 2000a: 285). Social exclusion—expressed, for instance, in limited access to justice—restricts the range of choices available to individuals in their everyday interactions.[40] Social degradation (i.e., the systematic practice of violating people's dignity) ruins people's self-respect and aspirations as well as their confidence in political institutions and the law. Along with economic inequality, these patterns shape the social conditions under which associational activity occurs. Their impact is simply too significant to be ignored. The more intense these patterns, the greater the tendency among organized citizens to be cynical about institutions and the legal system, to distrust other citizens beyond their immediate circle, and to tolerate violent solutions to societal problems and conflicts.

Let me now discuss the role of personal relations, violence, and underlying forms of social exclusion in the analysis of the rule of law within society. First, arbitrary and illegal state practices reinforce hierarchical social interactions, where "the use of personal relations" becomes a vital device for social navigation (da Matta 1987: 320). The law tends to be replaced by informal rules that are dependent upon patronage, clientelism, and kinship. This pattern feeds a form of "relational citizenship" that determines strategies of social negotiation in everyday life. As noted, these social strategies mirror and strengthen patterns of unfairness embedded in state practices. As Roberto da Matta (1987) argued in his study of Brazil, "Who you know versus who I know, is the fundamental fact in the . . . social calculus" (p. 322). It is not the nature of the law that is challenged in this context, but its applicability to certain individuals (da Matta 1987: 320–21, 328; Jelin 1996: 108). In other words, connections to actors or institutions of higher "prominence" in society confer superior status on some individuals, dispensing a "privileged treatment" that is usually manifested in the power to circumvent the law (da Matta 1987: 313–16).

In this type of setting, "relational citizenship" dominates everyday life and shapes society's culture of legality. Constitutions, legal codes, and other formal devices have only a limited ability to alter ingrained strategies of negotiation in the social sphere (da Matta 1987: 328, 330; Nino 1992: chaps. 1–3). When a person is in a disadvantaged position because of her race, gender, class, age, or other personal or group attributes, her relations with agents of the state and *private actors* are inherently discriminatory because they are not bound by legality.[41] The perverse outcomes of these interactions vary in their degree of severity. This is illustrated, for example, by the use of violence against vulnerable groups (e.g., women, indigenous populations, peasants, and the poor) by private actors in positions of power (see below). While society as a whole suffers when practices that reinforce illegal actions are extensive, the costs to underprivileged groups are disproportionately high (Leeds 1996: 65).

Second, the phenomenon of violence in society represents a central deficit of the rule of law. In Latin American democracies, violence is not limited to police abuse. Rural workers, squatters, and indigenous groups living in areas where land conflicts are widespread have suffered unusual levels of extralegal violence in recent years. In the 1990s, death squads—often funded by landowners and acting in complicity with local politicians—were responsible for numerous massacres in northern Brazil (de Almeida 1996: 2–9; Pinheiro 1996: 21). Reports found brutal practices, including "shooting the back of the neck, shooting point-blank after the victim has been immobilized, shooting in the back after the victim has been handcuffed, [and] violation of corpses" (de Almeida 1996: 9).

Rural violence became a common phenomenon in other countries too. In Mexico, particularly in the states of Guerrero, Chiapas, and Oaxaca, illegal violence by state and private actors has been used to deal with land and labor conflicts (Acosta 1999: 163). Assassinations of indigenous leaders and human rights activists escalated in Colombia in the late 1990s as a result of conflicts over land tenure that involved indigenous peoples (the U'wa, for example), large landowners, and foreign oil companies (see Mondragón 2000). Other forms of violence such as rape represent ingrained social practices, as in rural Argentina, where the practice of raping preadolescent girls of indigenous descent is still found in the country's northwestern provinces (see, e.g., *Clarín.com* 2003).

Where historical trends of ethnic, racial, and cultural hatred and subordination have permeated social interactions—as in Latin America and Africa—social differences tend to be determined not only by economic inequality but also by complex social considerations that range from racial and aesthetic features to indications of one's social identification with people or institutions of power in society (Jelin 1996: 107; da Matta 1991: 144; Mamdani 2001: 98–100). Particularly under conditions of routine impunity, inequality and discrimination breed a "constant and humiliating reduction in the physical, intellectual and social life chances of people," which diminishes moral resistance against the use of violence and increases scapegoating, resentment, and hostile attitudes in society (Uvin 1999: 53–54).[42]

Feelings of kinship within homogeneous networks can ease within-group cooperation, but these feelings "may turn to hostility toward other groups," transforming associations into potential "vehicles for hatred, discrimination, or even extermination *vis-à-vis* outsiders" (Hadenius and Uggla 1996: 1626). In Rwanda, associations that reinforced cohesion in homogeneous communities and fomented hatred against other groups participated in the 1994 genocide (see Chapter 6). Increasing tolerance for violence may be observed also in the rise of lynchings of alleged criminals during the 1990s in Brazil, Mexico, and Venezuela, sometimes in close-knit neighborhoods (Acosta 1999: 164; Pinheiro 1996: 22). Support for this practice can be widespread, as in Venezuela, where a nationwide survey conducted in 1995 revealed that 57 percent of the people approved of lynching (Ungar 1996: 41).[43]

Third, social interactions embedded in networks as well as norms, values, and habits dominated by clientelism, racism, and various forms of socioeconomic and cultural exclusion are prone to breeding forms of association with undemocratic orientations (Ospina 1999: 8; Yashar 1999: 85–96). Civil society reproduces these patterns of interaction and sometimes reinforces them. As the cases of Weimar Germany and the United States will show, ethnic, religious, and racial divisions—which interacted with cleavages of class, age, and gender—played an important role in shaping civic engagement in those settings. Indeed, civil society participants often face "competing loyalties"; that is, "the commitments of one organization might strain activists' ties to another, disrupting the broader network of affiliation" (Clemens 2001: 271).

Loyalties are often based on existing cleavages within society and changes triggered by broader political and economic developments.

While there are examples of empowerment of vulnerable groups through participation in civil society, often such outcomes result from the creation of institutional mechanisms that address structural impediments for the effective participation and broader influence of underprivileged groups. In the absence of these mechanisms, systems of interest intermediation such as clientelism, which are characterized by methods of distribution of public goods that are highly particularistic and discretionary, tend to have a negative impact on the capacity of the underprivileged to organize for the promotion of their common interests. These populations have to count on networks of subordination—both personal and political—for access to public goods and resources (Heredia 1997: 6–7; Ndegwa 1996; O'Donnell 1996a). In other words, dense clientelistic networks based on the "distributive capacities" of political brokers and other individuals in positions of power are often the only problem-solving devices for poor and marginalized groups (Auyero 2000: 60, 66; 2001: 89–91; Rossetti 1994: 100).

We can gather from this discussion that where patronage, clientelism, racial and ethnic hierarchies, and violence among citizens become organizing principles in society, they tend to shape the rules of social interaction, which influence a society's forms of association (see Rossetti 1994; Alvarez, Dagnino, and Escobar 1998). Under conditions of economic inequality, such rights as freedom of speech, association, and assembly are likely to be insufficient for promoting civil society groups empowered to democratize state-society relations and for the widening of the public sphere, primarily in settings where structural conditions sustain severe gaps in bargaining power across social sectors (Fraser 1993: 14–15, 20, 24). As the case of Argentina will show, organizations working under adverse conditions (lack of resources, corrupt and confrontational governments, low levels of trust in society) find it difficult to establish horizontal and vertical alliances that can strengthen their position. In fact, the observed trend is toward deepening fragmentation and distrust within civil society and toward the state.

As noted in the earlier discussion of the role of associations, groups address different issues that affect the quality of democracy. When considering how civic associations address the problem of socioeconomic stratification, we should distinguish between organizations that work to improve conditions for a particular group (usually their own) and organizations that challenge the overall socioeconomic structure. This is important both nationally and internationally, in rich and poor countries, as more and more organizations protest neoliberal policies and globalization. This raises at least two related problems. First, often "those social groups that are in greatest need of collective action (i.e., those with numerous, dispersed, and relatively impoverished individuals as potential members) are the least likely to be successful in attracting these members on a rational and voluntary basis" (Schmitter 1992: 436). In contrast, privileged groups—usually smaller, more concentrated, and with better access to resources—face fewer organizational obstacles. Second, the ability of groups to establish broad alliances across and within national boundaries as well as across class, gender, race, and other divisions may help to place questions of social rights on public agendas around the world. However, horizontal links are usually unstable and generally biased against groups with scant access to resources. There are recent transnational experiences that might lead to innovative alliances (such as the World Social Forum), but the potential benefits of these experiences for the underprivileged are still uncertain.[44]

## Conclusion

The phenomenon of civil society encompasses a variety of associational forms. Only if we take into consideration this diversity can we examine the different ways in which association is expected to influence democracy. Making sense of the mechanisms that connect civic engagement and outcomes is necessary, but it is also vital to understand that these outcomes are specific to certain contextual configurations. The previous discussion suggests—and the empirical analysis will show—that institutional and societal factors have different impacts on civic engagement at different levels of aggregation.

Civic engagement and democracy are intimately entwined with the effectiveness of the rule of law in both the state and in society. Among the most important considerations is the capacity of the state to guarantee the rights of citizens. "For better or worse," Putnam (2000) argued in his study of civic engagement in the United States, "we rely increasingly—we are forced to rely increasingly—on formal institutions, and above all on the law, to accomplish what we used to accomplish through informal networks reinforced by generalized reciprocity" (p.

147). My emphasis on the role of institutions and the law challenges the idea that voluntary associations and social networks per se can "make democracy work" for different sectors of the population. Putnam's analysis neglects the vital role that the law, the courts, and government institutions play in ensuring equal legal protection and rights for citizens "long left out of those informal networks, or not recipients of that 'generalized reciprocity'"—not only in the United States but in other democracies as well (Murphy 2001: 411).

Dominant patterns of interaction within society play a fundamental role in the construction of the rule of law. This is particularly relevant in new democracies, where democratic transitions have brought about more formal rights while the capacity of individuals (largely the poor and marginalized) to exercise many of these rights has remained unchanged or has even diminished (Foweraker and Landman 1997: 24 n. 32, 27; Yashar 1999: 80; Oxhorn 1999: 141). Political, civil, and social rights should be seen as interdependent (which does not imply a natural development from one type of right to another, as T. H. Marshall argued) and constantly in flux (which means that they can be reversed) (Yashar 1999: 79–80 n. 5).[45] The expansion of political rights (such as suffrage) can be accompanied by the decline of social rights (such as minimum labor standards) and civil rights (such as protection against arbitrary state violence), as has happened in many Latin American countries.[46]

The state and society, particularly in countries with a long history of authoritarian rule, must "tame" each other (Caldeira and Holston 1999: 719).[47] From the viewpoint of civil society, the articulation between state action and modes of social interaction shapes patterns of civic engagement and the outcomes of association. Both the state and the socioeconomic structure are important determinants of patterns and orientations of citizen participation (Migdal 1994: 7–30; Yashar 1999: 101–2). The analysis in the following chapters produces some counterintuitive results that challenge established assumptions about the link between civil society and democratization.

CHAPTER 2

# The "Serpent's Egg": Civil Society's Dark Side

SOCIAL TIES do not necessarily produce democratic norms and behaviors. Indeed, civil society is likely to intensify characteristics of the broader sociopolitical context. This applies to contextual traits that both support and are inimical to democracy. There is a critical difference between arguing that some organizations may be adverse to democracy (which Putnam admits in *Bowling Alone*) and claiming that more civic activity necessarily strengthens democracy (or, vice versa, that the decline of associational activity harms democracy). As noted in the Introduction, neo-Tocquevilleans have argued that the creation of associational ties generates prodemocratic social capital across different contexts. This claim, however, comes into question when we consider "crucial cases" that confound the civil society-democracy thesis. How do we account for circumstances in which civil society blossomed before the collapse of the democratic regime—as in pre-Nazi Germany, where civic engagement helped to delegitimize parliamentary democracy? Or how do we explain northern and southern civic movements against desegregation in the United States, which strengthened white social ties and networks while defending racism, opposing dissent, and limiting access to rights for blacks?

It is important to stress that civic engagement can have democratic effects on participants, political institutions, and the public sphere. Sometimes civic mobilization successfully expands grassroots participation in policy-making, integrates excluded sectors, and improves institutional performance.[1] However, civic involvement may also be linked to undemocratic outcomes in state and society, the presence of a "vital" civil society may fail to prevent outcomes inimical to democracy, or it may contribute to such results. Advocates of the civil society–democracy thesis have acknowledged that certain groups are clearly "uncivil" and thus do not promote democracy. However, as this chapter shows, it is not only society's small extremist groups—such as civilian militias, prison gangs, or vigilante groups—that have a dark side. Indeed, in very different national and historical settings, the most seemingly inoffensive civic groups can turn into forces that erode existing institutions and democratic practices and prevent further democratization (Berman 1997b: 567).

In this chapter, I focus on the link between civil society activity and *undemocratic* orientations and outcomes. I present two examples that demonstrate the antidemocratic nature and objectives of powerful civil society movements in a new democracy, Weimar Germany, and a well-established one, the United States. The case studies I use were produced by historians and present evidence that confounds the civil society–democracy thesis (Rogowski 1995: 470). I concur with Gary King, Robert Keohane, and Sidney Verba's (1995) belief in the usefulness of the descriptive case study literature for the purpose of evaluation, explanation, and generalization in social science (pp. 477–78).

## Undemocratic Civic Engagement

The cases of Germany and the United States illustrate how political and economic factors reinforced social divisions and exclusionary features of society, creating the conditions for the emergence of organizations and movements that undermined democracy (in Germany) and opposed democratization (in the United States). Civil society legitimated antidemocratic ideas and political discourses, demanded that the state favor some groups over others (violating the rule of law if necessary), and mobilized individuals and resources to promote hostility, confrontation, polarization, and even violence.

The interaction between institutional factors, economic dislocations, and underlying divisions in society created the conditions under which social groups adopted strong defensive postures (for or against the status quo, depending on the setting) and offensive ideas (involving the general organization of society and the reconfiguration of social identities). Patterns of rejection (e.g., antipoliticism, failure to make changes at the local level) and proactive ideas (e.g., Nazi ideology, racism) related in different ways to different social sectors, depending on their position within the broader socioeconomic context. As institutional and economic factors reinforced strains and conflict in society, the appeal of antidemocratic beliefs and attitudes across the sectors of civil society intensified.

Both patterns of rejection and offensive objectives are vital to understanding the emergence of these expressions of civil society's dark side. Nazism in Germany was fed by the rejection of party politics, anti-Semitism, and, increasingly, economic chaos, but it was also gradually legitimized by community leaders and social networks based on trust that communicated Nazi ideas. This led to the acceptance of an extreme ideology in an educated society. In the United States, an underlying racism (part of the societal context) galvanized whites on specific issues such as housing and school segregation, but the movement against integration was also motivated by a defensive middle class and homeowners committed to protecting their most valuable investment. Patterns of association inimical to democracy were encouraged not only by long-term objectives of general racial separation but also by short-term goals such as housing restrictions. An important corollary of this duality is the fact that these movements were not cohesive but experienced divisions across gender, religion, and class. In the southern antidesegregation movement there was an ideological breach between the rural middle class and the urban working class (e.g., the rift over the anti-Semitic and violent attitudes of the latter in the case of Alabama's Citizens' Councils) and in Detroit different levels of resistance to racial integration in Jewish and Catholic neighborhoods.

## Weimar Germany

In Weimar Germany, the sociohistorical context consisted in delegitimized political institutions, a weak party system, a deep economic crisis, and intensely confrontational citizen mobilization; together they created an explosive mix that led to the collapse of democracy and the emergence of totalitarianism. Indeed, this wave of civic activism was part of a broader process of social and political dislocation in the 1920s. I discuss very briefly a few aspects of the economic crisis and the party system, the question of governance, and the fragmentation within society.

In Weimar Germany, political parties reproduced a trend of social and political decay brought about by, among other things, a series of economic debacles between 1914 and 1933 (Jones 1979: 144).[2] Inflation and the currency reform of 1923–24 depleted the savings of the average German. These crises hit the middle class particularly hard, though the impact of the most destructive of these catastrophes (hyperinflation) was not uniform across this social sector. As one author explained, the major result of the hyperinflation "was not so much to seal the social and economic decline of the German middle class as to intensify the social and economic antagonisms that already existed within the German middle strata and to create new antagonisms where previously none had existed" (Jones 1979: 145–46).

In this setting, nonsocialist parties failed to provide "the more traditional elements of the German middle class with the effective political representation they needed in order to maintain their social and economic position in the face of mounting economic adversity" (Jones 1979: 144). The government's handling of revaluation (the stabilization of the currency) angered and alienated important sectors of the middle class, who witnessed how key provisions of the government's revaluation legislation (which were enacted by decree, without approval from the parliament) favored "big business, agriculture, and those economic interests that had profited from the inflation in the first place" (pp. 151–52, 162). Discontent with the government's handling of the economy and the lack of legitimate political parties that could effectively address this pressing issue on behalf of those affected by the crisis promoted a middle-class disengagement from political society and increasingly ardent rejection of the status quo.

Other political tensions also intensified the disaffection of large middle-strata sectors. An example of these political rifts was the political decay at the local level that resulted from the post-1918 process of decentralization that gave local authorities "greater autonomy and leeway in the running of their day to day affairs without the interference from central organs" (McElligott 1993: 18). This process entailed a substantial transfer of political and economic influence to the local level, allowing the working class to exert unprecedented control over the political process at this level. Intensified by the depression and the issue of the Reich's reparations obligation, municipal budgetary troubles, accusations of economic mismanagement and corruption, overtaxation, and the rapid delegitimation of local governments led to mounting social and political conflict. In this context, displaced local elites, conservative business groups, and especially large sectors of the middle class became increasingly hostile to local administrations and, as the central government failed to solve the crisis, these sectors turned against parliamentary democracy, opening the door for "the reconfiguration of bourgeois politics" around the Nazi project (pp. 18–23).

German society was highly fragmented. In addition to underlying ethnic / religious, gender, and other tensions, such as anti-Semitism, individual groups advanced their demands with increasing tenacity in a highly confrontational environment (Hagtvet 1980: 67). The worsening economic crisis in Weimar "made all groups more jealous of their socioeconomic interests and more strident and narrow in their political demands" (Berman 1997a: 415). Interest groups were aggressively involved in promoting sectoral demands, which potentiated conflicts not only across but also within class lines (Abraham 1981: 25). The typical middle class joiners in Germany grew more and more hostile toward corporate interests and the working class, who were viewed as the primary recipients of government policy at the national and local level (Berman 1997a: 415). This perception, mixed with a feeling of political impotence, fed the cynicism of the middle classes and made them more willing to accept nondemocratic solutions to the crisis.

Under these conditions, civil society emerged as an alternative to politics and a realm for the circulation of antisystem ideas (the rejection of the democratic regime) and the legitimation of specific proposals (the Nazi ideology). A postwar sense of national humiliation, economic fears, and political impotence combined to nourish deep uncertainty and resentment among middle-class sectors while traditional intermediary mechanisms of participation (political parties) failed to integrate conflicting social interests and adjust to the diverse demands of the electorate. Associational activity helped reinforce the climate of social tension, lower moral restraints against authoritarian alternatives, and increase disaffection with the regime. But this role was a function of factors external to associational life itself. In fact, civil society activity mirrored, and deepened, the contradictions of viewpoints and attitudes among key social groups (Abraham 1981: 27–28, 282). A defensive middle class found in civil society not only a space in which to express and circulate their anger and frustration but also an arena in which to confront others by defining and altering, over time, their identity in relation to other groups within and outside this social stratum.

## The United States

Putnam (2000) has argued that the postwar years represented a "golden age" of civic activity in the United States. In spite of racial, gender, and class divides, the World War II generation represented, Putnam has suggested, a model of civic-mindedness (pp. 268, 358). This assumption is not without challenge; there are competing views of the nature of civic-mindedness in the 1940s and 1950s in the United States. Putnam's concern with the decline of civic engagement since the mid-1950s is built upon the assumption that this nation enjoyed high levels of civic virtue in those years, at least when compared with the second half of the twentieth century (Putnam 2000: chap. 3). This claim, as Cohen (1999) puts it, is "bizarre" when one thinks of racial discrimination and white opposition to desegregation, McCarthyism, and the centrality of gender bias in American society in the 1940s and 1950s (pp. 82–83 n. 35).[3]

Beyond the debate over the civic nature of society in the post–World War II years, the social movements that I discuss in this chapter illustrate some of the ways in which civic engagement in a democratic but exclusionary society can buttress racism, intolerance, and violent action as social groups resist unwanted changes in their communities. In urban centers, rapid changes in race relations were often perceived by white groups as a threat: integration with blacks was viewed as dangerous for group identity, economic status, and political influence.[4] In some cases, white ethnic communities that practiced discrimination were motivated by perceptions of economic, social, and cultural vulnerability more than by virulent and violent racism. For instance, in the movement against residential integration, newcomers to the standing of "white Americans" (e.g., southern and eastern Europeans) were strongly driven to assert their whiteness as a way to defend their newly gained prerogatives (Gerstle 1995: 585; see also the discussion of the antibusing movement below).

In the homeowners' movement in Detroit, grassroots engagement resulted from strong and vital communities. In these close-knit communities, the concurrent processes of structural changes in the productive sector—triggered by recession, automation, industrial decentralization, and global competition, among other factors—and African-American mass migration to the city generated a perception of urgency and uncertainty among middle- and working-class white homeowners. Indeed, as a result of global trade patterns and new Cold War imperatives, the U.S. industrial sector experienced, in the postwar years, a contraction in such areas as auto production, textiles, and electronics (see Stein 1998a; 1998b).[5] In this setting, the perception of racial integration was even more worrisome, especially for working-class whites. These people felt that their homes—which represented the core of their economic life—and their shared identity as property owners were at risk. In this conjuncture, white homeowners resorted to civic organizations to defend, as Thomas Sugrue (1996) put it, "a world that they feared was slipping away" (pp. 5, 11, 125–52, 213–14). Fear has been also an important motivation behind the boom of gated communities in the United States since the 1980s (see discussion later in the chapter).

It is important to mention that defensive postures among middle- and working-class groups need to be placed in a broader context of "racialized" state-society interactions. A fine illustration of the role played by race and racial discrimination in state-society relations is the crafting of governmental housing policy during the 1930s, which set the boundaries for fundamental inequalities and tensions in the following decades. The vast changes in the racial geography of many cities from 1915 to 1930, a result of the massive migration of southern blacks to urban centers in the North, led to the emergence of "various legal devices, including zoning, deed restrictions, and racially restrictive covenants to impose and increase racial residential segregation" (Gotham 2000: 300–301). Racial restrictive covenants ("private agreements barring non-Caucasians from occupying or owning property") spread rapidly across the country in the early 1920s and were successfully enforced until their fall in the 1940s (Jones-Correa 2000–2001). In brief, broad changes in the racial composition of many cities (including Chicago, New York, Detroit, Philadelphia, Cleveland, and Los Angeles) influenced "the political mobilization of real estate interests and the subsequent formulation of New Deal housing legislation" (Gotham 2000: 300, quotation on 292). As one study has explained, "From the turn of the century on, the mainstream opinion among real estate agents, appraisers, brokers, and mortgage bankers was that the movement of African Americans into white neighborhoods would undermine property values, contribute to neighborhood deterioration, and lead to other negative consequences" (Gotham 2000: 301).

By the early 1930s, this view had not only influenced the establishment of a number of legal devices to enforce segregation but also shaped the formulation of the Housing Act of 1934 and the design of the Federal Housing Administration (FHA) (Gotham 2000: 302–7). The resulting regulatory guidelines, appraisal rating system, lending policies, mortgage insurance, and home-building subsidies "disseminated a segregationist philosophy that equated racially mixed and predominantly minority neighborhoods with declining property values and deteriorating housing conditions" (p. 310). In the United States, racial discrimination played a key role in structuring the housing and lending industry. State policy and the racial configuration of society shaped each other (p. 293). In this way, state agencies and governmental policy institutionalized racial discrimination and, in turn, contributed, first, to setting up segregationist norms that guided the behavior of major actors in the housing market and, second, to distributing resources to social groups along racial lines (pp. 310–11). This is an example of the "norm-setting" function of state institutions as well as the role of law-making and policy-making in the legal sanction of racial inequality. As explained in the previous chapter, these features influence the effectiveness of the rule of law and thereby the actual rights of different social groups.

Other societal cleavages also factor into an analysis of civil society. Whereas for working- and middle-class whites the defense of their right to homeownership included a racist component (a defense of both property values and their community's identity), for middle-class blacks the "outsiders" to be resisted were the poor, the African-American poor included. Therefore, while race was the central issue for white homeowners' associations, class was key to the perspectives and attitudes of black homeowners (Arnesen 1998: 46). Class and other issues also played a role in the white resistance movements to housing and school integration, creating rifts and undermining their cohesiveness. Thus both institutional and societal patterns influence civic participation. Without acknowledging the role of state structures in sustaining discriminatory patterns *and* the role of social cleavages in shaping social meanings for different groups, we cannot understand variations in the nature and orientations of civil society activity.

The mobilization of anti-integration activists suggests that we should give special attention to the analysis of civil society as an arena where social actors confront each other for "real or imagined" gains and losses in rights and power. For instance, the question of the relationship between civic engagement and democracy cannot be properly addressed without considering patterns of social exclusion. As massive resistance to integration in the United States illustrates, the attempt to change these patterns generated opposition within civil society. Thus, we need to ask, what is the impact of intolerant communities on democracy? (see Krygier 1997: 82–83, 86, 88; Janoski 1998: 11). Civic engagement, I argue, is potentially inimical to democracy when it is oriented to preventing the full realization of citizenship rights for certain sectors of the population. Civil society is then an arena where historical practices involving discriminatory modes of inclusion and distribution of resources are subject to challenge and counterchallenge by different social groups.

Having introduced the two case studies, I focus in the rest of this chapter on some of the most significant aspects of the dark side of civil society in Germany and the United States.

## Associational Life in Weimar Germany

Historical studies have shown that associational life was widespread, intense, and grew quickly in Weimar Germany, but that it contributed to the erosion of democracy. The case of Weimar contradicts the thesis that there is a universal positive relationship between the strength of civil society and that of democracy. If Germany in the 1920s and early 1930s enjoyed a vital and dense associational life, then, according to the neo-Tocquevillean thesis, it should have produced democratic results. But it did not. Shaped by dramatic changes in the social, political, and economic arenas, civil society not only helped the Nazis gain access to power but also planted the seed of its own destruction. Weimar Germany fits so well the neo-Tocquevillean characterization of what associational life should look like that its "unexpected" outcome cannot be taken to be purely accidental (Rogowski 1995: 468–69; see also Eckstein 1975: 118–19). On the contrary, it suggests that the neo-Tocquevillean theory needs to be revised.

Focusing on different dimensions of civil society in various regions of Germany, historical studies have shown that civic mobilization and participation in voluntary associations only decreased *after* the Nazis assumed power (Rogowski 1995: 468). More important, these studies have revealed that exactly the same type of participation that Putnam highlights as critical for democracy—involvement in voluntary associations that stimulate face-to-face interaction—contributed to the Nazi expansion.

The case of Weimar Germany is particularly useful because it shows how the same social mechanisms that, according to neo-Tocquevilleans, serve to produce democratic results can, under certain circumstances, have the opposite effect. Methodologically, an analysis of civil society at the micro level helps us to understand how contextual factors influence social interactions. This case illustrates, in particular, two dimensions of civil society. First, it shows that civil society tends to absorb broader attitudes prevalent in society: the phenomenon of associational life is inherently "neutral"; that is, rather than being an independent source of norms, values, or attitudes, it reacts to and amplifies the sociopolitical background in which it exists—for example, by amplifying conflicts that result from social cleavages (Hagtvet 1980: 94; Abraham 1981: 25, 284–87, 301–18; Berman 1997a: 415, 427; 1997b: 565, 569–70). Associational life shows a high level of adaptability to contextual conditions. In Germany, voluntary associations absorbed and, in turn, heightened the disaffection, hostility, and resentment of citizens against the republic.

The second dimension refers to the networks and ties through which people interact—that is, grassroots networks of "quotidian sociability." These networks can foster undemocratic views, as in Weimar. Evidence from Germany has shown that social bonds were strengthened by intense debates in such places as local taverns, living rooms, social clubs, and university halls—very much the arenas identified by neo-Toquevilleans as key sites for the production of democratic social capital. These social bonds played a crucial role in the insertion of the Nazi Party (National Socialist German Workers' Party, NSDAP) into everyday networks of social interaction. As Rudy Koshar (1986a) found in his study of Marburg, most members of the local Nazi Party had become acquainted with National Socialism through their associational activities and informal interactions with other townspeople (pp. 209, 220, 236–37, 279; 1986b: 29).

In Marburg, most Nazi Party members came from clusters of participants in ostensibly nonpolitical local clubs (such as student associations and sports clubs).[6] These activists were a small group within a large minority of Germans involved in voluntary associations. Their civic engagement was not different from that of ordinary members of local associations: they were all active in local social networks. Most Nazi Party members became involved in associational life before their incorporation into the party—they came to the party with an abundant stock of social capital in the form of personal contacts, organizational and leadership skills, and experience in the voluntary sector (Koshar 1986a: 185–86, 210–13).[7] This social capital was fundamental for the expansion of Nazi local networks.

Another detailed analysis of civic engagement—William Allen's (1984) examination of the microcosm of another German town, Northeim—offered additional insights into the social processes that characterized associational activity before the Nazi takeover. In the early 1930s, Nazi activists in Northeim acted as extraordinary "social capitalists"—to use the term crafted by Putnam (2000) for those who promote the creation of social ties that generate networks of reciprocity in a community (pp. 19, 362). As Allen described in his study, Nazi activists successfully promoted citizen involvement in Northeim.

Nazis used their creativity, effort, and organizational skills to produce an array of civic activities that allowed townspeople to spend a great deal of time in face-to-face interaction with fellow citizens. In the period 1930–33, the local Nazis organized an average of almost three public meetings per month.[8] This promotion of associational activity took place in a context of already active joiners. In Northeim, formal membership organizations such as veterans' clubs, choral societies, and gun clubs coexisted with informal social gatherings such as the *Stammtisch* and the "beer clubs" (Allen 1984: 18–19).[9] The interpenetration of associational life and the Nazi Party played a central role in the propagation of Nazi ideology (Hagtvet 1980: 94, 104; Allen 1984: 18–19; Koshar 1986b: 28–29; Berman 1997a: 415).

Northeim's Nazis used the arts and cultural activities as vehicles to gather broad and diverse groups of citizens. In addition to parades, rallies, assemblies, and soup kitchens, NSDAP activists organized spectacles, concerts, "film showings, plays, acrobatic acts, lotteries, dances, sport exhibitions, military displays, recitals by children," and many other social events (Allen 1984: 63, quotation on 142).[10] Also, the Nazis organized meetings appealing to specific occupational groups—such as rentiers, pensioners, war veterans, businessmen, artisans, and civil servants—and created a variety of associations specifically designed for boys, girls, and women (Allen 1984: 18, 74, 76–77, 98, 135, 142; see Koshar 1986a: 193–94, 204).

The "Hitler Youth," for example, originally served as a vehicle for boys to bond with other boys in town. "There was no pressure put on me by my father or anyone else to join the Hitler Youth—I decided to join independently simply because I wanted to be in a boys club where I could strive towards a nationalistic ideal. The Hitler Youth had camping, hikes, and group meetings," explained a former member of the organization who joined the Hitler-Jugend in 1930. The popularity of the organization was reflected in the growth of its membership in Northeim, which increased from nine members in 1930 to some seventy-five in late 1932. Before Hitler's rise to power, the group did not serve as an instrument of explicit political indoctrination, but as an organization similar to the Boy Scouts (Allen 1984: 76–77).[11]

As in Marburg, Northeim's Nazi leadership had direct access to the social resources necessary to facilitate their collective enterprise. Nazi leaders belonged to a network of middle-class townspeople, mostly businessmen, which was strategically located in the town's social networks (Allen 1984: 143–44). As in Marburg, these party joiners were already active before their incorporation into the Nazi movement. In this sense, they were endowed with plentiful social capital because, given their class status and their professional background, they had access to broad social networks of influence.[12] The incorporation of this group of activists was a precious resource for the marginal Nazi Party. Indeed, the qualitative impact of these supporters—especially because of their social connections—transcended their numerical relevance (Koshar 1986a: 223–24).[13]

Regional variations and multiple patterns of civic engagement make Weimar Germany a rich and complex case. My aim here is to concentrate on certain characteristics of associational life that highlight important aspects of the dark side of civic engagement. I focus on two themes to illustrate the interaction among context, civic involvement, and outcomes. One is the connection between civic engagement and antipolitical orientations, which played an important role in creating a social space for the propagation of antisystem and Nazi ideas. The second is the link between civic participation and social cleavages, especially class, age, and gender divisions.

## Civic Activism and Antipoliticism

A common effect of civic engagement was the reinforcement of people's rejection of conventional politics. In fact, civic organizations reinforced antipoliticism, an attitude of disengagement based on the assumption that public decision-making could function without an established party system, interest-group lobbying, and intermediary networks.[14] In this setting, the Nazis were able to assume a position of political leadership, mainly by using the interests of the disaffected middle class to their advantage (Koshar 1986a: 52, 150–66, 200; Berman 1997a: 401–29; 1997b: 562–74). This process took place amid a high level of local mobilization.

As Peter Fritzsche (1990) showed in his study of middle-class civic activism in Lower Saxony between 1918 and 1930, urban middle classes were involved in a variety of civic associations—such as social clubs and patriotic groups—which integrated them in a way that political parties did not (pp. 9–11, 83, 217–19). An outburst of middle-class activism also took the form of crowds bursting into the streets and public squares, and citizens organizing public assemblies and marches. Civil society provided a social space detached from the arena of traditional party politics, where middle-class activism stressed the rejection of party politics and the "political class."[15] Associational life became an alternative to political society.

This wave of mobilization was part of a broader process of social and political dislocation in the 1920s. The ascension of the Nazis also took place alongside the progressive corrosion of long-standing political allegiances among middle-class voters and the new dynamics of popular mobilization in the 1920s (Childers 1983: 262). Even though tensions across classes dominated in the context of the political and economic crisis, processes of socioeconomic diversification—in particular, industrialization, urbanization, income concentration, and the development of an increasingly secular culture—had created tensions within classes as well. In fact, the interests of the middle class were heterogeneous and thus difficult to subsume under a single party agenda (Hagtvet 1980: 96, 103).

Case studies of this period have shown that civic engagement among white-collar workers and farmers helped increase the antagonism of varied sectors of civil society toward Weimar's political regime while helping the Nazi Party to expand its electoral support base (Berman 1997a: 420–22; Kolb 1988: 101–3). As noted, there was a dynamic, reinforcing interpenetration between the local associational sphere and the Nazi movement. Often, town civic leaders legitimated the acceptance of the Nazis as a viable alternative to the traditional parties (Kolb 1988: 102–3; Koshar 1986b: 24). This social process took place also in rural areas, as in Bavaria, where the Nazi Party's acceptance among the peasant population was greatly facilitated by the conversion of leaders of agricultural interest organizations. As in urban settings, these associations were not infiltrated from without, but their support for the Nazis often resulted from the influence of community leaders who served as local opinion brokers (Zofka 1986: 60).[16]

Social networks at the local level served as vehicles of mobilization for the Nazi project (Koshar 1986a: 187, 200, 204; Hagtvet 1980: 104). In addition, the Nazis promoted the creation of voluntary organizations for specific professions and occupations: lawyers, teachers, physicians, manual workers, farmers, small businessmen, and so forth.[17] The simultaneous development of informal networks and formal organizations helped Nazi ideas to permeate existing civic associations locally and regionally, reaching both leaders and the rank and file (Kolb 1988: 102–3; Koshar 1986a: 202, 204).

Civil society offered a map to community rifts. Participation in voluntary associations contributed to social divisions—especially between the middle and working classes (Fritzsche 1990: 82–83). Clubs, for example, which played a central role in the life of many middle-class Germans, delimited social boundaries, especially because loyalty to one's organization became a vital matter for members (Koshar 1986a: 148–49). "The channels of social life were the impress of mutual hostilities," Fritzsche (1990) explained. "It was as club members that Germans understood and internalized the fractured community" (p. 82). Social clubs, patriotic societies, and other civic groups contributed to the development of networks of particularized trust, which deepened societal fragmentation, and to the cementing of hostility toward the democratic system, gradually undermining the stability of the institutions of the republic.[18]

In Marburg, for instance, deepening fragmentation in society was reflected as an increase in the number of organizations and a simultaneous decrease in the number of participants per organization. The number of voluntary organizations in Marburg increased steadily in the period 1914–30 while the membership per organization decreased. There were 223 associations in 1914 (a density of 10 associations per 1,000 residents and 99.6 individuals per organization), 257 in 1920 (density: 11.3; members per group: 88.5), 319 in 1925 (13.7; 73.0), and 407 organizations in 1930, with a density much higher than in 1914 (15.9) and a much lower average number of members per organization (63.0) (Koshar 1986a: 136–37, 276, 298, table A-2).[19]

Civic activists and leaders construed party politics as morally corrupt and detrimental to Germany's national interest. Civic participants viewed voluntary associations as an alternative to the unpatriotic behavior of economic interest groups and party bureaucracies. Voluntary associations, they claimed, offered a buffer to political hostility because they could counteract ideological and partisan conflict. However, civic associations proved unable to cushion political strains, and the divide between civil and political societies intensified along with the polarization in associational life. There was a natural convergence among antipoliticism, social fragmentation, and the National Socialists' emphasis on a society "beyond parties" (Koshar 1986a: 156–57, 160–61, 163–66, 277–78; 1986b: 22).

From 1924—when the Nazis entered the electoral scene—to the Reichstag elections of 1932, the National Socialist constituency was never stable or socially fixed. The NSDAP, according to Thomas Childers (1983), represented a "catchall party of protest, whose constituents, while drawn primarily from the middle-class electorate, were united above all by a profound contempt for the existing political and economic system" (p. 268).[20] Voters cast their ballots in protest against a system that they perceived as helpless to deal with the grave problems facing the country. Theirs was not an ideological commitment to the Nazis, but a profound disenchantment with the traditional party system. This heterogeneous mass of voters had in common their economic and political grievances against the Weimar regime (see Childers 1983: 5, 262, 268; 1986: 253–54). Discontent with the government's handling of the economic crisis (policies that were perceived as biased and unfair by large middle-class sectors) and the array of tensions involving local governments contributed to the perception that institutions were no longer legitimate. These tensions, coupled with serious rifts within society and middle-class parties incapable of offering effective political representation, galvanized citizens around patterns of rejection of democratic institutions and the legal order. Civic groups served as building blocks for political mobilization against the regime, but they could not offer the political leadership and proactive agenda that a party organization could provide. In a context of low levels of institutional legitimacy and rejection of "politics as usual," the Nazis emerged as a viable alternative to the status quo.

## Class Cleavages

Associational life may become open to antidemocratic appeals because of deepening social cleavages. In Weimar Germany, cleavages of class, ethnicity and religion, region, and occupation were already intense, and political parties were not effective mechanisms for bridging those divisions. Society was fragmented, and competition among groups was fierce. Germany's vital civil society was characterized by dense networks within classes but very few connections across classes (as noted, there were also serious divisions within the middle class). Each class had its own network of voluntary associations, which intensified their isolation from other sectors of society.[21] Civic engagement then contributed to the fragmentation of society and, in a context of heightened antipoliticism, to give legitimacy to an antidemocratic movement. The appeal of the Nazis, then, was largely abetted by a context in which social cleavages—especially those of class—created intense societal conflict (Hagtvet 1980: 67–68, 78, 99).

The protracted economic crisis in Germany had important effects on the political orientations of the middle class. Income differentials between social segments decreased rapidly: "The ratio between wages of skilled and unskilled workers diminished from 1914 to 1922, from 145.9 to 106.8" (Bresciani-Turroni 1953: 313; see also Holtfrerich 1990: 81–88). The inflationary process benefited speculators in the stock market and those who had borrowed large amounts of money, whereas traditional sectors of the economy (e.g., the so-called "old rich" and the primary sector) and small investors were the ones hardest hit by the economic crisis (Bresciani-Turroni 1953: 296, 298; Hughes 1982: 385; James 1986: 49–51).[22]

The hyperinflation of 1922–23 exerted a heavy toll on large sectors of the middle class. After 1924, stabilization failed to help retailers, professionals, and small businesses. But the middle class, positioned between "the two poles of big business and organized labor," was hardly a uniform victim of the economic catastrophe. "Of the various social and economic groups that constituted the German middle strata," one analyst argued, "the one affected most directly by the collapse of the German currency was the millions of small investors who over the course of the past two or three decades had systematically set aside a major portion of their income in private savings of one form or another" (Jones 1979: 148). As noted, the economic crisis precipitated a long process of "disintegration of the German bourgeoisie as a homogeneous social force" that began with the country's industrialization in the later part of the nineteenth century (p. 146).

Other developments accentuated the impact of the crisis on the middle stratum. Soon after Germany's central bank announced that it would restrict credits, bankruptcies increased by 160 percent (Childers 1983: 66).[23] Salaries and employment in the white-collar sector followed similar trends (Lepsius 1978: 50–61). Tensions between social groups intensified as wages of unskilled workers increased 20 percent in 1924 and white-collar wages did so by only a very modest percentage (Childers 1983: 87–88). Civil servants suffered additional losses as their salaries were cut by 23 percent between 1930 and 1931 (James 1986: 69; see also Bresciani-Turroni 1953: 326–27).

Following the Great Depression, the banking crisis of 1931 provoked more discontent with the financial system and the government's eco-

nomic policies among upper and middle sectors of the population
(James 1986: 323). The impact of the economic crisis on the middle sectors forced them to make a number of major changes in their lifestyle.
Middle-class Germans used various strategies to protect themselves
from further economic and social decline. For example, many sold personal property—furniture, jewelry, artwork—in the stores that proliferated at the time. Many tried to protect their savings by taking their
money to Switzerland themselves—which prompted the government
to restrict foreign travel to control small-capital flight (Bresciani-Turroni
1953: 330; James 1986: 301). This situation, as a number of studies have
argued, had a profound impact on the political views of middle-class
Germans.[24] Millions of them perceived that the boundaries between
classes were disappearing; thus the threat was not just economic decline, but decreased *"social* distance" from the working class (Hagtvet
1980: 102). This was a fundamental factor in the deepening of social tensions and the acceptance of antisystem ideas.

Indeed, middle-class citizens, though with different interests and different demands, experienced as a whole a serious threat to their identity. Class polarization, then, should be understood in both economic
and social terms. This understanding reveals why civil society in
Weimar Germany served as a mechanism of "social defense" in a context of increasing social fragmentation and in the absence of other
mechanisms (such as political parties) to protect class interests. The antisystem attitudes of the middle class thus were rooted in "its ideology
of social protectionism" (Hagtvet 1980: 78–79, 100, 102–3). From the
perspective of important segments of the middle class, the Nazis became an instrument to contain the workers and the Social Democratic
Party as well as a device to protect their identity as a group—that is,
their "social existence" (Allen 1984: 296; Kolb 1988: 102; Hagtvet 1980:
93, 103).

## The Cleavage of Age

Even though the average middle-class citizen provided the core following for the NSDAP, the support of sectors of the upper middle class was
also crucial for the Nazis' ascension to power. Even before the onset of
the Great Depression in 1929, the National Socialists were expanding
their influence over these sectors of society. In the second half of the
1920s, newly created professional associations linked the Nazi Party to
influential sectors of German society (Kater 1986: 147, 171). These asso-

ciations facilitated the diffusion of the National Socialist discourse within the traditional professions—lawyers, physicians, academics, and civil servants.[25]

The Nazi Physicians' League (NSÄB) illustrates the incorporation of well-educated joiners into the Nazi movement and also provides an example of the role of nonclass cleavages—in this case, age—in the development of voluntary associations that supported the NSDAP. German doctors experienced their own crisis after World War I. This was a crisis of varied dimensions. Especially after the harsh economic stabilization that followed the hyperinflation crisis, "medico-ethical issues were closely tied to the economic ones by an acrimonious inter-generational conflict in the ranks of the medical profession" (Kater 1986: 149). While established doctors benefited from the public health care system (for instance, by taking advantage of the system of lump-sum compensations), younger physicians worked in substantially inferior conditions, which fed animosity toward their older colleagues (p. 150).

The Nazi Physicians' League did not invest energy in the recruitment of young doctors at first, but began to exploit this generational conflict in the early 1930s (Kater 1986: 148–50). It lowered its membership fees in 1930 as part of an effort to entice young practitioners to join the organization. Interestingly, this decision gave the league an advantage over the more established physicians' association, the Hartmannbund. Soon the traditional lobbying association started to lose the support of groups of young physicians formally associated with it (such as the Emergency League of Junior Doctors), which veered toward the Nazis. The Nazi Physicians' League also benefited from the generalized disillusionment among young professionals with the traditional political parties and their affiliated organizations (pp. 152, 160–62). In other words, younger doctors turned toward the Nazis because of their discontent with both traditional politics and interest organizations, which they felt did not address the serious generational conflict in their profession.

The league encouraged its members to run for office at all government levels as part of a strategy focused on electoral gains. Particularly important was the group's objective to compete against the Hartmannbund for access to the political decision-making process. Even though few physicians actually became elected officials, this strategy had other important effects. The league urged its members to promote the Nazi project in their offices and social gatherings. As Michael Kater (1986) explained, socialist doctors complained that Nazi physicians sought to influence "their patients, especially the workers, handing them propaganda leaflets during office visits and urging them to attend Nazi rallies" (p. 167). At the same time, networks of sociability linked physicians with other well-off sectors of society. Some of these contacts were occupational, such as those with pharmacists and other health professionals; others were purely social, such as those with high-level bureaucrats and lawyers. These social connections were important for the diffusion of Nazi ideas.

The ethnic and religious cleavage (discussed below) was another important division that shaped the associational networks of physicians in Weimar. Gradually, anti-Jewish sentiment permeated the Nazi Physicians' League and, toward the end of the republic, the doctors' organization incorporated an increasingly anti-Semitic discourse. The organization began to attack Jewish doctors as part of a strategy to attain greater legitimacy in the profession and to overpower the Hartmannbund. The emphasis on "racial hygienics" played a major role in this effort (Kater 1986: 162–64).[26]

## Gender and Religious Divides

The role of anti-Semitism was obviously important in several other organizations of civil society in pre-Nazi Germany. The interaction between the ethnic and religious divide and other cleavages is a good example of how solidarities in civil society changed dramatically as a result of contextual transformations. The experience of middle-class women in the feminist movement demonstrates the interconnection between ethnic / religious and gender cleavages. As Marion Kaplan (1984) has argued, "within a broad, middle-class context women shared common gender-specific experiences across ethnic / religious lines and yet suffered divisions created by these same identities" (p. 174). Whereas voluntary associations of German and German-Jewish women actively collaborated in the advancement of a feminist agenda—the defense of women's rights—the limitations of such cooperation became apparent in a society that grew increasingly anti-Semitic.

Civic organizations proved unable to buffer the fragmentation of society along religious lines and its effect on the rights of citizenship in Germany. Jewish women involved in the feminist movement "suffered from the double burden of being women in a sexist society and Jews in a racist one" (Kaplan 1984: 174, 192). These social cleavages defined, in a dynamic way, the identities of women activists in the transition from the republic to Nazism. The relative prominence of each of these cleavages dictated the patterns of social organization available to these women at different times.

Gender and ethnic / religious cleavages interacted in different ways and shifted as a result of changes in the broader political context. Feminist solidarity—as expressed by horizontal cooperation between the League of Jewish Women and the German feminist movement, especially the Federation of German Women's Associations—gradually eroded as anti-Semitism increased following the Great Depression. (The league and the federation had an important presence throughout the country: the League of Jewish Women included twenty provincial associations and nearly 500 locals. The Federation of German Women's Associations had a membership of around 900,000 in the 1920s.) The league was a member of the women's federation, and both organizations enjoyed decades of cordial relations—in fact, for years the league had viewed the federation as a partner in the struggle against anti-Semitism in Germany (Kaplan 1984: 180–86).

From the point of view of organized German women, the struggle for the rights of Jews and women was essentially one, because both Jews and feminists fought for a democratic and pluralistic society. However, while the German and German-Jewish women's organizations largely concurred on gender and class matters, the German women's organization often exhibited derogatory and hostile attitudes toward the Jews, which fluctuated from mild intolerance of Jewish distinctive traits to open anti-Semitism. These attitudes reflected patterns found in the broader society (Kaplan 1984: 185–89).

By the early 1930s, anti-Semitic trends strengthened within the German feminist movement. This caused serious tensions within the movement. Following the National Socialist seizure of power in 1933—which forced the German women's federation to choose the path of dissolution—the broad social networks developed in the previous years also disappeared (Kaplan 1984: 174–75, 180–82, 185–89, 192). The notion of gender loyalty was rapidly weakened by the primacy of the ethnic / religious divide in society.[27] Long-standing networks of cooperation and trust among women dissolved at a dramatic pace as the political conditions in Germany changed.

As this example illustrates, situating associational activity within underlying social and political conditions shows that organizations and movements offer both opportunities and risks for building alliances to pursue specific goals (e.g., women's rights). As Clemens (2001) found in her work on women's associations in the United States from the 1880s to the 1920s, the women's movement offered activists the possibility to decide "which kind of woman" they would identify with while supporting a specific cause, but this very possibility forced every participant to face competing allegiances (p. 217). The resulting tensions limited the construction of broader networks and alliances in favor of women's suffrage in the United States. In Germany, before the Nazi takeover, involvement in the women's movement also challenged individual participants to choose memberships that reflected their own identity, with obvious consequences for the nature of the movement.

The account of associational life in Germany presented in the first part of the chapter has shown that civil society contributed to the collapse of the democratic system, and indeed helped to hatch Germany's "serpent's egg."[28] As emphasized earlier, I have focused on the civic engagement of average Germans and explained, in particular, the role played by organizations that fit the "Putnamesque" profile. The second half of the chapter continues the emphasis on average forms of participation, now shifting the attention to the United States.

## Contesting Desegregation in the U.S. South

Following the U.S. Supreme Court's school desegregation ruling in 1954 (*Brown v. Board of Education*), southern whites rapidly organized to resist integration. Across the South, they created a network of associations committed to preserving white supremacy (Bartley 1995: 200). Increased civic participation in the South represented a swift reaction to a crisis that affected the status quo. In other words, whites organized to prevent any major transformation of race relations and the potential social changes that desegregation would bring into their communities. The Citizens' Councils were part of a broad effort to present a common front against integration in the southern states.[29] Voluntary organizations became the backbone of a movement to create a network of legal mechanisms throughout the region that would obstruct the Supreme Court's decision (McMillen 1994: 361). When chapters of the National Association for the Advancement of Colored People (NAACP) filed petitions calling for the desegregation of public schools, such demands for compliance with federal law were met with strong reaction by white activists (Bartley 1969: 82–83, 105; 1995: 199).

The Citizens' Councils that spearheaded lawful organized resistance to desegregation began in Mississippi and rapidly expanded to the other southern states.[30] Most councils and kindred groups explicitly condemned the use of violence, but opposed democratization by aggressively contesting the expansion of civil rights for blacks.[31] The movement grew dramatically immediately following the Supreme Court's ruling. By early 1956, councils and allied groups had enrolled between 250,000 and 300,000 members (Bartley 1969: 84; 1995: 199, 201; McMillen 1994: 152–54).[32] Informal networks—characterized by strong links of interpersonal solidarity—were vital to the movement's rise.[33] Associational growth in a community was directly related to the perceived threat posed by blacks and the NAACP. First, there was a positive relationship between the creation of council chapters and the percentage of African Americans in a county. In Mississippi, for instance, council chapters flourished in counties where blacks constituted at least 50 percent of the population. Second, council growth was largely a function of a surge in black mobilization. That is, it was directly related to the emergence of concrete challenges to white supremacy (e.g., petitions to desegregate schools) (McMillen 1994: 27–31).[34]

Making effective use of social networks to mobilize members, political connections, and resources, the council movement had substantial political influence at the state and local levels, particularly in Mississippi, Alabama, Louisiana, and South Carolina (McMillen 1994: 362). By late 1955, the network of councils dominated all other interest groups in the South. A combination of competent leadership and organizational effectiveness placed the movement in a strong position of power in the debate over race, within the white community and in the policy-making sphere (Bartley 1969: 83–84). Data on the number of blacks enrolled in integrated public schools eight years after the Supreme Court's 1954 decision suggested that organized resistance to desegregation succeeded in slowing down integration. By spring 1962, only 0.1 percent of black students attended integrated public grade schools in the South (Cook 1962: 3).

The first Citizens' Council was organized in July 1954 in Mississippi, where 253 councils emerged in less than a year. Membership was 60,000 by August 1955, and increased to 85,000 by late 1956. Council chapters represented a truly grassroots movement, which became one of the most influential forces in Mississippi's politics. Since its beginning, the council leaders agreed that a successful movement of resistance required direct influence over the political power structure at the local level. Indeed, the network of Citizens' Councils in Mississippi became powerful throughout the state, influencing the local media, the educational system, and policy-making. The councils, sometimes working closely with the American Legion and civic organizations, advised PTA groups on effective anti-integration campaigns, censored films and educational materials, blacklisted activists and civic associations perceived to support civil rights, and created files on potential "agitators"—both black and white (McMillen 1994: 26, 236–62, 239–54, 319–54; Muse 1964: 176–77). "The very presence of a strong and active Council in any given community," Neil McMillen (1994) has explained, "was usually sufficient to silence dissent" (p. 252). The Citizens' Councils also exerted strong influence in Mississippi's legislature, where the "Dixiecrat–Old Guard" led by the House Speaker assumed an activist role in the antidesegregation movement (Bartley 1969: 85–86).[35]

From Mississippi, councils expanded to Alabama, Louisiana, and South Carolina, allowing the movement to make important social and political inroads.[36] In Alabama, for example, support from state senators gave the council movement a high degree of political influence. Council members included mayors, police commissioners, state senators, businessmen, and civic leaders. In Louisiana, the Citizens' Council established links with various civic associations, including Louisiana State University and the state medical association. In South Carolina, council members included top leaders of the State Farm Bureau Federation, the bar association, and higher education institutions (Bartley 1969: 87–91, 93).[37]

The wave of mobilization in the South was abetted by caste solidarity, racial fears, and a strong desire for retaliation. While the opposition to integration was deeply embedded in southern society, association provided the means to carry out resistance more effectively. Even though councils resorted to many forms of intimidation, most of them rejected secrecy and violence explicitly.[38] They emphasized "legal" forms of defiance to integration, using political influence and legal instruments to challenge school desegregation (Bartley 1969: 83, 200). The movement was presented as an alternative to the Ku Klux Klan model, especially because of its commitment to fighting integration with legal devices (Bartley 1995: 201, 204; McMillen 1994: 360). Choosing to distinguish the movement from the Klan, the councils sought to open a new space in southern conservatism.

Council leaders promoted the grassroots character of the movement and attempted to recruit "respected" and "responsible" members who would represent all major sectors and interests of the white community. These included business, industrial and labor interests, the agricultural sector, religious groups, and social organizations. The recruitment of politicians (including governors and legislators), judges, lawyers, industrialists, bankers, physicians, and professors provided the movement with valuable resources in the form of political influence, funding, and social capital. Members were involved in civic activities that promoted face-to-face interaction and debate on issues of public concern. As in Weimar Germany, these activities were not different from those identified by contemporary neo-Tocquevilleans as mechanisms for the promotion of democratic norms and practices. Participants attended meetings, did volunteer work, collected signatures for petitions, planned mobilization strategies, supported allied groups on organizational matters, and discussed politics, among other activities (Bartley 1969: 98–99, 102; McMillen 1994: 11, 21). According to the historical narratives cited here, the segregationist movement was very effective in multiplying the existing stock of social capital throughout white southern communities.

## The Use of Social Networks

While rural towns and villages provided the mass of the movement's middle-class activists, the urban working class was also drawn into the Citizens' Councils and other segregationist groups. The leadership of the movement came mainly from the urban business and professional sectors. In rural areas, "whites at the lowest socio-economic level who wished to protect the white man's prerogatives were apt to find the Ku Klux Klan more to their liking" (Bartley 1969: 104). As Numan Bartley (1995) explained: "The alliance of middle-class black belt whites and metropolitan working-class whites was logical enough: they were the two white social groups that would in practice do most of the integrating" (p. 203). Eventually, serious disagreements between rural and urban groups contributed to the decay of the segregationist movement. For example, the Citizens' Councils of Alabama, a group with a rural constituency, severed links with the North Alabama Citizens' Councils in Birmingham because of ideological differences. The Citizens' Councils of Alabama rejected the extremist attitudes of the Birmingham-based group, which espoused anti-Semitic and violent tendencies (Bartley 1969: 104–5).

From the point of view of civic engagement, one of the most interesting aspects of the Citizens' Councils and other similar organizations was the close connection between these segregationist groups and associations that have been seen as the backbone of the "golden age" of U.S. civic activism in the 1950s and early 1960s, such as the Rotary Club and the Exchange Club (see Putnam 2000). This illustrates an important aspect of the dubious link between civic engagement and democratization: the "dark side" of civil society may not be easily set apart from the "bright side." In the process of recruitment for the councils, for example, the organization of local chapters was aided by civic activists from the Rotary Club, Exchange Club, Kiwanis, Lions, Civitans, and the American Legion, among other groups (McMillen 1994: 20; Bartley 1995: 201). In fact, many chapter members came from the ranks of these civic associations (Bartley 1969: 104). Social connections eased the process of creating new council chapters:

> Typically, an organizer . . . would be invited by a sympathetic member to address a Rotary, Kiwanis, Civitan, or Exchange Club luncheon in an unorganized locality. After explaining the Council's nature and purpose, he met with interested individuals to arrange a second and larger meeting. At this second meeting a temporary chairman and a combination steering-nominating committee were chosen. The committee, in turn, drafted a proposed charter and bylaws and prepared a list of nominees for the board of directors. (McMillen 1994: 20)

This network of social ties was very effective at creating obstacles to desegregation attempts in many southern communities. The Citizens' Councils and allied organizations played a central role in the implementation of mechanisms for "economic retaliation" against those who supported integration (Bartley 1969: 83, 193; McMillen 1994: 209–15). "We intend to make it difficult, if not impossible," a council leader stated, "for a Negro who advocates desegregation to find and hold a job, get credit, or renew a mortgage." Economic pressure was found to be a forceful response to blacks who dared challenge white supremacy. "Don't let him eat at your table, don't let him trade at your filling station, and don't let him trade at your store," urged a former governor of Georgia to council members (as quoted in Bartley 1995: 204, 205).

The use of economic pressure to "discourage" petitions for integration illustrates a resource seldom mentioned in studies of civil society. The councils played a fundamental role in paving the way for the use of economic retaliation to crush dissent. Through their Legal Advisory Committees, they often recommended economic pressure as an instrument to hinder NAACP petitions to desegregate schools (Bartley 1969:

193–94). Accordingly, the councils advertised in the local newspaper the names of blacks who had signed NAACP petitions and displayed the lists in stores, banks, and other public places (McMillen 1994: 211). Soon after such campaigns were launched, the number of petitioners would decrease dramatically.

As noted in Chapter 1, civil society often functions as an arena in which different groups confront each other over the distribution of rights and resources. In the U.S. South, privileged citizens made effective use of their resources to deny citizenship rights to African Americans. Segregation was one of many expressions of a broader system of domination and subordination. This system hindered the rights of blacks because it limited their role as workers, consumers, residents, and participants in public affairs. Whites' efforts to maintain the status quo permeated political society, the public sphere (especially through the role of the media and other opinion molders), and economic society. In fact, economic intimidation proved to be as effective as lobbying, propaganda, demonstrations, and other forms of mobilization to challenge integration. As a council spokesman in Alabama said: "The white population in this county controls the money and this is an advantage that the Council will use in a fight to legally maintain complete segregation of the races" (as quoted in Bartley 1969: 193).[39]

Even though African Americans tried to use their power as consumers to retaliate against economic discrimination (for instance, by launching boycotts against white businesses), the Citizens' Councils' strategy worked in small towns where this form of economic "lynching" was difficult to counteract.[40] Its effectiveness was demonstrated once again in the 1960s, when a second wave of white economic retaliation against black petitioners followed the boycotts of the 1950s, affecting an even larger number of African Americans than the first wave (Bartley 1969: 194–95).

To exert political pressure, the councils engaged in a variety of activities that sustained the massive opposition to integration. Across the South, councils often functioned "as a self-appointed clearing house for political aspirants" by screening the "segregation credentials" of candidates for public office (McMillen 1994: 306–7). In some states, Citizens' Councils administered questionnaires asking candidates for public office their opinions about segregation, black voting, and closing public schools in order to prevent integration. The councils disseminated these political questionnaires to the media.[41] Councils also lobbied intensely in state legislatures, and a few of their leaders ran for public office (Bartley 1969: 197–99; McMillen 1994: 306–9).

Council members understood that black voters could have a stronger influence on many southern communities than school desegregation petitions. Therefore, council chapters engaged in an organized backlash against voter registration for blacks. In Louisiana, for example, council activists used voter qualification criteria (the literacy and understanding clause in the state constitution) to challenge the qualifications of already registered black voters; they called this campaign "operation clean-up" (Bartley 1969: 200–201; McMillen 1994: 215–28). "On the basis of this provision," Bartley (1969) said, "Council members in thirteen parishes succeeded in removing some eleven thousand Negroes from the voter lists during the winter of 1956–57, and other purges followed during the late 1950's" (p. 201). Councils also harassed local registrars to "persuade" them to reject black applicants. Following the enactment of the Civil Rights Act of 1957, council leaders "briefed parish registrars, district attorneys, sheriffs, and police jury presidents on ways and means of evading federal voting laws" (McMillen 1994: 225–26). These tactics cemented the social and political influence of the councils in many southern communities.

## Links with the State

In the Deep South, council and government activity often complemented each other. While councils carried out tactics of intimidation—targeting both blacks and whites—state governments frequently used their power to defeat prointegration initiatives. State power was consistently oriented to harass organizations and individuals who pursued integration agendas. A central focus of this campaign was the NAACP. Southern states employed different harassment tactics against the NAACP. These included the creation of investigating committees to uncover "communist infiltration" in the organization, the dismissal of state employees who were NAACP members, the biased application of laws governing tax exemptions, and the attempt to restrict NAACP freedom to promote litigation. In this way, state authorities waged a war against the African-American organization, at times shutting down its activities completely, as in Alabama, Arkansas, and Texas (Bartley 1969: 212–36; McMillen 1994: 269).

Across the South, state and societal actors established strong networks for the promotion of a prosegregation agenda.[42] Because the boundaries between state and society tend to be elusive and fluid, it is often difficult to identify the limits and interests of state and society as distinctly separate (see Mitchell 1991; Nugent 1999). In Louisiana, for example, the Citizens' Council was a de facto extension of the state's Joint Legislative Committee to Maintain Segregation. As Bartley (1969) explained:

Throughout the decade Council activity outside the New Orleans area was hardly distinguishable from that of the committee. State Senator William M. Rainach, chairman of the Joint Legislative Committee, was president of the Association of Citizens' Councils of Louisiana. State Representative John Sidney Garrett, committee spokesman in the lower chamber, became president when Rainach stepped down. William M. Shaw, general counsel for the legislative committee, was executive secretary of the state Citizens' Council organization. (p. 90)

Networks connecting government officials and anti-integration activists blossomed in the 1950s. Congressmen and local authorities actively collaborated with the councils' activities—and also joined council ranks—in several states. While state authorities and council activists converged in the effort to mount a vast campaign of legal opposition to the *Brown* decision and the intervention of the federal government, they also succeeded in crushing local defiance. In a context of generalized white opposition to desegregation, civil society activity (i.e., intense pressure from the councils) combined with public pressure from state authorities to create a climate that seriously limited the freedom of dissent in many southern communities (Bartley 1969: 201).[43]

Close cooperation with legislators and government officials facilitated many of the councils' activities. In Mississippi, the Citizens' Council established close alliances with policy-makers to the point that council leaders "so thoroughly blurred distinctions between public and private authority that they virtually dominated many areas of public policy" (McMillen 1994: 319). A fine example of council-state cooperation was the propaganda campaign mounted by Mississippi's Citizens' Council. Its numerous publications reached vast audiences; by 1956 the association's newspaper, *The Citizens' Council*, had a monthly circulation of 40,000.[44] In early 1957 the council started a weekly telecast in Jackson. Soon the program began to be broadcast by stations throughout Mississippi and also in Alabama, Louisiana, Georgia, Texas, and Virginia. Radio tapes were even more widely distributed. Crucial to this rapid expansion was the fact that telecasts were offered at no cost to radio and TV stations across the country. This was made possible through the assistance provided by Mississippi's congressional representatives in Washington, D.C., who opened the congressional recording studios to the council for the production of its propaganda series. This kind of support gave the organization access to a wider national audience and bolstered its appeal throughout the South (pp. 37–39).[45]

In contrast, other state actors, especially at the national level, played a fundamental role in promoting more equitable race relations (with some important exceptions, as I explain in the next section). Agencies of the U.S. government, the Supreme Court, and the federal judiciary promoted progressive change at the community level in the South. In several ways, which ranged from legal action to laws and federal grants, national authorities opposed white racism and the inflexibility of southern governments (Button 1989: 235). Several local conflicts, such as school desegregation battles, were finally decided in federal district courts. States, as this case illustrates well, pull in multiple directions (Migdal 1994: 8). Indeed, while citizens confronted each other in the realm of civil society, political institutions collided over fundamental questions of citizenship rights—as illustrated by the fierce clashes between federal and state courts over the implementation of desegregation rulings.

## Antiblack Community Activists in the Urban North

The Citizens' Council movement in the South should not be considered an anomaly; it was only one outcome of politics that represented broader patterns in the United States (Gerstle 1995: 579). Massive resistance to racial integration also took place in Detroit, Chicago, and other northern cities. As explained, the Citizens' Councils emerged from the informal networks and associational fabric already present in southern communities. In turn, the northern homeowners' movement to be discussed in this section developed out of close-knit communities, such as middle- and working-class neighborhoods.

After the U.S. Supreme Court ruled in 1948 that states could not enforce restrictive covenants ("clauses incorporated into deeds which had as their intention the maintenance of 'desirable residential characteristics' of a neighborhood," which could stipulate restrictions against certain racial, ethnic, or religious groups), blacks in several cities stepped up their search for better housing in white neighborhoods (Abrams 1955: 170–72; quotation from Sugrue 1996: 44).[46] For civil rights organizations, the court's ruling represented a victory in the fight against racial discrimination. In Detroit, civil rights groups and city authorities, later joined by religious organizations, played a central role in contesting the city's racial divisions, challenging residential segregation, and establishing the foundation for a vigorous open housing movement (Davis 1990: 161–63; Sugrue 1996: 182–83, 193).

With the expansion of property ownership among the white working class, neighborhood associations blossomed from the mid-1940s through the mid-1960s in number and influence. These "civic," "protective," "improvement," and "homeowners'" associations came to constitute a dominant force in Detroit's public life, overshadowing other groups and forms of political participation.[47] Thus, while blacks and liberal whites organized to champion housing integration (sometimes with the full support of public officials), they were confronted by a movement that mobilized tens of thousands of white homeowners against public housing and open housing in Detroit. Similar associations whose purpose became the exclusion of blacks from white neighborhoods were active in other cities too, such as Chicago (Abrams 1955: 97, 181; Sugrue 1995: 211, 557, 560, 563, 578; 1996: 207, 209–213).

Originally, the purpose of most of these homeowners' associations was not to promote racial exclusion. They were concerned with improving communities and with socialization. But later, neighbors turned their social capital to the task of protecting their homes from the threat of black "invasion" (Massey and Denton 1993: 35–36). The makeup of these groups was diverse, encompassing different ethnic groups and activists with multiple memberships (Sugrue 1995: 557; 1996: 215; Gerstle 1995: 582). These associations socialized individuals into cooperative behavior and provided tangible services to their communities.[48] They gathered complaints and informed the city of zoning violations, lobbied for the improvement of public services, organized social events, disseminated neighborhood news, and promoted safety and home improvement. The neighborhood was a central part of the life of white Detroiters, especially among the working classes, and the idea of homeownership was inseparable from the notion of neighborhood. Strong social ties resulted from physical closeness—small lots, little privacy, strong networks of daily sociability—and from common religious beliefs (neighborhood associations in predominantly Catholic communities developed out of parish social groups) (Sugrue 1996: 212–13).

As judicial challenges to restrictive covenants and other exclusionary practices multiplied, homeowners turned to collective organization and the creation of coalitions to expand their influence in city politics (Sugrue 1996: 220–21). Bipartisan federated organizations of white homeowners exerted considerable influence over city officials and political leaders (Abrams 1955: 183). These groups sought to patrol the selling of properties to African Americans and to influence the real estate market in order to discourage blacks from moving into white neighborhoods. One way to do so was to inflate house values. Also, they lobbied intensely for zoning restrictions and for public investments in their communities to raise property values beyond the means of potential black buyers. Associations often raised money to buy any property (such as a vacant home) considered to be appealing to African Americans (Massey and Denton 1993: 36).

Some groups developed extralegal tactics to fight the legal attacks on restrictive covenants—they distributed, for instance, "mutual reciprocal agreements" among homeowners that avoided any reference to exclusion based on race, but in actuality precluded the selling of houses to blacks. For example, some associations required their members to "sign a contract promising to sell their houses only through approved real estate brokers and to offer the association the right to match the offer of any prospective buyer" (Sugrue 1996: 222). Other groups harassed or boycotted brokers who sold properties to blacks—and sometimes resorted to vandalism against blacks who dared to cross the racial divide (Massey and Denton 1993: 36; Sugrue 1996: 221, 226, 229). In 1963 the homeowners' movement in Detroit launched a proposal to create a "Homeowners' Rights Ordinance" that would allow whites to prevent racial integration in their communities. The proposed ordinance was framed as a statement on rights guaranteeing freedom to choose one's social life and surroundings as well as the right to be free from government interference in one's privacy and the use of one's property. A year later the ordinance was approved by 55 percent of the voters, but soon after it was declared unconstitutional and thus never enforced (Sugrue 1996: 226–27).

Embracing their "whiteness" and their "rights" as citizens, these Detroit activists worked to prevent the incorporation of blacks into their communities. Their wealth of social capital was key to their becoming a major force in Detroit politics. They helped split the Democratic Party and managed to get segregationist Republicans elected time and again (Gerstle 1995: 582). Through civic engagement, alienated white home-owners exerted a powerful influence over mayoral elections in Detroit. They also targeted "adversary" city government agencies with great success. One example was the neighborhood associations' highly effective campaign against the city's race relations agency, the Detroit Mayor's Interracial Committee (MIC), which was engaged in an active defense of the rights of African Americans in Detroit (Sugrue 1995: 569, 573–74; 1996: 191, 224–25; see Abrams 1955: 96, 99).[49]

With the support of Mayor Albert Cobo (elected in 1949), the home-owners' movement obtained key positions in Detroit's housing, urban development, and race relations commissions. This close cooperation with city authorities set up the conditions for a fierce battle within civil society. The homeowners' associations identified civil rights organizations, liberal religious organizations, and prointegration government officials as their enemies. White homeowners rejected integration as a project of particular interest groups, claiming that it eroded their rights as homeowners and thus democratic standards (Sugrue 1996: 222, 224, 226; see Abrams 1955: 97). Interestingly, this perception paralleled the view held by rural middle-class and urban working-class sectors in the South, who saw themselves as the major victims of the northern liberals' agenda of social engineering.

## Stratified Societies

The problem of black segregation falls within the larger question of social stratification. In Detroit and other cities, black communities suffered from economic, political, and social inequality.[50] Residential segregation was a major element of this bleak picture of exclusion. The impact of segregation on the well-being of African Americans was thus a function of structural conditions. In the specific case of housing, residential mobility for blacks was restricted by systemic obstacles, including discrimination in the apportionment of home loans and discriminatory practices by government agencies such as the FHA and by the real estate business.[51] Residential segregation sustained other processes of racial discrimination that affected the workplace, the interaction of blacks with government authorities, their power as consumers, and so on. This form of segregation was crucial in supporting a consistent system of subordination based on race.

This system limited the ability of the black population to navigate social structures both through the state and in society. For example, even if African Americans could overcome the FHA discriminatory practices and obtain a home loan package, real estate agents would not sell them houses outside "black" areas; and even if they succeeded in moving into a white neighborhood, they would be received with harassment, intimidation, and violence by their white "neighbors." The series of obstacles black citizens had to face were a structural feature of the U.S. context (Massey and Denton 1993: 2, 8–11, 49–51; Gotham 2000: 300–307).

In Detroit, changes in economic structures (e.g., plant automation and deindustrialization), government policies (e.g., federal and local housing policies), and patterns of social exclusion (e.g., multilayered forms of racial discrimination that influenced the workplace, residential opportunities, and so on) yielded winners and losers (Sugrue 1996: 3, 5–9, 122–23). These structural factors had a disproportionately negative effect on blacks, restricting their rights in various ways (Massey and Denton 1993: 69). In housing, for example, controlling for education and occupational status, African Americans could purchase "fewer goods distributed through housing markets with their income than other groups" (Rosenblum 1998: 147).

The importance of social stratification as a structural framework illuminates the relationship between social inequality and social capital. Generalized trust and reciprocity across cleavages are not likely to emerge in a society ripped by conflicts of class or race (Wilson 2001: 226). Most important, social capital is not merely the aggregate of individual choices—the decision to cooperate with others—but the outcome of a complex interaction between structure and agency. In this respect, the cases discussed in this chapter present interesting similarities. In both Germany and the United States, civil society reflected ongoing conflicts between social groups—these struggles were played out in neighborhoods, streets, clubhouses, and other terrains. These examples show that citizenship does not emerge only through confrontations between organized citizens and the state, but also through contention within civil society. This contention, however, may take unusual forms, as the next section explains.

## The "Right" to Segregation

The civic engagement of Detroit white homeowners shows that civic engagement inimical to democratic norms is not necessarily expressed in terms of hate. White homeowners' associations in Detroit viewed their purpose as consistent with the values and practices of democracy. These civic activists saw themselves as defending an inclusive model of participatory democracy. The protection of one's home (the most important investment for the working and middle classes), the defense of neighborhood and family from crime and the social threats perceived to be associated with a black invasion (often expressed as sexual fears), and the emphasis on rights and responsibilities associated with home-ownership were, for white activists, goals clearly aligned with democratic participation. For these activists, whiteness, citizenship, and patriotism were interrelated values (Sugrue 1996: 211–12, 216–17; Hirsch 1983: 196; McMillen 1994: 185–86).

Other confrontations over civil rights in the United States displayed similar characteristics. For instance, white resistance to busing in the 1970s—which united concerned parents to defend their "alienated rights"—blossomed in Boston and other cities. Antibusing sentiment permeated most realms of white civic life—from bumper stickers to massive petitions to local newspapers (Weisbrot 1990: 288–91). For many white citizens, defending their neighborhoods and schools was a way of protecting their communities, their country, and their freedom. For them, this type of civic engagement was a civic duty. As an activist in Charlotte, North Carolina, put it: "I served in Korea, I served in Vietnam, and I'll serve in Charlotte if I need to" (p. 289).[52] These participants saw themselves as fulfilling the democratic responsibility of protecting their rights as citizens.

To the anti-integration activists, homeownership was intertwined with the notion of entitlement (Arnesen 1998: 46). Homeowners shared a common identity; homeownership was the "glue" that brought together whites across ethnic and class cleavages. Their mentality as a group triggered both a sense of "inclusiveness" (originating in ownership) and racial fears. For them, a home was more than just an investment: it was "the repository of family values and the center of community life" (Sugrue 1996: 213). A well-kept home and lawn represented not only a sound investment—the value of a house depended on others in the neighborhood—but also signified membership in the middle class (Rosenblum 1998: 119).[53]

One of the most interesting dimensions of Detroit's homeowners' movement was the discourse employed by these participants. This was a discourse centered on rights, linking homeownership to citizenship. While affirming their rights, white activists emphasized the perceived unfairness of state-enforced integration: they viewed themselves as good citizens (patriotic, anticommunist, hard-working Americans) who were victims of black activists and a social engineering project promoted by white elites at the commanding heights of the state. The discourse of neighborhood associations bound notions of rights, citizenship, and patriotism together into an effective rhetoric of demand-making. Interestingly, voicing demands in the language of rights was part of a broader process of empowerment of social actors initiated by postwar New Deal policies. While blacks demanded equal access to employment and housing as a right of citizenship, whites organized to defend their right to live in segregated communities. The notion of homeowners' rights was based on the assumption that citizens had been promised "racial homogeneity" by the government. As a "government-sanctioned" right, the abandonment of segregation represented a broken promise. Trust between represented and representatives was eroded, and therefore civic mobilization became a major, alternative way for white homeowners to defend their rights (Sugrue 1995: 564–66, 568; 1996: 10, 218–19, 225–26).

As already mentioned, neighborhood associations were endowed with high levels of social capital, which was the result of a reserve of social trust—a particularized form of trust—developed over time in these communities. These cases reveal that the production of social capital was not connected to democratic objectives. This is a fundamental revision of accepted views on the positive relationship between social capital and democratic outcomes. Indeed, as these cases have shown, social capital can serve as a lubricant for the transmission of antisystem ideas, as in Weimar Germany, or it may provide cohesion for collective action to prevent the expansion of rights for other social groups, as in the United States.

## Chicago and Los Angeles

The undemocratic associational activity that characterized Detroit in the postwar years existed in other areas of the urban North too. In Chicago, groups of white homeowners mobilized, sometimes violently, against the establishment of African-American families in their neighborhoods—as in Chicago's Trumbull Park in the early 1950s. Emphasizing their rights to "racial homogeneity," antidesegregation activists in Chicago's ethnic neighborhoods organized to preserve the "whiteness" of their communities—"White People Must Control Their Own

Communities" was a popular slogan among these groups (Abrams 1955: 182, 184; Hirsch 1995: 548). Supported by homeowners and local businesses, groups such as Chicago's Southtown Planning Association urged whites to "Choose Your Neighbor" (Abrams 1955: 188).[54]

The Supreme Court's 1948 ruling was followed by a wave of associational activity in Chicago, where resistance to public housing became a unifying force among white homeowners. Residents' associations, community newspapers, and other local institutions converged around the antidesegregation effort. They sought the support of government officials, the police, churches, and other local civic organizations (Abrams 1955: 185–88). As in Detroit, associations lobbied for zoning ordinances that would contain no direct reference to race, but that nevertheless would exclude blacks from white neighborhoods. Whites mobilized to defend not only the value of their homes but also community life. The residents of Trumbull Park, as the *South Deering Bulletin* put it at the time, were fighting for the defense of the neighborhood's "property values, its morals, its children's future, . . . [and] the future of the older set who . . . cannot run away to a new neighborhood and start all over again" (as quoted in Hirsch 1983: 194). According to a 1955 study,

The migration of minorities prompted many of these organizations to mobilize against possible intruders or to oust minorities who have already settled. Meetings are now called by them to arouse owners to the "perils of invasion," urge them not to sell or rent to minorities, exert moral pressures and sanctions against owners who have done so, and often engage in intimidation and violence. They are also an important factor in the discouragement of builders from venturing into minority housing. (Abrams 1955: 181–82)

As in Detroit, whites' reaction against integration was primarily nourished by fear of the breakdown of their communities. If the introduction of blacks into white neighborhoods entailed the disintegration of traditional communities and loss of property values, then whites would be forced to move to the suburbs, which many of them (particularly immigrants) viewed as a threat to their livelihood and social life. "Communities like South Deering displayed close ties between residence and jobs, and the loss of the former, many steelworkers believed, meant the loss of the latter," Arnold Hirsch (1983) explained. "And the dispersal of the traditional neighborhood threatened extended kinship networks (especially the links between aging parents and their children) and provided the prospect of 'isolation, loneliness, and insecurity'" (p. 196). As perceived by white homeowners, the level of the threat posed by African Americans provided them with a strong motivation for organization.

Similar antiblack mobilization at the grassroots level emerged in Washington, D.C., Baltimore, Miami, Houston, San Francisco, and Los Angeles (Abrams 1955: 184–85). In Los Angeles, homeowners' associations acting as enforcers of deed restrictions (or restrictive covenants) and engines of "block restrictions" played a key role in insulating white middle classes from the threat of minority invasion, thus safeguarding social and racial uniformity in suburban areas. In southern California, this process started during World War I and acquired greater relevance in the 1920s when homeowners' associations channeled white activism against attempts by African Americans to purchase homes in white neighborhoods. In the 1920s, the combination of deed restrictions and block restrictions secured for whites 95 percent of Los Angeles's available housing. During World War II, pressures for access to housing outside of the Los Angeles ghetto intensified as black workers moved to the area. As in Detroit and Chicago, black access to white neighborhoods was strongly contested by homeowners' associations (Davis 1990: 161–63).

From the 1920s to the 1960s, homeowners' associations in southern California were mostly concerned with the establishment of residential communities of single-family homes characterized by racial and economic homogeneity. Beginning in the mid-1950s, their attention centered on the protection of suburban neighborhoods as enclaves protected not only from industrial, apartment, and office buildings, but also from minorities. These homeowners' groups did not resort to a racist discourse; instead they employed a discourse of "urban environmentalism" to defend their communities. White homeowners organized and mobilized to defend their property as well as "a way of life," and in doing so they were struggling to limit the expansion of rights for blacks (Davis 1990: 169–70).

Along with industrial lobbies and public sector labor unions, associations of middle- and upper-class white homeowners supported the process of municipal incorporation and fiscal zoning.[55] The wealthy were able to make demands more effectively than other groups because, among other reasons, they succeeded in creating powerful homeowners' associations that arranged the incorporation of their communities. Economic and political resources mattered because most incorporations were based on "the existence of a sharp gradient of home values between the inclusive community and the area intended for exclusion" (Davis 1990: 166–67). The result of this massive organizational movement was a broadening of the race and class disparities in the Los Angeles area—expressed, for example, in residential segregation and housing shortages for minorities.

Effectively organized, middle- and upper-class homeowners obtained the right to incorporate their suburban communities with zoning authority and control over the use of land without the load of public expenses commensurate with those of older urban areas. This meant that communities of well-off citizens were allowed to get their public services at prices below the standard cost. Thus all taxpayers in a given county would indirectly subsidize all vital services for middle- and upper-class communities. These neighborhoods also utilized zoning as an exclusionary mechanism to limit the entrance of minorities. This type of incorporation had a negative impact on the tax resources of Los Angeles. As a result, it triggered intense conflicts between well-off homeowners in the suburbs and a rising underprivileged population in the inner city which relied on public services (Davis 1990: 165–67, 169; Rosenblum 1998: 141–42). As in other cities, civil society organizations of well-off homeowners became a fundamental vehicle for the promotion of their interests at the expense of those of less-privileged citizens without the resources, capacities, and above all, social capital, for effective organization.

## Gated Communities

Patterns of spatial differentiation and separation between social groups built in the urban environment constitute an important phenomenon in the United States and, increasingly, in other countries. Seeking to escape crime, social ills, and government inefficiency, millions of homeowners have opted to live in gated communities. This massive process of spatial reengineering, which has transformed major U.S. urban and suburban areas, has its roots in historical trends of racism and racial segregation (Low 2001: 46; Webster 2001). Gated communities are "residential areas with restricted access in which normally public spaces are privatized. They are security developments with designated perimeters, usually walls or fences, and controlled entrances that are intended to prevent penetration by nonresidents" (Blakely and Snyder 1997: 2). A brief look at gated communities in the United States shifts the emphasis to the cleavage of class.

Following their emergence in the 1960s and 1970s as residential alternatives for middle-class retirees, gated communities became increasingly popular, first among the wealthy and, since the end of the 1980s, among the middle class. Appealing to fears about street crime and other urban ills engulfing the city and older suburbs, gated communities became an attractive form of community for middle-class homeowners. Spatial separation also gained appeal among lower-income populations, who have increasingly turned to physical barriers to shut out crime and violence from their neighborhoods (Blakely and Snyder 1997: 102–5, 114–17).[56] Still, gated communities represent a middle- and upper-class phenomenon, even in California, which contains the highest number of gated communities (indeed, Los Angeles has one of the highest concentrations of gated communities in the country) (pp. 4–7). This phenomenon has steadily grown in the last two decades. According to the Census Bureau's 2001 American Housing Survey, approximately 6 percent of all U.S. households (more than 7 million) are in residential developments separated by walls, fences, and security mechanisms.

Gated communities are typically run by homeowners' associations, which help guarantee social uniformity as a way to protect residential values.[57] Increasingly, in California and other states, gated communities resort to "civic secession" from a city or county. This model, which allows the "winners" to separate themselves from the "losers," has a number of implications pertaining to social interaction, urban services, fiscal and environmental interests, crime control, and local governance. For instance, "the new jurisdictions can pass regulatory ordinances that restrict new entrants." They can also "direct publicly collected taxes to locally specific goals rather than allowing them to be used over a larger area" (Blakely and Snyder 1997: 25).

While this type of community may create strong networks of trust and reciprocity among members, they "impose a variety of harms on nonmembers, who are affected by exclusion, discrimination, and a disintegrating tax base" (Kennedy 1995: 793). Nonmembers not only lose access to public spaces, but they also "must forfeit their right to live in certain areas, their right to move about freely, their constitutional guarantees of equal protection and due process, and their right to a fair share of the public fisc" (p. 767).

Beyond the restrictions imposed on rights, some authors have argued that the growth of "walls, gates and guards produces a landscape that encodes class relations and residential ... segregation more permanently in the built environment" (Low 2001: 45). In this sense, gated communities generate new patterns of residential segregation and reinforce social exclusion and existing cleavages in society. The barriers imposed by these communities, which express socioeconomic inequalities and various forms of prejudice, are strengthened by "planning practices and policing, implemented by zoning laws and regulations, and subsidized by businesses and banks" (pp. 45–46, quotation on 47).

Gated communities and other residential enclaves (for example, in São Paulo, Brazil, where the rich live in "fortified" residential complexes close to the poor) shape the production and orientations of social capital. For example, the process of spatial segregation in urban and suburban areas has implications for social interaction: it promotes a "public sphere that accentuates class differences and strategies of separation" because it promises, for instance, "total security" for some (Caldeira 2000: 213, 215, 266). The presence of "monitored spaces for residence, consumption, leisure, and work" shapes public space, networks of trust, access to resources, and people's cognitive maps of everyday social relationships (pp. 213–14). It is difficult to imagine how social capital produced within these spaces—indeed, within walls—can be aggregated into broader networks of generalized trust and reciprocity. In many ways, intra-urban boundaries imposed by "fortified enclaves" and "golden ghettos" define a new type of border at the subnational level that sets winners and losers apart from each other (Holston and Appadurai 1999: 16; see Svampa 2001; Low 2003).

## Resistance to Busing in Boston

A brief look at antibusing organizing, with a focus on the city of Boston (where the movement was sustained and intense), completes the analysis of the U.S. case. This example, which returns to the racial divide and anti-integration efforts, offers another viewpoint to understand how defensive postures in civil society can lead to undemocratic dispositions (and sometimes even violence) among participants. The case of Boston highlights the importance of ethnic cleavages in society and their interaction with political decisions perceived as illegitimate by social groups. The cleavage between Irish Americans and the white Protestant majority in Massachusetts dominated the struggle against desegregation. Because of previous discrimination, Catholic Irish Americans in Boston had "a much higher level of resentment against the elite power structure, and school desegregation was regarded as an assault by this power structure" (Taylor 1998: 6). Like other grassroots movements of the 1970s, the antibusing movement reflected "rampant citizen alienation from impersonal government, drawing on an in-grained, deeply felt sense of injustice, unfairness, and deprivation of rights" (Formisano 1991: 3).

There was a measurable rift between the Irish-American politicians who dominated the city of Boston and the white Protestant politicians who dominated the judicial power structure of the state. Irish-American neighborhoods in particular resented the order for integrated bus-ing and saw the action as interference by elites (Taylor 1998: 167–69). The perception among anti-integration Irish activists was that their rights were being violated "by a hostile power structure that was try-ing to victimize the Irish community by imposing unwanted reforms" (p. 168). Feeling discriminated against, they resented the liberal re-formers who, in their view, sought to burden the Irish-Catholic com-munity with the costs of redressing what these outsiders perceived as social ills and imbalances (p. 169). Indeed, working-class groups, Irish Americans in particular, who rebelled against the integration plan im-posed by the federal courts, resented not so much the black commu-nity, whom they saw as mere pawns in this power struggle, but the outsider political establishment that sought to impose social dictates upon them (pp. 206–7).

Thus, antibusing resistance was, to a large extent, fueled by the per-ception of ethnic groups that they were being forced by out-of-touch suburbanite politicians and judges to take part in a social experiment whose effects the latter could comfortably escape (Taylor 1998: 67–83, 168–69). Residents saw in this kind of social restructuring an inappro-priate, unnecessary, and intrusive role for the government. Frustration with "the media, liberals, and the establishment connected also to a widespread distrust of politicians and alienation from politics," which supported confrontational, intolerant, and sometimes violent forms of organizing (Formisano 1991: 158). In fact, many leaders and activists of the antibusing movement did not see this issue as different from a num-ber of other "reforms" that white Protestants had tried to impose upon them before.[58] As noted, other groups opposed to school and residential desegregation in the United States had a similar reaction to externally promoted social engineering.

The ethnic enclave of South Boston (as well as Charlestown, East Boston, and the North End) provided working-class residents a "de-fended neighborhood," that is, a community in which "most inhabitants feel personally safe and interact with neighbors on a relatively intimate basis" (Buell 1982: 7). These tightly knit and highly homogeneous communities bred parochialism, particularistic trust and suspicion of outsiders, and strong resistance to change long before the federal courts decided to employ integrated busing as a way to attack discrimination in public schools (p. 55). Civil society activity was a fundamental vehicle for the intense defense mounted against unacceptable change.

The core of the antibusing movement was South Boston, where the city's most effective antibusing group originated. Restore Our Alienated Rights (ROAR) was established in 1974 in response to the federal court ruling that ordered mandatory busing. The group organized to resist the judicial decision and quickly began efforts to get it overturned. ROAR staged a number of successful boycotts (especially in South Boston, Hyde Park, and East Boston) in response to what they regarded as "judicial tyranny" (Formisano 1991: 75; Taylor 1998: 85–88). ROAR and similar groups used tactics ranging from civil disobedience to violence. For the most part, they held marches, rallies, boycotts, sit-ins, sleep-ins, motorcades, and demonstrations. Some radical splinter groups resorted to violence (e.g., destruction of public and private property and various forms of harassment) to promote the antibusing cause (Formisano 1991: 143). At the same time, the group provided members "a sense of community, with meetings bubbling with conviviality, singing, and socializing" (pp. 158–59). Existing organizations, such as labor unions, supported ROAR and other groups in the antibusing resistance. Initially, ROAR functioned as a bridge uniting Italians and Irish Americans, but ultimately rifts developed as a result of leadership struggles and a highly confrontational style, among other factors (pp. 83–84, 160).

In brief, the antibusing movement shows that underlying racial and ethnic tensions—part of the societal context—galvanized average citizens over shared opposition agendas. However, when seen in tandem with the previous analysis, it becomes clear that virulent racism was not always the driving force behind the dark side of civil society. Ethnic cleavages within the white community and other factors that defined a "defensive" posture among activists (such as the desire to safeguard their neighborhoods from outside influence) also shaped civil society activity in cities such as Boston.

The defensive actions against school busing also show how identity influences the character of associational life. In Boston, for example, working-class Irish Americans identified themselves as a minority group rather than as part of the white majority (Buell 1982: 54–56). The perception of this separate identity is well illustrated in the intense struggle over South Boston High. Despite its rundown structures and poorly equipped classrooms, the school was valued by its working-class residents. For them, "the high school functioned as a socializing experience, reinforcing neighborhood values and identity" (Formisano 1991: 115). The fierce struggle over busing at this school went beyond racial separation: neighbors organized to defend their own enclave from outside interference. Boston public schools (or an expensive private school) were the only option for those who could not afford to flee to the suburbs (Buell 1982: 152–54)

The Boston press (e.g., the *Boston Globe*) called attention to the activities of the antibusing movement, conveying "an inflated view of the costs of desegregation"—for example, by covering violent incidents in particular—and thus influencing the public against integration (Taylor 1998: 84–85). According to observers at the time, the national media, in turn, painted the antibusing mobilization in general and Manichean terms, without attention to the real motivations of protesters, their background, and the actual characteristics of their communities (pp. 83–85).

## Conclusion

Undemocratic civic engagement can take different forms. In this chapter I have analyzed patterns of associational activity whose effect was inimical to democracy by looking at the intersections between social cleavages, political conditions, and their link to civic engagement. Events in Weimar Germany challenge the assumption that civil society necessarily leads to democracy. As Max Weber argued in the late nineteenth century: "The quantitative spread of organizational life does not always go hand in hand with its qualitative significance" (quoted in Koshar 1986a: 4). Active involvement in social clubs and other voluntary associations, work-based networks, religious organizations, and informal social connections may be linked to the production of social capital, but there is nothing inherent in these dimensions of civic engagement that connects them to democratic outcomes. In the Weimar Republic, Nazi voters and supporters (outside of the party's activist core) were not ideological zealots. The growth of the Nazi project was facilitated, using Putnam's (2000) terminology, by both *machers* and *schmoozers* (pp. 93–95). "In Yiddish," Putnam explains, "men and women who invest lots of time in formal organizations are often termed *machers*—that is, people who make things happen in the community. By contrast, those who spend many hours in informal conversation and communion are termed *schmoozers*" (p. 93). Weimar citizens organized at an unprecedented rate, leadership skills became available to wider sectors of the public, and membership in voluntary organizations increased dramatically, but German *machers* and *schmoozers* conveyed antipolitical beliefs and antidemocratic ideas (see Koshar 1986a: 161, 276). German civic activists built networks of reciprocity and sociability, but these networks did not produce democratic results.

The analysis of civic engagement requires that we understand not only political processes at the level of the state, but also social processes pertaining to the unmaking (and remaking) of collective identities and social boundaries (across class and other social cleavages) (Koshar 1986a: 282). Berman (1997b), for example, has argued that one "factor to examine in determining when civil society activity will bolster or weaken a democratic regime . . . is the political context within which that activity unfolds" (p. 567). Emphasizing the importance of strong political institutions for successful governance, Berman focused on institutional variables in her assessment of the impact of context on civil society activity. However, the political sphere (e.g., political institutionalization) does not account for the interaction between conflicts in society and the characteristics of the political regime, which in turn influences patterns of civic engagement. As the case of Germany illustrates, the intersections of class, gender, ethnicity, religion, and age—analyzed in light of the broader political context—are critical to understanding participation in civil society. This is a case in which civil society contributed to corroding democracy to the point of its breakdown in a context of fragile political institutionalization, heightened social polarization, and severe economic dislocations. By contributing to (rather than breaking) a "vicious circle," civil society offered a venue for disaffected citizens and this participation in turn deepened their dissatisfaction with political institutions, hardened their grievances, and made them more willing to support antisystem solutions.

The conflict over desegregation in the United States illustrates how, under certain circumstances, organized citizens opposed efforts by other sectors of civil society and segments of the state to democratize society and expand citizenship rights for excluded populations. While the civil rights movement pressed for democratization, organized white resistance attempted to maintain the status quo and impede changes in race relations.[59] The movement of resistance to desegregation shows that conflicts over the democratization of social relations are often waged in civil society. In sum, this is a case of a sector of civil society undercutting the democratic character of a liberal state.

Resistance to racial equality movements defended a system that per-petuated inequality. Specifically, the promotion of racism is not just a matter of hatred, but "rather the defense of a system from which ad-vantage is derived on the basis of race" (Wellman 1993: 210, cited in Nelson 1996: 358). In this respect, when social capital is produced in op-position to a redistribution of power in society, then such capital and the civic networks creating it are likely to maintain—and possibly in-tensify—social disparities.

Studies of civil society have paid little attention to the exclusionary dispositions of groups and communities in general (Sugrue 1998: 61). As explained, sometimes the expansion of rights for marginalized sec-tors is perceived by other groups as an infringement upon their rights. Examples of this type of counterdemocratic civic engagement were not restricted to the U.S. South, as most accounts of the myth of post–World War II "liberal consensus" have argued (Gerstle 1995: 579). Northern grassroots activity against desegregation demonstrates that the Citi-zens' Councils in the South cannot be considered an "anomaly." As in Detroit and Boston, the creation of community often involved the erec-tion of territorial, economic, or political borders aimed at insulating so-cial sectors perceived as a threat to dominant collective identities. The more recent gated communities are new forms in which these borders are built.

The political attitudes, votes, and organized actions of antidesegre-gation white groups in the urban North restricted the process of demo-cratic change in the 1950s, opposed the civil rights movement, and lim-ited the expansion of citizenship rights to blacks. In Detroit, the networks of working- and middle-class whites, which mobilized to pre-vent African Americans from moving into their communities, devel-oped into one of the most powerful civic movements in the history of that city (Sugrue 1995: 551, 557–58). The risk of diminished home val-ues as a result of changes in a neighborhood's racial composition gave them a strong motivation to mobilize. Employing a seemingly "demo-cratic" repertoire of activities, organizational models, and discourse, these civic activists defended what they considered the "right" of whites to live in segregated neighborhoods. In southern California, homeowners' associations fostered the rise of suburban communities marked by racial and class exclusionism. Affluent homeowners organized to defend their privileges under the banner of "home values and neighbor exclusivity." Suburban incorporation as a form of "separatism" benefited privileged groups (e.g., by lowering their public expenditures) at the expense of less-affluent minorities and entailed the creation of communities empowered to make authoritative decisions over zoning and the use of land (Davis 1990: 153, 158–59, 164–66). As noted in the discussion of gated communities, this form of organization can deepen social fragmentation and even inflict damage on nonmembers, ranging from discrimination to a deteriorating tax base.

Confrontations in civil society do not only entail clashes between cohesive groups. The interaction of gender and ethnicity / religion in the German women's movement before Nazi totalitarianism illustrates how social cleavages triggered divisions and conflicts within civil society, leading to dramatic shifts in the allegiance of different social groups. In the United States rifts, tensions, and competing interests split blacks, as race intersected with class or occupational divisions. In Detroit, class cleavages within the black community helped perpetuate inequality patterns. While civic organizations such as the NAACP and the Urban League challenged the government, industries, and labor unions over workplace and housing equality issues, many well-off African Americans actively opposed, along with white homeowners, public housing projects, and when possible they moved to peripheral areas to escape all-black neighborhoods (Sugrue 1996: 12; 1998: 61). Thus, while race solidarity sustained collective action for civil rights, common class interests across racial divisions served as a basis for organization oriented toward the social exclusion of underprivileged blacks. As noted earlier, the perception of African-American homeowners with respect to underprivileged groups (the poor blacks included) is another aspect that illuminates the problem of cleavages, identity formation, and their interaction with association.

White reaction to integration varied across ethnic / religious divides.[60] Detroit's Jewish neighborhoods responded to changes in racial composition in a different way than Catholics did. Jewish residents, though still espousing racial prejudices, showed a relatively flexible attitude regarding blacks as neighbors. A combination of factors accounted for the different reactions of largely Jewish neighborhoods and their Catholic counterparts—a higher rate of renters, a lower level of

geographic attachment to Jewish institutions, and a commonly supportive attitude toward civil rights (Sugrue 1996: 242–45). Though we
can only hypothesize on this matter, the Jews' own experience of discrimination did not result in higher levels of resistance to integration
with blacks, in contrast to the case of Irish American neighborhoods in
Boston. It is possible that Jewish neighborhoods, with a lower rate of
homeownership and less territorial attachment to centers of community life, did not fear that racial integration could translate into a dramatic change in their lives, personally or financially (p. 244).

The case studies presented here reveal two analytical truths. First,
the case of Weimar Germany shows that the civil society–democracy
connection must be considered in concert with the mechanisms associated with civic engagement. Critics of the neo-Tocquevillean perspective have emphasized that this approach does not explain what mechanisms link the production of social capital to democratic outcomes. But
as the case-study literature on Weimar has revealed, the Nazi project
was transmitted mainly through networks of trust embedded in formal
and informal interactions at the local level (Koshar 1986b: 29). Cross-af-
filiations linked the NSDAP to civic groups and helped in the diffusion
of the Nazi project by providing direct inroads into local social life.[61]

The swift growth of the Nazis' popularity was largely explained by
the role that grassroots networks played in the dissemination of National Socialist ideas. Indeed, "word of mouth propaganda" was much
more important than any partisan campaign because it was carried by
individuals who could be trusted, and it took place in ordinary, famil-
iar places such as home, the workplace, and the local tavern. Trusted
doctors, neighbors, and fellow club members presented the Nazi project as a suitable political alternative to the traditional parties of the
bourgeoisie, fierce interest-group competition, and unpatriotic politics
(Koshar 1986a: 284). In the United States, the efforts to organize council
chapters in opposition to civil rights rulings were abetted by the social
connections of average civic activists: Rotarians, Civitans, and Kiwani-
ans, among others (Bartley 1995: 201). The Citizens' Councils also made
effective use of informal social networks to mobilize members and resources.

Although people's social networks transmit attitudes and behaviors
across society, these mechanisms do not guarantee democratic results;
in fact, they produce different results in different settings.[62] As Rosenblum (1998) has argued, the orientations of civil society cannot be predicted on the basis of associational features such as decision-making
structures (pp. 155–56). An exclusive focus on associational life does

not allow one to determine which direction the dispositions nurtured in civil society will take.

Second, civil society plays an important role in the confrontation between winners and losers, as illustrated by the dispute between blacks, who demanded more rights, and white homeowners, who fought to preserve their hard-won position in the urban environment. If we do not take these inequalities into consideration—and just examine the link between civil society and democracy without attention to context—then crucial cases such as the vast white grassroots mobilization against racial integration in the United States are pushed to the margins as mere outliers. More broadly, we cannot disregard institutional and economic conditions, government policies, and embedded social and cultural dynamics in the analysis of organizational patterns and their objectives. As the example of antibusing resistance illustrates, short-term defensive actions against policies may respond to long-term patterns of discrimination against certain communities (such as Boston's Irish-Catholic population) and not, primarily, to virulent or violent racism against African Americans. The examples provided here make the case for this contextually embedded analysis of civil society activity. More research will allow us to understand other nuances of this complex question.

The process of defending and expanding rights implies conflict, and thus civil society emerges as a pivotal field in the struggle to define citizenship rights and political agendas. As the case of the neighborhood movements in the United States has illustrated, civil society groups may generate a discourse on the notion of rights, but it may be inherently antipluralistic and intolerant. Indeed, organized average citizens can perceive that "civil rights for blacks were won only at the expense of white rights" (Sugrue 1995: 567; 1998: 61). Thus, rather than looking at civil society as a pristine reservoir of democracy, we should look at it as a realm where major conflicts over the definition and meaning of civil, social, and political rights are played out—sometimes with an active presence of the state and other times at the periphery of institutionalized politics.

There are, of course, other wrinkles in this analysis. The next two chapters address some of them by examining a third-wave democracy, Argentina. Employing a multimethod approach that seeks to capture the diversity of associational life, I explore whether and how civil society influences democracy in a context also found in many other new democracies around the world. As I will show, the findings are intriguing.

CHAPTER 3

# Association and Context in
# a Third-wave Democracy

ARGENTINA was among the first in Latin America to make the transition to democracy as part of the "third wave" of democratization that began in southern Europe in the mid-1970s and then expanded throughout the world. The demonstration effects of Argentina's democracy, particularly in the context of the global changes triggered by the third wave, have had a special impact in the Latin American context. As of this writing in 2003—when Argentina is struggling with the impact of an unprecedented socioeconomic and political crisis—the country has revealed the various dangers and problems that arise throughout transition and post-transition processes.[1] In this respect, Argentina continues to be an important test case for examining the nuances of "making democracy work." A study of civil society and its relationship with democracy in this country provides lessons that can be applied to other Latin American nations and to third-wave democracies in other regions as well.

This chapter first describes recent contextual trends and patterns in Argentina so as to provide some empirical background for the case analysis in Chapter 4. Then it outlines a map of civil society and identifies the organizations included in my ethnographic study and some relevant methodological aspects of the fieldwork. Chapter 4 introduces the questions, hypotheses, and conceptual categories that guide the empirical analysis (which employs data drawn from ethnographic field research, public opinion polls, congressional activity, and other sources) and presents my findings regarding the relationship between civil society activity and democratization.

Broadly, the data show that civic engagement in Argentina simultaneously facilitates and hinders democratization. When the effect of civic engagement is assessed at different levels—for example, individual and institutional—one can see that the contribution of civil society to democratic politics and practices amid a weak rule of law and increasing levels of social stratification is paradoxical at best. The role of civic engagement in the development of democratic dispositions and individual capacities is not as positive and universal as neo-Tocquevilleans have argued. Moreover, the potential of civil society to support the equal defense of interests in the public realm and individual rights guarantees is seriously constrained when access to justice is limited and when there are high levels of violence, widespread corruption, and a vast gap between the letter of the law and its implementation.

## Recent Trends

This section briefly discusses four topics that provide a background for my discussion of association and context in democratic Argentina: first, the social movement that resisted the military regime's human rights violations and then demanded truth and justice for those crimes; second, the underlying authoritarianism in some sectors of Argentine society, particularly during the last period of authoritarian rule; third, economic inequality and the growing gap between rich and poor, as well as the decline of the middle class; finally, the rising crime rates and the government's response to this pressing issue. I then examine the varying effectiveness of the rule of law at the state level, in state-society relations, and in interactions within society.

### The Human Rights Movement

The explosion of social movements during the demise of authoritarianism and the transition to democracy in Latin America received vast attention from students of the region, who viewed these movements as evidence of the critical role of popular organizational activity in processes of democratization. As Latin American countries went through democratic transitions in the 1980s, contentious actions emerged in the region, generated not only by traditional labor unions, but also by new movements of women, peasants, relatives and victims of state repression, squatters, gays and lesbians, environmentally concerned citizens, and so on. The region developed, in the eyes of many observers, a "movement society" populated by highly mobilized social actors committed to political and social transformation. By most accounts, the sphere of social movements became a central arena of civil society.

The interplay between society and state changed dramatically in the new democratic setting. The weakening and collapse of authoritarian regimes brought freedoms that stimulated popular mobilization, but some of the conditions that had facilitated mobilization—such as the social cooperation that resulted from a struggle against a common adversary (the authoritarian state), the space for competing ideologies in coalitions opposed to the regime, and the effectiveness of expressive actions that appealed to moralistic and universal notions (such as human rights)—changed substantially under the new political structures. Social actors needed to find new motivations, contenders, repertoires, and audiences to advance their interests and demands (Roberts 1997: 140; Brysk 1994: 156–57, 164; Krygier 1997: 75–76).

As Alison Brysk (1994) found in the case of Argentina's human rights movement (which emerged in response to the repression launched by the military dictatorship of 1976–83), the effectiveness of this social movement was sometimes greater during the transition than during the everyday interaction with political institutions after the transition was completed. Indeed, as she noted, this social movement, like others in Eastern Europe, found it hard to move from opposition against authoritarianism to participation in democratic politics. Even though the human rights movement in Argentina successfully disseminated a discourse of human rights in the public sphere, it was unable to prompt institutional changes that would have transformed the organization of state power in Argentina (Brysk 1994: 21, 108, 136).[2]

Indeed, a nondemocratic regime establishes conditions that will not be replicated in a democratic system. It has been argued that changes at the level of the regime affect the nature of civic engagement. For instance, when confronting a totalitarian state, as happened in Poland during the development and zenith of Solidarity, coordinated group action in civil society was facilitated by a well-defined enemy: the state. Once the communist system collapsed, the character of civil society changed. The social coordination facilitated by a single, common enemy dissipated, as did the capacity of the movement to include a multiplicity of ideologies without undermining its organizational strength. Indeed, competing ideologies can become incompatible when the opponent is not so clearly defined (Krygier 1997: 75–76, 78). Once a transition to democracy is completed, the nature of civic participation often changes substantially because antistate strategies tend to lose their effectiveness and civic coalitions often break up (Brysk 1994: 22, 90, 160). Under some conditions, civil society—acting as a "counterweight" to a democratic state—may grow increasingly hostile to state forces, thus becoming a "burden" to democratic governance (Foley and Edwards 1996: 39; Krygier 1997: 81).

What happened to Argentina's human rights movement from the mid-1980s to the end of the 1990s? First, public attention shifted to other issues, mainly the serious economic crisis of the late 1980s. Also, the public was wary of taking too much power away from the security forces amid sociopolitical uncertainty. Second, the human rights movement was weakened by some of its initial strengths: a strong and resolute leadership, a focus on non-negotiable demands, and an emphasis on symbolic strategies of protest. Later, these same features limited the movement's capacity to establish cross-sectoral alliances and to bargain with democratic state institutions. The ability of human rights organizations to maintain, strengthen, and expand horizontal links in civil society was made more difficult by the fragmentation of Argentine society, which resulted from long-term social and political cleavages as well as from the legacy of fear and distrust generated by the traumatic experience of authoritarianism in the 1970s and early 1980s (Brysk 1994: 10–13, 19–22, 109, 124–25). Finally, finding effective ways to cooperate with the institutions and agencies of the democratic regime proved to be notably difficult for groups accustomed to a strategy of confrontation. These factors indicate the importance of studying the new human and civil rights groups in Argentina during the 1990s in the climate of a new democracy. I discuss these groups—and other manifestations of civil society—in the second half the chapter.

## Society and Authoritarianism

While Argentina produced a world-renowned human rights movement in the 1970s, there were many indications that large sectors of its society repeatedly accepted authoritarian solutions. As O'Donnell (1973) argued in his classic study of bureaucratic authoritarianism, key organized sectors of Argentine society supported the termination of democracy in the 1950s and 1960s (p. 153). For example, business organizations and other special interest groups welcomed the military coups that overthrew the civilian administrations of Perón, Frondizi, and Illía in 1955, 1962, and 1966, respectively. Survey data collected in Argentina in late 1965, a few months before the 1966 coup, showed that close to 40 percent of all interviewees agreed with the idea that "a few strong leaders would do more for this country than all the laws and talk" (Kirkpatrick 1971: 217, table 9.5). Support for the military as the only institution with the capacity to save the country from chaos was considerably stronger among the upper and middle classes (31.2 percent and 21.5 percent, respectively) than among the working class (9.1 percent) (Kirkpatrick 1971: 134, table 6.11). In fact, under conditions of political instability and increased mobilization of the popular sectors, important segments of the middle class aligned with the elites, encouraging a turn toward authoritarianism.

Several studies have acknowledged the contribution of segments of civil society to legitimate the military regime of 1976–83 (see, e.g., Romero 1994; Malamud-Goti 1996). The social control imposed by the military regime could not have been as pervasive or effective as it was without the collaboration of important sectors of society. "For such control to occur," O'Donnell (1999a) has argued, "there had to be a society that patrolled itself" (pp. 54–56, 59–60, quotation on 54). As some researchers have pointed out, a large portion of the citizenry gave their implicit or explicit support to the military regime's "antisubversive" campaign because they accepted the idea of order advanced by the armed forces (see Malamud-Goti 1996: 23).[3] Certainly some civic organizations courageously confronted the military government, but others supported the regime or defended it against external "distortions" of the country's image. An example of the latter posture was the campaign in domestic and foreign newspapers underwritten by more than three hundred civic associations representing Argentina's social, scientific, and business sectors in 1978. This campaign was launched against "those who attempt to distort the country's image from abroad" (as quoted in Bayer 2001, my translation). The signatories included the major umbrella organization of Jewish associations in Argentina (DAIA), the Argentine Catholic University, the Rotary Club, the Argentine Association of Magazine Publishers, the Argentine Cancer Society, and the German Club (Bayer 2001).[4] The public relations campaign responded to an advocacy effort by international human rights organizations and political exiles to denounce human rights violations in Argentina.

Following the dictatorship, most of public opinion focused on the military as the sole cause of Argentina's ills (Malamud-Goti 1996: 188).

Argentines "sought to convince themselves that the military dictator-ship and everything that went with it had been a phenomenon isolated from the *real country*; something comparable to the occupation of the national territory by foreign forces" (Neilson 1993, as quoted in Mala-mud-Goti 1996: 192). Without condoning the military's central respon-sibility in the horror experienced in Argentina in the second half of the 1970s, it is important to note that the proclivity to find single-factor ex-planations to national tragedies has been long present in Argentina's social and political discourse, regardless of its ideological bent (see Ar-mony 2001: 309–11).

## Economic Inequality

Besides dealing with the legacies of authoritarianism, Argentine society has been confronted with new sources of social tension since the return to democracy. Increased economic inequality, rising levels of crime, and abuse of power by government officials were among the predominant problems in the 1990s. In the last quarter of the twentieth century, the middle class in Argentina suffered a striking economic decline—as Fig-ure 3.1 shows. The middle class, which represented 65 percent of the population in the mid-1970s, shrank to 45 percent by the turn of the century—three out of every ten members of the middle class joined the ranks of the "new poor" in Argentina. As the middle class shrank, ab-solute class differences grew. The gap between rich and poor widened dramatically. While in the mid-1970s the richest 10 percent of the popu-lation received a share of the national income twelve times larger than that of the poorest 10 percent, by the beginning of the twenty-first cen-tury this figure had more than doubled.[5]

In the first half of the 1990s, Argentina experienced considerable eco-nomic growth while income distribution deteriorated. Even though poverty rates decreased from 40 percent in 1990 to a low of 22 percent in 1994, poverty increased after 1995 as gains went mainly to the more trained and educated workers. Simultaneously, unemployment in-creased, hitting the poor in particular, many of whom were underem-ployed or survived on temporary jobs (World Bank 2000b). Particularly important was the expansion of the informal sector, which grew steadily throughout the 1990s. While this is not a new phenomenon in most of Latin America, where the rate of informal self-employment has been growing since the 1950s, it does represent a new trend in Ar-gentina (which started in the early 1980s). Argentina's rate of informal

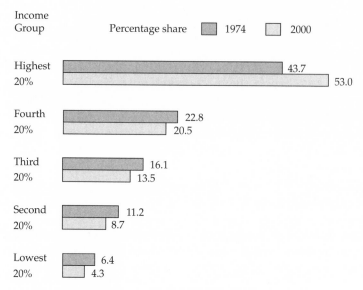

FIGURE 3.1    Distribution of Income in Argentina
SOURCE: Data from Equis in *Clarín.com*, available at http://
old.clarin.com/diario/2002/01/28/pag12.jpg.

self-employment increased steadily from 17.2 percent in 1990 to 33.5 percent in 1998 (see Table 3.1). That year, 42.3 percent of the economically active population was either unemployed or informally self-employed. This figure increases when we add to this rate the proportion of the economically active population that falls into the categories of underemployment, unemployment due to the discouraged worker effect, and government work programs (which provide an insufficient salary). Adding up these five categories shows that, as of 1998, 54.6 percent of the economically active population in Argentina was excluded from the modern sector of the economy (Carbonetto and Brites 2001: 157).

The reason for looking at the informal self-employed sector (instead of focusing on the unemployed only) is twofold: first, the informal sector indicator provides a much more accurate measure of the actual portion of the population that has been pushed to the margins of the economy (lack of access to credit, capital, or technology and low productivity), and second, a focus on the informal sector allows us to account for a dimension of social exclusion not easily seen through other types of evidence. Indeed, in addition to the economic and technological deficiencies associated with this sector, informal self-employ-

TABLE 3.1

Employment Trends in Urban Areas of Argentina, 1990–1998

|  | Economically Active Population (EAP) (thousands) | Employed EAP (thousands) | Rate of Unemploy- ment (%) | Rate of Informal Self- employment (% of employed EAP) | Unemployed and Informally Self- employed (% of EAP) |
|---|---|---|---|---|---|
| 1990 | 10,823 | 9,892 | 8.6 | 17.2 | 24.3 |
| 1991 | 11,138 | 10,370 | 6.9 | 17.0 | 22.7 |
| 1992 | 11,432 | 10,644 | 6.9 | 21.0 | 26.4 |
| 1993 | 12,144 | 10,941 | 9.9 | 23.0 | 30.6 |
| 1994 | 12,251 | 10,940 | 10.7 | 23.4 | 31.6 |
| 1995 | 12,996 | 10,579 | 18.6 | 28.5 | 41.8 |
| 1996 | 12,682 | 10,528 | 17.0 | 30.5 | 42.3 |
| 1997 | 13,265 | 11,129 | 16.1 | 31.0 | 42.1 |
| 1998 | 13,609 | 11,813 | 13.2 | 33.5 | 42.3 |

SOURCE: Carbonetto and Brites 2001: 168.

ment exposes individuals to noneconomic risks and uncertainties, which sustain a level of precariousness that threatens their autonomy and personal capacities. These risks and uncertainties include legal insecurity (persecution, confiscation, and payment of bribes to police officers, municipal officials, and other government agents), personal insecurity (no fringe benefits, vulnerability to the police or mafias), and exacerbated individualism and isolation (in general, absence of sustainable sectoral organization) (Carbonetto and Brites 2001: 173–75).

In Argentina, as in Germany and the United States, the economic context is important for understanding orientations in public opinion and practices in civil society. Even though income inequality and poverty increased throughout the 1990s, the halt of inflation, the initial investment boom, and the promise of a better future (reinforced by the international exaltation of the "Argentine miracle") kept much of the population guardedly supportive of the Menem administration's neoliberal policies, up until the recession hit particularly hard in the latter years of the decade. However, the progressive deterioration of the distributional gap, in combination with other factors, such as the weakening rule of law, reinforced tensions and conflict in society, which were translated to the realm of association (see Chapter 4).

It is necessary to emphasize, as I did in Chapter 1, the important role of other forms of inequality beyond economic disparities. These forms include discrimination, social exclusion, and the systematic humiliation of individuals by the state and powerful private actors. I explore some of these patterns of inequality in the discussion of the rule of law within society later in the chapter.

## Crime and Police Response

It is not surprising that, in a context of increasing inequality, social exclusion, and (as I show below) ineffective law enforcement, criminality has become a major problem in Argentina. Crime levels steadily increased in urban centers in the 1990s. For example, in the second half of the decade (from 1995 to 1999), the crime rate in the city of Buenos Aires increased by 65 percent. A study showed that, as of 1999, 40 percent of the residents in Buenos Aires province had been victims of crime—22 percent had been the victims of violent crimes (Tedesco 2000: 534; see *Economist* 1999: 33–34). A 1999 report from the Ministry of Justice's National Directorate for Criminal Policy stated that 82 percent of murders since 1996 had been committed by people without a previous criminal record. The percentage of murders involving people younger than 18 (as victimizers) increased from 2 percent in 1991 to 10 percent in 1996 (Tedesco 2000: 536). According to another source, in the period 1991–97, the rate of reported crimes (per 10,000 inhabitants) in greater Buenos Aires went from 78.2 to 156.5, a 100 percent increase (Palmieri, Filippini, and Thomas 2001: 7, citing Bulat and López 1999: 4).[6]

The rise in crime triggered promises of a "tough hand" by public officials. However, the actual capacity of the police to deal with mounting crime has been limited. Late 1990s data showed that merely one in four crimes (violent and nonviolent) reported to the police in the city of Buenos Aires was investigated, and only one in eight crimes was the focus of a police investigation in the province of Buenos Aires.[7] The police leadership—both federal and provincial—repeatedly expressed to the media that they preferred to kill criminals rather than try to arrest them. As the then-chief of the Buenos Aires Provincial Police said: "If there is a shootout as a result of a crime and the lives of citizens and policemen are at risk, I do not care at all if a criminal dies."[8] The message was that to kill a criminal was "positive" for society, particularly in light of the inefficiency of the justice system, which the general public viewed as partly responsible for the government's failure to control crime.

Police corruption and inefficiency received increasing media attention during the 1990s, triggering a debate about appropriate responses to rising crime levels. Experts on law enforcement argued that the police lacked the training, expertise, and information needed to generate an efficient response to crime. In fact, these experts maintained that police brutality did nothing to deter crime; it only made criminals more violent. In 1997 the government of the province of Buenos Aires started a program to reform the province's infamous police force in an attempt to make it more accountable and less violent and corrupt. However, the reform was soon crippled as the leadership of the province changed hands (Palmieri, Filippini, and Thomas 2001: 24–27). The new governor, Carlos Ruckauf from the Peronist Party (the same party that had started the reform), had expressed in his election campaign that "the thieves must be shot, fought against without mercy" (Tedesco 2000: 540, citing *Clarín*, August 4, 1999).

The crime crisis often nurtured public attitudes conducive to the acceptance of unlawful actions by state agencies for the maintenance of "law and order." In fact, many Argentines showed that, under conditions of insecurity (e.g., increasing crime), they were ready to tolerate the use of arbitrary violence by the state (public opinion surveys captured these attitudes; see below). For example, instead of demanding more efficient law enforcement, people were willing to support extralegal measures to fight crime. These measures provided reassurance in the face of widespread societal insecurity. According to one study, citizens in several provinces were even willing to elect former authoritarian leaders as majors, governors, and legislators if they promised, among other things, to curb crime and corruption (see Seligson 2001). As we shall see, increased acceptance of extralegal violence has detrimental effects on state-society relations and interactions within society.

## Variations in the Rule of Law

Even a cursory examination of institutional and societal patterns in Argentina indicates that the rule of law in this country was fragile during the 1990s and that inequality, social exclusion, and humiliation were part of everyday life for many Argentines. The discussion in this section is organized following the conceptual analysis presented in the second half of Chapter 1. As I argued there, the fluctuation in adherence to the rule of law can be found at different levels, namely, the state, in state-society relations, and in citizen-citizen interaction. The discussion is by no means exhaustive; it aims to give the reader a general sense of the Argentine context by employing illustrations that capture some aspects of the (un)rule of law in this setting.

## *The State Level: General Patterns*

Institutionally, Argentina's democracy has been characterized by low levels of transparency and accountability. Respect for the law has been low. Throughout the 1990s, the administration of Carlos Menem ruled without attention to constitutional and congressional limits, thus seriously weakening the rule of law. Menem's style of governance weakened the principle of constitutionalism by making an abusive exercise of the presidential decree, which, for example, conferred legislative powers to the president. Indeed, in only a few years (1989 to 1996) Menem issued thirteen times more decrees than his predecessors did in the previous 136 years (most of these decrees, particularly early on, addressed economic issues). Most of the president's decrees remained in effect, though only a small percentage were fully ratified by Congress, as the constitution mandates (Linz and Stepan 1996: 201; Ungar 2002: 147). In fact, while the executive power overstepped its formal boundaries, legislative acquiescence (a product of clientelism, among other factors) reinforced the erosion of the principles of separation of powers and horizontal accountability. It is important to point out that the Menem administration's economic reforms—which were influenced by international trends (generated in highly industrialized nations) toward deregulation, increasing financial openness, and heightened concern with low inflation—were largely implemented without serious attention to the rule of law.

The executive's political influence on the judiciary was another element that weakened the rule of law in Argentina. The politicization of the judiciary permeated all levels of the system of justice, often influencing appointments, budget allocations, and rulings. Still, major judicial reforms—such as a new penal code—brought several needed improvements to the administration of justice, in spite of limitations due to politicization (Ungar 2002: 151; see also Larkins 1998; Prillaman 2000: chap. 5).

The executive's influence on the Supreme Court of Justice was especially negative for the rule of law. In 1990, President Menem proposed to expand the Supreme Court from five to nine members. He needed a partisan court to ratify his administration's structural reform of the state and to support his decision to terminate all trials against former members of the military regime (Verbitsky 1993: 36). In spite of the strong opposition to the president's scheme by influential segments of society, the court-packing plan was promptly sanctioned by Congress.[9] Analysts have agreed that this type of extraconstitutional action drastically reduced the possibility of making the judiciary accountable to the law in Argentina (see Negretto and Ungar 1996: 8–9).

Menem's decision to pack the court was one of the darkest components of the government's scheme to place the justice system at the core of its partisan agenda. Indeed, fourteen days after the House of Representatives passed the resolution to expand the court, the Senate confirmed—in a seven-minute "record time" session—all the nominees submitted by the president. The new magistrates were close to Menem and his entourage via personal or political connections (Verbitsky 1993: 18–22, 28–30, 52–68). This was not an isolated event, but part of a pattern that Philippe Schmitter (1994) has called "Argentinization": a democracy operating under weak formal rules, extraconstitutional action, personalistic and centralized executive rule, and mutual distrust between political actors (pp. 60–61).

Beyond the specific case of Menem's government, the public administration sector in Argentina has been characterized by serious deficiencies in the compliance with formal standards, weak mechanisms of control and information, and an inadequate disciplinary system for public employees. At the turn of the century, the state's capacity to combat corruption continued to be hindered by a number of factors, including the absence of a clear governmental anticorruption plan, the lack of independence of such control agencies as the Anti-Corruption Office (OAC) and the General Accounting Office (SIGEN), the politicization of the judiciary, and the inadequacy of formal mechanisms designed to guarantee civil society's monitoring of state agencies and the decision-making process (CIPPEC 2001: 11–23).[10]

Table 3.2 summarizes the most significant deficiencies found in the public administration sector in terms of accountability and transparency. These problems pertain to the quality of rules and regulations and their implementation in the contracting of services by the state and in the functioning of the state apparatus itself. Major corruption exposés in Argentina—ranging from the tainted privatization of public

TABLE 3.2

Horizontal Accountability and Transparency in Argentina:
Public Administration Sector

| | Rules and Regulations | Information | Mechanisms of Control |
|---|---|---|---|
| Planning and contracting | • Deficient models and unclear formal norms<br>• Agencies lack independence from political power<br>• Organizational flaws (poor coordination mechanisms) | • Poor description of norms and procedures<br>• Inadequate information for decision-making (e.g., scarcity of databases)<br>• Deficient channels for communication within and across agencies | • Absence of a system of evaluation for state contracts<br>• Existing mechanisms encourage abuse or corruption<br>• Lack of follow-up studies (public works and projects) |
| Human resources | • Absence of regulations on hiring employees<br>• Clientelism (e.g., personal contacts, partisan decisions)<br>• Deficient system of promotion | • Lack of information on personnel<br>• Inefficient recruiting practices<br>• Poor coordination in resource-sharing across agencies | • Insufficient and poorly trained personnel<br>• Inadequate methods of personnel evaluation<br>• Low levels of sanction |

SOURCE: CIPPEC 2001.

enterprises, such as Aerolíneas Argentinas, to the IBM–Banco Nación scandal (the American-based company paid bribes to be the provider of its equipment to the bank)—were only the tip of the iceberg.[11] Other corruption scandals erupted at the provincial level too (in Formosa, Chaco, and other provinces). State agencies also operate with substandard levels of information, which has crippled the capacity of the state to design, plan, and evaluate public policy. In turn, mechanisms of control do not work properly because of political pressures, poorly trained personnel, and the absence of an effective system of sanctions, among other reasons. As a result, the state falls prey to cartels, public officials have strong incentives to engage in corruption (the cost of violating the law is very low in this setting), existing human resources are ill-used, and policy design and implementation are generally flawed (CIPPEC 2001: 11–12).

*Executive Agencies.*   The state is not a single entity with a defined "interest," but a collection of agencies with often contradictory approaches and expectations of and by society. In the 1990s the practices of some government agencies in Argentina contrasted sharply with the trends outlined above. Some agencies encouraged institutional accountability, access to justice, and concern for the rights of citizens. For the purpose of describing the role of state institutions in the promotion of the rule of law, it is important to distinguish among executive agencies (in their commitment to the rule of law), since they are central to the state's coercive side. These agencies illustrate the regressions and advances in the effectiveness of the rule of law.

In the 1990s the role of the justice and interior ministries was shaped by their dependence on the executive. This dependence hindered their capacity to improve criminal policies, to increase citizen security, and to make the administration of justice more effective. In spite of these limitations, the Justice Ministry, for example, was responsible for implementing programs that improved access to justice for poor sectors of the population—mostly focused on the resolution of community disputes. The Social Program of Juridical Service, launched in 1995, established "community justice centers" in several poor neighborhoods in the city of Buenos Aires. The centers handled disputes concerning "unemployment, wages, social service cuts, and high prices resulting from currency parity with the U.S. dollar" as well as rent conflicts, and family and neighborhood disputes, often with satisfactory resolutions (Ungar 2002: 220–21). Nationally, these mediation mechanisms increased access to justice for underprivileged sectors: "about 90 percent of users of the country's mediation centers were poor people and about 60 percent were female" (Ungar 2002: 205, citing Blair 1994: 42–43).

The creation of the nation's Office of the Ombudsman represented a fundamental reform toward the strengthening of the rule of law in democratic Argentina, especially in the promotion of accountability. This independent agency, among other duties, receives and investigates complaints from citizens and initiates legal recourse. The Menem administration, however, appointed a political crony to the position of ombudsman, "negating the neutrality that gives the body its authority" (Ungar 2002: 40). This decision undermined the ability of this agency to contribute to the rule of law for most of the 1990s.[12]

The Argentine Federal Police, under the authority of the Interior Ministry, has been characterized by deficient training, corrupt practices, and weak mechanisms of accountability. Like the rest of the police forces in the country, the Federal Police has a militarized organizational structure, in spite of being a body under civilian supervision. This structure shaped the security practices of the police in the 1990s, making it largely impermeable to control by other sectors of the state or civil society (Palmieri, Filippini, and Thomas 2001: 3–4). The judiciary found its power to limit the police restricted, not only by features inherent in the police structure, but also by pressures from the executive, unclear parameters concerning the legal bounds of police power, and the disorder characterizing the judicial system itself (Ungar 2002: 84–85).

There have been, though, some improvements in police activity and law enforcement during the democratic period. These include the new penal code, new guidelines regulating detention procedures for the Federal Police (see Chapter 4 for details), and police reforms triggered by public concern with higher crime rates. In the case of the Federal Police, reforms included the removal of officers accused of abuses and the incorporation of human rights courses in the training curriculum (Ungar 2002: 82–83). The government's 1997 reform of the police force in the province of Buenos Aires included the removal of the entire leadership of the force, the dismantling of the command structure, and the mandatory retirement of more than three hundred police commissioners (Palmieri, Filippini, and Thomas 2001: 12).[13] This reform effort ended when the new governor of the province adopted a "tough hand" approach to crime. Indeed, the outcomes of these different reforms have been mixed—thus their long-term impact on the rule of law is still uncertain. As Mark Ungar (2002) has explained,

The executive's repression and the judiciary's disarray led to new laws, a new penal code, and major alterations for both the Buenos Aires provincial police and the PFA [Federal Police]. These changes have already reshaped police relations with the state, judiciary, and society. But to function properly in the long run, functioning oversight of the new limitations on police actions will be needed. Without such oversight, public pressure over crime, continuing judicial disarray, police strength, and executive politics will allow old practices to continue even within reformed structures and laws. (pp. 96–97)

Conversely, one executive agency that has advanced the rule of law is the Subsecretariat of Human Rights, of the Interior Ministry. Its leadership and most of its staff were largely drawn from activists in this area, especially from the old-line human rights groups (e.g., the Ecumenical Movement for Human Rights [MEDH] and Relatives of the Detained-Disappeared).

In addition to its role in the reparations process for victims of state terrorism, the subsecretariat sought to develop broad networks of cooperation across the country. Under the leadership of Alicia Pierini, the agency established links with provincial state and society actors at various levels. Institutionally, it developed working relationships with the Federal Council, counterparts in the provinces' executive governments, and rights commissions in the provincial legislatures. These connections served to (1) formulate national policies and programs, (2) respond to demands for technical training from the provinces, (3) update debates and knowledge on human rights issues, (4) provide information to legislators, and (5) address specific problems at the provincial level.

The subsecretariat designed human rights courses for the command of the Federal Police and training programs on human rights for police officers. This agency also established links with civil society: national universities, civic associations, and regional networks of grassroots organizations. Through these connections, people were intended to share information, discuss human rights policies, collaborate with civic organizations in the investigation of state abuses, and draw on civil society's expertise.[14]

The Justice Ministry's bureau for public legal aid was created in 1993 to provide legal assistance to citizens. Though very small and largely unnoticed within the ministry's bureaucratic structure, this office carried out an impressive range of activities. Like the Subsecretariat of Human Rights, its staff was largely drawn from civil society organizations—in this case, labor unions. For example, the bureau provided legal assistance in the form of complaints against federal prosecutors suspected of bias. These complaints followed institutional channels and usually led to satisfactory outcomes for the plaintiffs. The bureau also investigated irregular acquittals and advised victims or their relatives on the proper legal channels for seeking redress for abuses committed by state agents. More informally, the bureau helped relatives of victims in cases of police violence, providing them with legal experts (often through personal contacts) to guarantee a fair investigation. Most of the bureau's clientele belonged to the lower-income sector, and many asked this office for help obtaining food, health care, and shelter. The staff often used formal and informal connections within the state to find solutions to these problems.[15] As we shall see, despite the positive features of this bureau, its relations with some rights groups in civil society were often problematic.

## State-Citizen Interaction

The state's weak "norm-setting" function is a result of the executive's insulation from constitutional and legislative controls, corruption, and other illegal activities involving public officials, and the inability of state agencies at various levels to enforce the law for all citizens, among other factors. In this context, most people believe that institutions do not need to be obeyed. Indeed, public opinion data shows a dramatic decline in trust in political institutions since the inauguration of democracy. There has been a drop in citizens' trust of Congress, the judiciary, and political parties. Gallup data from 1984 to 1996 (before the Menem administration's economic program began to run into problems) document this trend. Trust in Congress declined from a high of 72 percent in 1984 to 16 percent in 1991, and to a chilling low of 10 percent in 1996. Trust in the judicial system decreased from 57 percent in 1984 to 26 percent in 1991, and to 11 percent in 1996. Finally, support for political parties was already very low in 1991 (12 percent), and it declined to 4 percent in 1996—that is, 96 percent of respondents already distrusted political parties five years before Argentina reached the unprecedented political and economic crisis that forced Fernando de la Rúa out of the presidency in December 2001.[16]

The practices of citizenship are eroded when individuals are consistently mistreated by agents of the state. This is illustrated most clearly by the interaction between citizens and the police in Argentina. Indeed, while the oversight face of the Argentine state is weak, its repressive face has remained strong (Stillwaggon 1998: 121). Following the transition to democracy in 1983, the armed forces represented a threat to the new democratic system: there were several military uprisings from 1987 to 1990. In that context, the government did not consider the police forces to be a vital component of the democratization process, despite the high levels of police violence (Palmieri, Filippini, and Thomas 2001: 4). In fact, since Argentina's return to democracy, domestic and international NGOs have reported systematic patterns of police violence by both the Federal Police and the Buenos Aires provincial police in the form of deadly force in preventive or repressive police procedures, executions, disappearances, and death or torture under police custody

TABLE 3.3

Police and Judicial Behavior in Argentina in Cases of Police Brutality:
Main Patterns

| Police | Judiciary |
| --- | --- |
| • Formulate a false version of events | • Is negligent in the supervision of police investigations |
| • Hide, destroy, or counterfeit evidence | • Fails to investigate incriminating evidence |
| • Threaten, harass, or torment victims and witnesses | • Creates unnecessary delays in the investigations phase |
| • Lack effective mechanisms of internal control | • Imposes light sentences or absolves guilt in questionable circumstances |

SOURCES: CELS/Human Rights Watch 1998: 111–44; CELS 2001: 136–46.

(CELS/Human Rights Watch 1998: 111–44). Not only is the police institution responsible for physical abuse and arbitrary killings (often the result of "trigger-happy" behavior), but it also prevents victims or their relatives from seeking redress for these illegal actions, often in concert with the judiciary. Field research visits allowed me to observe several instances in which judges violated procedures and acted in connivance with corrupt police authorities. These patterns were particularly serious in the provinces.

Table 3.3 summarizes the principal patterns found in cases activated by police brutality in the 1990s. Most relatives of victims of police violence—especially those active in civil society (as I found in my ethnographic study)—have experienced the patterns outlined in this table. Many are middle-class people who thought that "this nightmare could only happen to political activists during the military regime or to the poor," as one of them told me. Narratives of relatives of victims of police violence in the 1990s described devastating ordeals, including death threats, violation of victims' bodies, and humiliation at the hands of judges and police authorities. The experience of seeking justice revealed, for many of these individuals, the limits of their citizenship rights. This speaks to a broader pattern, the disjunctive character of democracy (see Chapter 1), which has been manifested in Latin America as extensive political rights (unparalleled for the region) and increasingly weak civil and social rights for most of the population (Ox-horn 1999: 141).

A public opinion survey conducted in the mid-1990s by the Permanent Assembly for Human Rights (APDH) showed that the civil rights of citizens were violated even in ordinary, everyday interactions with the police. Asked about their assessment of the quality of police behavior in regular interactions with citizens (e.g., traffic violations, reporting of a crime), 95 percent of interviewees said that the police treated them in an arbitrary and authoritarian way. According to the survey, police abuse was exercised, first, in the form of shouts, insults, and threats; second, as requests for bribes; and third, in the form of physical abuse (violence). Maltreatment by police officers in ordinary interactions with citizens (at police stations or on the streets) was much more frequent among those in the lower social strata (APDH 1995). A survey conducted in 1992 showed that 47 percent of respondents viewed the police as corrupt, and 60 percent gave poor marks to police performance in prevention activities. In 1995 only 23 percent of the city of Buenos Aires and greater Buenos Aires residents expressed trust in the police. A year later, this figure declined to 15 percent.[17]

Abuse against young people by the police, especially among marginal sectors, is prevalent. In the 1995 survey, over half of the interviewees younger than 20 reported having been harassed by the police when stopped on the street or detained (APDH 1995). Also, a report on civilians killed by the police under democracy (1983–98) revealed that the average age of victims of "trigger-happy" violence by the police was 17.[18] It is interesting to note that those between 15 and 24 years old in Argentina were severely affected by the dramatic increase in the gap between rich and poor in the 1990s. As of 2000, about 40 percent of Argentines in this age group lived below the poverty line (this situation worsened considerably in 2001–2). Nearly 30 percent of them neither worked nor studied (Rojas 2000).

The poor are continuously exposed to police abuse. This abuse ranges from maltreatment to assassination. During the 1990s, for example, shantytown residents were a preferred target of police violence (Brinks 2002). Darker skin, which is associated with low social status in Argentina, makes an individual more likely to experience abuse. Observers have coined the expression "portación de cara" (which can be loosely translated as racial profiling) to denote the common police practice of violating the civil rights of the underprivileged (see Saidon 2002).

Crime victim surveys confirm the generalized lack of trust in the police among Argentines. A 1998 survey conducted by the National Directorate for Criminal Policy showed that in greater Buenos Aires only 34.6 percent of crimes concerning property (e.g., theft, vandalism) were reported to the police; the figure for the city of Buenos Aires was 37.3 percent (Fernández and D'Angelo 1999). More important, the 1998 survey revealed a large divide between rich and poor in reporting a crime to the police: whereas 42 percent of upper-income victims reported crimes to the police, only 29 percent of lower-income victims did so. When victims who did not report a crime were asked why, 43.3 percent responded that "the police would not have done anything" (Fernández and D'Angelo 1999). This evidence concurs with the results of the APDH survey, showing that the distribution of law enforcement is uneven across social cleavages.

Questions about trust in the judicial system revealed a similar pattern. In a 1994 survey conducted in the city of Buenos Aires and greater Buenos Aires, only 9 percent of those interviewed had a favorable opinion of the judiciary in Argentina. For 84 percent of interviewees, the judicial system consistently favored the wealthy and powerful. Eighty-eight percent said that access to justice was not equal for all in Argentina. Also, 84 percent of interviewees said that the justice system in Argentina was inefficient, and 78 percent considered the Supreme Court to be heavily influenced by political power. People did not feel protected by the courts in Argentina: 82 percent opined that the courts did not protect their interests, and 88 percent said that the justice system did not offer adequate protection to the underprivileged (CEJURA 1994: 7–17, 37–39).[19] These views concur with data that show a negative relationship between an inegalitarian social structure and the robustness of the rule of law. This relationship, as we shall see in Chapter 5, is confirmed at the cross-national level for both new and well-established democracies.

## Citizen-Citizen Interaction

Increasing crime rates, abuse by the police, and an inefficient and biased system of justice[20] have promoted a generalized sense of insecurity and impotence among citizens. The lack of adequate state oversight and constant abuse of the rights of citizens lowers moral restraints and often encourages abusive behavior by private actors, such as job supervisors, security guards, producers of foodstuffs, and landlords. In this context, the costs of violating the law are low. In general, the culture of legality is weak in Argentine society. Widespread tax evasion and everyday corruption are two important expressions of this weakness, but there are other serious manifestations, such as regular discriminatory practices and a favorable predisposition toward violence.

If it is difficult to expect concern, respect, or veracity from others, it comes as no surprise that social trust is extremely low in Argentina.[21] It is simply not rational to trust others in a context in which there are no effective mechanisms for enforcing compliance with formal rules. This is often translated into patterns of social navigation that allow those with economic resources or personal contacts to operate above the law. It is also expressed in everyday forms of abuse among private actors in the workplace (workers are treated arbitrarily and forced to work in dangerous conditions), home and neighborhood (contractors disregard building codes, industries dump toxic wastes in poor areas), healthcare (disregard for basic standards of practice in hospitals), and other spheres of daily life (e.g., consumption of contaminated or adulterated food, exposure to pesticides and other harmful chemicals) (Stillwaggon 1998: 121–40). Those who possess fewer resources are the ones most exposed to this kind of abuse. But this is a reinforcing process, which affects individuals regardless of their position in society. As a professional in his forties commented to me:

When I was a teenager, I thought that the abuse at school had to do with the military regime. In my early twenties, I thought that the harassment at the hands of the police was because I was young. A decade later, I believed that the humiliation at work was simply a result of my professional inexperience. Now in my forties, I am tempted to think that the abusive behavior of a private security guard or a bus driver is a consequence of the generalized crisis. But it's not: the practice of mistreatment is inseparable from one's day-to-day experience. You abuse me, I abuse others.

Low levels of social trust are not something new in Argentina. In 1965, Jeane Kirkpatrick (1971) conducted a national public opinion survey in Argentina which revealed that "interpersonal relations outside the family" were characterized "by mutual suspicion and distrust" (p. 119). Eighty-four percent of respondents agreed with the statement, "If you don't watch yourself, people will take advantage of you," and 69 percent agreed with the observation, "No one much cares what happens to you, when you get right down to it" (p. 120, table 6.1).[22] These figures challenge analyses that view low levels of trust in Argentina as a phenomenon primarily associated with the traumatic experience of the 1970s "dirty war."

Increasing crime rates and citizen insecurity have been perceived by large segments of society as a manifestation of the state's "weak authority," thus triggering demands for "tougher" forms of social control (see Caldeira 1996: 202). Public opinion data have revealed a broad perception (across social classes) that the justice system protects criminals more than it protects victims of crime. According to a public opinion survey conducted by Gallup Argentina in 1994, 83 percent of interviewees said that victims did not receive as much protection from the courts as criminals did. Many people expressed their willingness to support extralegal measures to fight crime. A survey conducted earlier in greater Buenos Aires found that nearly 40 percent of the population condoned the use of torture by the police to extract information from suspects.[23] This is not a pattern exclusive to Argentina. In Brazil, for example, polls showed public support for a harsh approach in the fight against "undesirables," even if such an approach entailed the use of deadly force.[24]

Citizen-citizen interaction in contemporary Argentina is characterized by high levels of discrimination. This phenomenon is common throughout the country, and most clearly seen in major urban centers such as Buenos Aires city and greater Buenos Aires. Even though discriminatory practices are common in these urban areas, discrimination has been generally ignored in public debates. Argentina has been traditionally imagined as a white country and Buenos Aires as a homogeneous European metropolis. Nonwhites have been made "invisible" in the media and in political, educational, and other institutions, or if acknowledged, they have been relegated to a subordinate status. Also, those who suffer discrimination in this setting tend to deny it—consciously or not—as some studies have shown (indeed, discrimination has become a naturalized aspect of their everyday interactions) (Margulis 1999b: 148, 150; see Margulis et al. 1999).

Discrimination, racism, and social exclusion are closely related. In Argentina, the basis for rejecting the "other" is based primarily on physical, ethnic, cultural, class, and nationality traits (Margulis 1999a: 47). The most common patterns of discrimination are those that construe the other as a *negro* (a derogatory term, which carries a meaning similar to "nigger") or *villero* (shantytown dweller). These discriminatory categories are applied to internal migrants (especially from the northern provinces), immigrants from countries such as Bolivia and Peru, and dark-skinned people in general.

There are few systematic studies of discrimination in Argentina. But one survey conducted among residents of the city of Buenos Aires and greater Buenos Aires in the mid-1990s revealed some interesting trends.[25] In this study, only 12.3 percent of interviewees did not express any discriminatory views: 66.7 percent of them were women and 55.3 percent had a college education. In the rhetoric of discrimination, the "other" (the *negro* or *villero*) was excluded because he or she was viewed as unhealthy, lazy, brute, backward, ignorant, ugly, dirty, smelly, promiscuous, and dangerous. Discriminatory views were more common among groups with middle and low levels of education who lived in middle-class neighborhoods. At the time, these middle classes were undergoing a process of social decline, which strengthened their prejudice against foreign and internal migrants as well as against the poor in general (Urresti 1999: 300, 315–16, 330–31).

Immigrants from Bolivia, Peru, and Paraguay were the central target of discrimination in the study, followed by internal migrants from the northern provinces and residents of shantytowns (Belvedere 1999: 282). In the discourse of discrimination, the "other" was (1) dehumanized (for example, immigrants from neighboring countries were described as "ignorant, animals, beasts"), (2) marginalized (the immigrant was placed in a group that had violated, in the eyes of the person who discriminates, a basic social norm, such as immigration laws, criminal laws, or rules of decency), and (3) effaced (Bolivians, Peruvians, and others were construed solely on the basis of negative or unacceptable features, such as being lazy, a drunk, an invader) (Szulik and Valiente 1999: 237).

Discriminatory discourse and practice are part of the same phenomenon in Argentina. Ordinary interactions are often shaped by social hierarchies constructed on the basis of several of the patterns just described. Discrimination can be deadly—shantytown dwellers are more likely to be killed than other social groups, as when the police use abusive force to deal with poor populations—but more often it is subtly embedded in routine social practices. In all its forms, discrimination erodes civil rights and sustains social stigmas and social exclusion. Discrimination incapacitates and diminishes the autonomy and potential of individuals, heightens distrust in others, and intensifies cynicism with respect to institutions and the legal system (Margulis 1999a: 37–38).

# Civil Society in Argentina

Having discussed the main conditions under which citizens organize and mobilize in Argentina, let me now focus on associationism. Civil society in Argentina has received much attention since the arrival of democracy in 1983. According to several studies, associational life exploded in the second half of the 1980s, involving rapid growth in the number of foundations, cooperatives, research centers, think tanks, watchdog groups, consumer associations, civil rights groups, and development organizations (Thompson 1992: 393–95; 1995b: 57–58; González Bombal 1995: 76–77).[26] It is very difficult to determine the number of civil society organizations in Argentina—and whether or not their number increased from the 1980s to the 1990s—because of lack of reliable data, a lack of consensus on what constitutes the universe to be studied, and an absence of clear guidelines in the agencies that measure this sector (Thompson 1995a: 48). CIVICUS, an international alliance focused on strengthening civil society around the world, estimated that Argentina had more than 80,000 civic organizations by the second half of the 1990s (see CIVICUS 1997). A study sponsored by the United Nations Development Program and the Inter-American Development Bank (1998) used government records to calculate that 78,800 organizations were legally registered in the country. Half of these associations were located in the city of Buenos Aires (19,000) and Buenos Aires province (20,000). Among the rest of the provinces, the ones with the most associations were Santa Fe (5,500), Córdoba (5,100), Tucumán (4,800), and Mendoza (4,500).

In the 1990s, a large portion of civil society participation—expressed as formal organizations and social movement activity—converged around the theme of civil rights. This activity was largely triggered by cases that exposed widespread patterns of police and military as well as judicial and political corruption (the media played a central role in investigating and publicizing scandals). This pattern of civic engagement was viewed by scholars as a burgeoning civic movement with the capacity to activate the question of citizenship rights in Argentina and thus help launch a new phase in the construction of democracy (Landi and Bombal 1995: 176). This wave of civic activity was influenced by the human rights movement that originated in the 1970s and by a new cluster of nongovernmental organizations that emerged in the 1980s and early 1990s under democracy (Campetella, González Bombal, and Roitter 1998: 22–23; Thompson 1992: 389–93).

## Trends in Group Involvement

Survey data offer information on trends of group membership and voluntary work in Argentina from the 1980s to the 1990s. These data are useful for describing general patterns of participation in formal organizations. Specifically, they can reveal changes in the level and intensity of people's participation (intensity understood here as involvement in various types of groups). In the World Values Surveys study for Argentina (World Values Study Group), respondents were asked if they belonged to or did voluntary work for different types of voluntary organizations, defined by issue (e.g., social welfare, youth work, human rights, sports). The data discussed here were collected in 1984 and 1991. The 1984 survey included ten types of organizations in the list. In 1991 the list was expanded to include six more. In order to compare both surveys, I employ an index of participation that includes the original ten types of organizations.[27] I am interested in establishing a general picture of participation in the early 1990s because it was when most of the groups in my qualitative study began to emerge.

The surveys showed that most of the interviewees did not belong to any of the formal civic organizations included in the list. Indeed, in 1984, the first year of democracy, nearly two-thirds (65.3 percent) of the population were not members of any of these groups. Seven years later, in 1991, there was a statistically significant increase in nonparticipation; that is, four-fifths (81.4 percent) of those interviewed did not belong to any of these organizations.

If we examine the level of participation by aggregating the number of different organizations to which individuals belong, it is possible to have a general sense of the changing density of cross-cutting involvement (across issues) in voluntary organizations in Argentina.[28] The results are shown in Figure 3.2. In 1984, 26 percent of respondents were members of only one type of organization, 6 percent were members of two types, and 2.7 percent belonged to three or more. By 1991 the general level of involvement in voluntary associations had decreased. In particular, while the proportion of members in one type of organization decreased to 14.3 percent, the percentage of nonparticipants increased. In other words, many individuals with a low level of involvement in different associations discontinued their participation completely (at least when measured as membership in formal groups). The proportion of those with multiple memberships also declined. If we create a measure of participation that includes all sixteen types of voluntary organi-

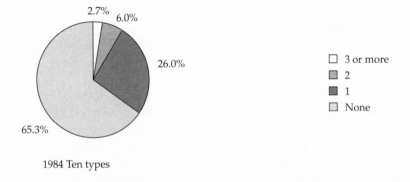

1984 Ten types

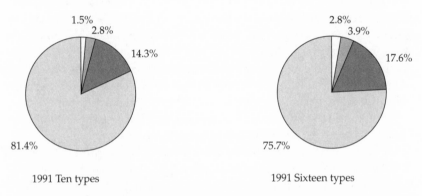

1991 Ten types                                1991 Sixteen types

FIGURE 3.2   Membership in Voluntary Associations
SOURCE: World Values Surveys (Argentina, 1984 and 1991).

zations (those asked about in the 1991 survey), the results are not very different from those obtained with the original set of groups. Participation in only one type of organization shows an increase from 14.3 percent (including the original ten types of groups) to 17.6 percent when all sixteen types are considered.[29]

In addition to asking about membership in formal associations, the World Values Surveys asked people whether they do "unpaid voluntary work" for civic organizations. It is possible to assume that doing voluntary work for an organization must entail some form of direct interaction with other members of that organization. In other words, such involvement is likely to provide the social connection that membership alone may not provide (e.g., if it is restricted to "writing a check for dues" or reading a newsletter) (Putnam 1995a: 71). Looking at those volunteering in Argentina, the survey revealed patterns similar to those found for membership, including a decline in participation from 1984 to 1991.

A 1992 survey conducted among residents of the city of Buenos Aires and greater Buenos Aires provides additional information on civic participation in the early 1990s. In this poll, 74 percent of interviewees said that they did not participate in any political or social activity at the time.[30] Eighty-one percent of these nonparticipants were young people, and 85 percent of them belonged to the lower income and educational tiers. Among nonparticipants, only 30 percent said that they had been participants in the past (these were mostly people over 60 years old, women, and upper-middle-class respondents). Of those who participated in social or political activities (26 percent), most were involved in parent-teacher associations, religious organizations, neighborhood associations, and political parties.

These low levels of participation in the early 1990s appear to reflect long-standing trends in civic engagement, at least when we look at people's involvement in political activities. When Kirkpatrick (1971) asked Argentines in 1965 if they had "ever participated in *any* type of political activity," only 7.1 percent responded affirmatively (pp. 170–71, table 7.11).[31] Participation was viewed by respondents as a responsibility of citizenship. Indeed, as Kirkpatrick reported, "almost half of all respondents asserted that citizens have a duty to participate in local affairs." However, the survey also showed that "the participant was not a widely admired personality type" among respondents.

## Social Movements and the Media

Survey data on group membership or voluntary work in formal organizations do not tell us about other arenas of civic engagement. Thus a description of main trends in social movement activity and an account of the role of the media in exposing major scandals involving public officials is necessary to provide a more complete picture of Argentina's civil society in the 1990s. Social movements, in particular, played an active role in the country's arrhythmic and contradictory process of democratization at the end of the twentieth century.

A new wave of social movements emerged in the 1990s, calling for justice, transparency, and accountability, among other demands. Neighborhood-based activism confronted authorities with protests and demonstrations against impunity, police violence, and corruption, but also organized forums to discuss reforms and mobilized to provide citizen-based solutions to problems of citizen security. For example, in the mid-1990s, middle-class movements such as Buenos Aires Viva organized to provide input to the reform process initiated with the new autonomous status of the city of Buenos Aires (Poggiese, Redín, and Alí 1999: 170–71). Various neighborhood organizations in Buenos Aires took on community policing to reduce crime. These experiences did not last long and achieved mixed results: most of the projects supported by Buenos Aires Viva did not materialize, but the movement provided a new space for citizen involvement in public debates; crime rates did not decline as a result of community policing, but neighbors' relationship with the police improved for some time (Poggiese, Redín, and Alí 1999: 174; Smulovitz 2001: 16–17, 46, 50).[32]

Three paradigmatic cases illustrate the new wave of prodemocratic social movements of the 1990s: the cases of María Soledad Morales (a schoolgirl murdered in the province of Catamarca); Omar Carrasco (a low-ranking recruit who died in an army post in the province of Neuquén); and José Luis Cabezas (a news photographer assassinated in a beach resort in the province of Buenos Aires). These civic movements originated in cases of wrongdoing by government officials. They mobilized thousands of people and attracted major attention in the media: "the original mobilization was initiated locally, generally by relatives and friends of the victims, and extended afterwards to include local and national NGOs and broad sectors of the population" (Peruzzotti 2002: 8–9).

María Soledad Morales was killed in 1990 in Catamarca, a province in northwestern Argentina. The son of a senator participated in the murder. The province's government and police attempted to cover the crime. Catamarca's civil society organized silent demonstrations to demand justice, and soon these extended to the entire country. As a result of this mobilization, seven months later Governor Ramón Saadi was removed from office by the national government. In 1991 the Saadi family lost the provincial elections for the first time, after having dominated provincial politics for more than fifty years. In the six years following the crime, there were more than eighty silent demonstrations in Catamarca and twenty-five in other parts of the country. The Truth and Justice Commission, created to monitor the investigation and the legal proceedings of the case, and extensive media coverage helped the demands for a trial succeed. The first trial was suspended for irregularities, and the second trial, which started in 1997, resulted in the conviction of two individuals accused of the crime (Smulovitz and Peruzzotti 2000: 154–56).

Omar Carrasco was completing the compulsory military service in Neuquén when he was killed. Military and police authorities were involved in the death and its cover-up. The media and public opinion were attracted to the case—mostly because it uncovered many of the arbitrary practices ingrained in the unpopular compulsory military service—and there were widespread demands for justice. Some human and civil rights NGOs were instrumental in moving the investigation forward. Of the three cases, the Carrasco affair was the only one that resulted in a concrete policy reform (Waisbord 2000: 214). Indeed, some of the suspects were convicted in a trial, and later, the mandatory military service was eliminated. Some analysts have argued, though, that the abolishment of military service could have been an electoral strategy by the government to attract young voters and their families in the 1995 presidential elections (Waisbord 2000: 214, citing Barcelona 1994). Yet it is hard to discount the pressure exerted by public opinion, the media, and several organizations of civil society.

Finally José Luis Cabezas, a photographer for a political magazine, was tortured, assassinated, and his body burned in 1997 in a coastal town in Buenos Aires province. The case appeared to have serious political implications. Cabezas was the first to photograph a leading businessman accused of being the head of a mafia group with connections to the federal government. Some police officers seemed to be linked to the murder, and the police investigation showed once again signs of deliberate mishandling of information and evidence. Cabezas's relatives and colleagues in the Argentine Press Association (ADEPA) started an informal media campaign to place the Cabezas case at the top of the public opinion agenda. They also organized several demonstrations, together with a dozen other groups. The Cabezas movement helped to speed up the investigation, which resulted in the imprisonment of some police officers and some minor criminals. Mobilization to demand justice for Cabezas's murder was sometimes linked to demands for justice in the 1994 bombing of the Argentine Israelite Mutual Aid Association (AMIA), a major civil society organization in Buenos Aires.[33] At one time, for example, "20,000 persons attended [a protest] to decry for the failure of the government to prevent or prosecute criminal and terrorist acts" (McSherry 1997: 79).

The Cabezas case is a clear example of the interaction among civic movements, formal organizations, and especially the media. Thus an account of developments in the public sphere in the 1990s cannot neglect the role played by the media in attempting to bring accountability to the democratic system in Argentina. The media conducted numerous serious investigations and denounced acts of corruption and crimes in the 1990s and had done so on a smaller scale earlier. The decrease of state violence against investigative journalism, a marked political cynicism and skepticism regarding politics and governmental institutions in public opinion, a demand for watchdog media by the public, and stronger journalistic ethics were among the factors that made this phenomenon viable (Waisbord 2000: 244–45). Some of the most resonant cases of "the journalism of exposé" in Argentina were "Swiftgate" (government officials bribing the Swift company to import machinery) and "Yomagate" (a drug money-laundering case involving the sister-in-law of President Menem). Other cases were the IBM–Banco Nación affair and the scandal involving the Argentine government's selling arms to Ecuador and Croatia. There were numerous media investigations of corruption and malfeasance involving state agencies such as the police, the social service agency for senior citizens (PAMI), the customs service, national legislators, Menem's cabinet, and even the president himself.

The unfavorable context of widespread corruption, co-optation, and clientelism in Argentina's society and government limited the impact of watchdog journalism on democratic politics. Journalists were often forced to use unreliable sources or informants who sought to discredit their enemies or opponents. The media concentrated almost exclusively on the government (there was little investigation of the corporate sector, for example), and thus, according to analysts, a feverish attempt to expose corruption finally saturated public opinion.[34] Few of the media exposés resulted in actual convictions. Of the seventy-one officials formally accused of corruption in the first Menem administration (1990–95), for example, none were convicted. By 1996, only 3 out of 108 cases of malfeasance resulted in sentences (Waisbord 2000: 212, 249).

Even though my analysis of civil society does not look specifically at the media, media contributions have two connections to the theoretical themes of the book. First, as happened in the province of Buenos Aires, the media can publicize and increase public awareness of crime and then of police abuse and corruption. Even though this role is vital in shaping the public agenda, one should not confuse it with the actual implementation of accountability. As explained in the analysis of the rule of law (Chapter 1), the principle of accountability is not satisfied if there is no sanction for demonstrated illegal or arbitrary acts by state and private actors (see Schedler 1999: 14–17). Second, the media, like other institutions of civil society, rely on contextual factors, which can restrict the discussion of certain issues and limit the re-creation of debate in the public sphere (see the discussion of the public sphere, Chapter 1). In addition to the contextual elements already mentioned, others include links between political authorities and the media, ownership concentration in mass media, governmental attempts to restrict the freedom of the press, and violent attacks against journalists, all of which limited the democratic role of the media and even media access by civil society organizations, especially human and civil rights groups (Park 2002).

Returning to the 1990s cases cited above, a closer look at some of these cases raises questions about the actual effect of mass mobilizations *after* public attention shifted to other issues (this problem also relates to the media, specifically to its inherent inability to sustain coverage of an issue over time). Although civil society may call for accountability, its actual realization—which should entail sanctions when appropriate—depends on government institutions and the courts. In the María Soledad case, for example, the important achievements did not end impunity in Catamarca. In fact, ten years after the popular mobilizations, thirty-three witnesses denounced for false testimony had not been investigated by the courts, and the nearly twenty police officers implicated in the vast operation that included destruction of evidence, mutilation of the victim's corpse, bribing, threats against witnesses and judges, and even torture of suspects and witnesses remained at large. Several of the police officers continued in their posts, and five were promoted to the rank of commissioner, including the officer suspected of planting the body of the victim where it was found (Osojnik 2000). Former governor and local caudillo Ramón Saadi was elected to the national Congress in 1999.

Civil society involvement contributed to the dispersion of power in Catamarca, strengthened popular participation, and successfully pressed for a trial and indictments. However, for the participants themselves, the outcome of this effort was not as positive as one might expect. Relatives of the victim and former leaders of the movement continued to accuse the courts and politicians of sustaining impunity for most of the individuals responsible for the crime (Messi 2000). They believed, a decade after their mobilization, that justice was yet to be served in Catamarca. As one of the organizers of the demonstrations recently said, "One has the feeling of having fought in vain" (as quoted in Osojnik 2000, my translation).

Ongoing research on these movements has revealed competing assessments, viewing their impact as successful, unsuccessful, or mixed for democracy, depending on the variables chosen or the time frame for the study. One important dimension illustrated by the three cases was the question of civil society's *reaction* to events. Indeed, in Catamarca, Neuquén, and Buenos Aires, the civil society organizing was largely in reaction to the killings, and most of it dissipated as the cases moved into glacial and corrupt judicial processes. The cycle of improvements and erosion in the efforts to control police power shows a similar process in which galvanizing events led to some type of reform (such as a reduction in the maximum time allowed for detentions on suspicion of criminal activity), which was later undermined when mobilization dissipated (e.g., the gradual renewal of police powers) (see Chapter 4).

The question of reaction, which has been an important characteristic of civil society activity in post-1983 Argentina, is pertinent to other societies, as the example of grassroots rebellion against busing in the northern United States illustrated. In new democracies, the problem of civil society's reaction is particularly relevant to understanding the contribution of civil society to the actual transition to democracy as opposed to the post-transition phase. Civil society organizations in southern cone countries were more effective at documenting and denouncing rights abuses by the military than they were at following through with effective influence on lawmaking and institutional reform after the military left power (see, e.g., de Brito 1997). Similarly, in the democratization of Eastern Europe, and more recently in Asian and African countries, many groups in civil society were connected to limited demands that contributed to the democratic transition but faded after these goals were met. If, as some analysts have argued, participation in voluntary associations is expected to create and disseminate throughout society a democratic political culture (among other things), then a sustained focus on long-term issues is an important condition for achieving that outcome. As the discussion of Argentina's institutional and societal conditions suggests, whether civil society groups are connected with temporary or long-term issues is determined, to a great extent, by the context in which they operate. Neo-Tocquevillean accounts of civil society have neglected this important aspect, which has major implications for new democracies.

## A Slice of Civil Society

The task of surveying organizations, movements, networks, and ties of civic engagement is very complex and requires using a combination of methods to capture the full dimensions of civic activity. However, we can explore certain trends by looking at a slice of civil society "at close range," that is, by examining civic involvement in its specific context, from various perspectives, and from micro interactions to broader exchanges within civil society and with the state. For Argentina, I focused on a new generation of associations linked to problems—such as police violence and citizen security—that took on considerable relevance in the context of democracy. As some scholars have argued, as authoritarianism receded and new democracies were confronted with serious problems associated with the coercive dimension of the state (particularly in the dimensions of day-to-day power, physical force, and legal abuse), groups such as human and civil rights organizations were viewed as potentially key players in the construction of more democratic societies. These organizations, it has been argued, could play an important role in restructuring authoritarian "reserved domains" (e.g., the police) and contribute to improving the legitimacy of the judiciary and other sectors of the state (see, e.g., Linz and Stepan 1996: 7–8).

In 1996, I conducted a detailed study of fifteen organizations in the human and civil rights area. All but one of these organizations were created in the late 1980s and early 1990s and belonged to a new generation of civic associations linked to the emergence of demands for minority rights (women, gays, indigenous peoples, and so on) and rights associated with democratic citizenship.[35] Students of civil society in Argentina saw this generation of associations as an important force in democratization, particularly in the dispersion of power to the citizenry, the democratization of political institutions, and the increase of governmental responsiveness to popular demands (see Thompson 1992; Landi and Bombal 1995). This cluster of organizations is useful for examining the democratizing potentials and limitations of a relevant sector of civil society in Argentina.[36] In 2000, I conducted a follow-up study with a subgroup of interviewees in order to examine attitude changes over time.[37]

The groups' members were mostly from the middle classes, though many were in the process of becoming part of the "new poor" in Argentina. Groups in my cohort were socially homogeneous. It was unusual to find individuals from very different social strata sharing membership in an organization. Sampling allowed as much variation as possible across groups about their specific goals and collective action forms. The sample can be divided into groups largely made up of victims or relatives of victims and groups constituted by professionals, though some groups combined both.[38] Groups of relatives in this wave generally followed the strategies of those in the human rights organizations created as a reaction to state terror, in which relatives initially form a group focused on self-help activities and later evolve into an advocacy organization, such as the Mothers of the Plaza de Mayo.[39] About a third of the groups in the sample had transnational connections and received funding from international organizations.

By focusing on formal organizations, the study selected only part of what constitutes civil society. However, the selection of a sample of organizations that are most likely to reveal a positive connection between civic engagement and democratization—simply because the promotion of democracy is their raison d'être—gives especial relevance to this slice of civil society. This cluster of organizations provides a "best case" scenario for finding a positive connection between associational activity and democracy. Stated differently, they provide a crucial test of the civil society–democracy link.

What is the place of this cluster of groups in the universe of formal organizations in Argentina? A study commissioned by the Johns Hopkins Comparative Nonprofit Sector Project (Campetella, González Bombal, and Roitter 1998) drew a map of the nonprofit sector in Argentina in the 1990s following the structural-operational framework developed by Salamon and Anheier (1996). As explained in Chapter 1, these researchers devised a set of standards for organizations to be included in the "third sector"—standards that range from a meaningful level of institutionalization to independence from the state and a high degree of volunteerism (Salamon and Anheier 1997: 33–34). Figure 3.3 shows a map of the nonprofit sector in Argentina outlined according to Salamon and Anheier's criteria.

The new human and civil rights organizations included in my study are nongovernmental organizations (NGOs). Not all of the NGOs were legally constituted as civil associations.[40] The term *NGO* is applied to organizations engaged in advocacy (e.g., human and civil rights, environmental protection), social development (often providing technical assistance to poor people's grassroots organizations), and watchdog activities (monitoring the state and entrepreneurial sectors) (Thompson 1994: 32, 50–51, 55). Legally constituted or not, NGOs make up a de-

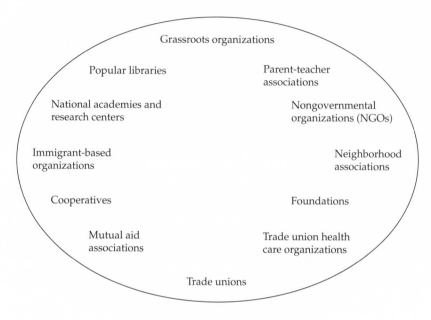

Grassroots organizations

Popular libraries

Parent-teacher
associations

National academies and
research centers

Nongovernmental
organizations (NGOs)

Immigrant-based
organizations

Neighborhood
associations

Cooperatives

Foundations

Mutual aid
associations

Trade union health
care organizations

Trade unions

FIGURE 3.3    The Nonprofit Sector in Argentina
SOURCE: Campetella, González Bombal, and Roitter 1998: 8–19.

fined universe, insofar as they have a public presence and remain active
in the public sphere (Campetella, González Bombal, and Roitter 1998:
12). These groups perceive themselves as part of the same segment of
civil society, whether they engage in mutual cooperation and establish
alliances or not.

Less visible NGOs, which proliferated in the 1980s and 1990s, responded directly to high-level public officials from different political
parties and sometimes received state funds without any proper
scrutiny. In 1996, for instance, the media uncovered that $33 million
was apportioned by the Ministry of Economy and Congress to about
thirty NGOs in various fields. The investigation revealed that the apportionment of funds responded to political decisions and that the only
criteria for such allocation appeared to have been the strong personal
contacts between leaders of these NGOs and high-ranking government
officials (Thompson 1996: 17–18).

The organizations that constituted the human rights movement in
the 1970s and 1980s continued to be active in the 1990s. Many of these

NGOs launched new programs in order to insert themselves into the rapidly changing democratic context. For example, the Peace and Justice Service (SERPAJ) worked in the area of education for human rights; MEDH developed programs on children's rights and domestic violence; and APDH worked on discrimination issues and offered free legal advice through cooperation with the University of Buenos Aires.

Finally, it is important to mention that a number of rights activists from the NGO sector accepted posts in the government at various times after the return to democracy, especially during the 1990s. A few of them assumed policy-making positions. In most cases, rights activists worked as advisers to different governmental agencies, though some assumed executive positions in such agencies as the Subsecretariat of Human Rights. Some of these activists told me that those who served as advisers were usually very discreet about this type of activity because of the generalized perception among the rights community of the state as an adversary. In other words, working for the government could erode someone's legitimacy and trustworthiness in the eyes of other activists and organizations.

## Conclusion

As Chapter 4 will show, several of the human and civil rights organizations in the ethnographic study were incapable of promoting social trust and tolerance among their members, and sometimes they even intensified attitudes at odds with democratic practices. Moreover, horizontal links among groups in this cluster—and between them and other sectors in civil society—were scarce, and individual groups' achievements did not strengthen the sector's impact as a whole. Vertical links with the state were weak and unstable. Even when a government agency offered a niche for cooperation, the unfavorable impact of the broader political and social context limited the possibilities of developing such cooperation.

In addition to the ethnographic study, my analysis of the different dimensions of the link between civil society and democracy employs evidence drawn from other sources. I employ survey data to test trends found in the qualitative study and use data on legal outcomes of criminal cases against police officers, legislative activity concerning police reform and related issues, and trends in police violence since the onset of democracy in 1983. In the analysis, I explore the impact of civil society beyond the realm of formal associations, looking at the ways in which social networks, public forums, and the media, among other manifestations of civil society activity, influenced the democratization of a specific area of the state. The goal of this study is, then, to examine the capacity of civil society not only to promote a more democratic political culture, but also to control and impose limits on the state's coercive side (more specifically, on its repressive power). As the following chapter describes, civil society's capacity to exercise this role, by means of influence on the judicial and legislative arenas, has been quite limited in Argentina.

While the data offer a multilevel view of the complex, and often paradoxical, connection between civic engagement and democracy in 1990s Argentina, they also unveil important undercurrents that would rise to the surface with the crisis of 2001–2. In this respect, the analysis of civil society in this country not only helps to broaden our understanding of the civil society–democracy link, highlighting elements that can be applied to other cases, but also illuminates some of the central aspects of the specific, intricate *problématique* of Argentina.

# CHAPTER 4

# Civic Engagement and Social Dysfunction

IN THIS CHAPTER, I examine the civil society-democracy thesis in democratic Argentina. My analysis is organized around three central issues. First, I look at the relationship between civic engagement and democratic dispositions at the individual level. This issue examines the potential effect of association on the political and critical skills of participants as well as on their civic virtues. The experience of participation in small groups may help not only in the development of democratic dispositions, but also in the promotion of important skills in the creation of "citizen-selves" (see Rosenblum 1998: 361; Foweraker and Landman 1997: 33; Janoski 1998: 228–30; Warren 2001: 61). The individual effect of civic engagement may also influence the level of social trust in participants. Thus I examine whether participation in a specific cluster of civic associations in Argentina (human and civil rights groups) breeds tolerance, habits of bargaining and compromise, belief in the legitimacy of institutions, organizational and leadership skills, and social trust in individuals.[1]

The second issue is civil society's horizontal and vertical links. At the group level, I investigate the extent to which civic engagement promotes networks of collaboration within civil society and connections with the state. Civil society groups, especially when they pursue similar goals and espouse parallel interests, may engage in a range of cooperative relationships, thus broadening and reinforcing participation. In turn, civic organizations may engage in mutually beneficial collaboration with various segments of the state, which would help these groups to influence institutions. Focusing on my sample of organizations, I explore the links among them (and with the rest of civil society) and their relationships with different sectors of the state. I examine patterns of interaction, strategic priorities, social networks, and the perceptions that shape the horizontal and vertical links of this cluster of groups.

Third, I explore the institutional effects of associational life, in particular, the capacity of civil society to control and impose limits on the coercive power of the state (specifically, everyday power, physical force, and legal abuse). Even though the capacity of civil society to build community and solidarity is important, the impact of civil society activity on the state apparatus represents a concern with pragmatism. This perspective recognizes the role in democratization of civic organizations, social movements, or other forms of association as a check to abuse of state power and as a source of accountability of public officials (see, e.g., Chazan 1992: 281–82, 287; Janoski 1998: 228–30; Brysk 2000a: 288).[2] This section then assesses the impact of various dimensions of civil society (civic groups, social networks, public forums, and the media) on the outcome of criminal cases against police officers involved in acts of brutality, legislation on law enforcement and individual rights, and congressional activity in the area of police reform.

## Dispositions among Participants

The tools of ethnographic research can be useful for investigating attitudes and beliefs that are not easily conveyed in public opinion surveys. They yield a multiplicity of observations that, when aggregated, suggest empirical patterns that are not easily identified in survey questionnaires. Initially, I expected to find that groups providing collective responses to state violence were promoting civic values and trust among their members. However, the data revealed a much different picture.

At the individual level, civic engagement in these groups was connected to four types of disposition. First, participants developed skills that improved their capacity to articulate their interests, make demands, and generate mechanisms of collective action to exhort responsiveness from authorities. Activities that fostered organizational skills included grant-writing, computer literacy (e.g., the use of e-mail and the Internet, as well as the creation of databases), planning activities and events, and developing an agenda for group meetings. Some participants were able to transfer these skills to other spheres of everyday life, primarily the workplace. For some activists, civic engagement opened access to conferences and debates in university settings and other spheres where ideas are produced and exchanged. This possibility often contributed to the development of professionalism among members—that is, a more strategic, informed, and less visceral approach to problem-solving. Civic activists with university education acknowledged learning that extremist positions—such as constant denouncing without proposing solutions—did not achieve concrete results.

The second type of disposition found in my ethnographic study was a heightened cynicism with respect to formal institutional channels to obtain justice or make demands. Interviewees talked repeatedly about their disappointment with specific institutions (e.g., the judiciary, police, Congress). This frustration was often expressed as disenchantment with institutions in general. The more they participated, the more cynical they grew regarding the possibility of improving government institutions. The implications of this pattern are important, particularly for the underprivileged. When people know their rights but do not have the resources and access to effectively demand them, they become increasingly disillusioned with democratic institutions. For many, asserting one's rights is not an easy task in a context such as that of Argentina. As one interviewee summarized this reality, "For the poor and those without access to the powerful, to defend one's basic rights often entails a high personal cost—even risking one's own life."[3] In general, frustration leads to paralysis and disengagement. This outcome was revealed, for example, in the high rate of "exit" in the organizations in my study.

In contrast to this trend, I found that some of the activists reinterviewed in 2000 had begun to use their newly acquired skills in other spheres of everyday life to object to everyday discrimination, authoritarian behavior, and arbitrariness at home, school, work, church, and in other spheres of civic life (see Rosenblum 1998: 362; Chandhoke 1995: 247). For some, this disposition ran parallel to a denaturalization of the condition of being a victim. In this sense, for a small number of participants, civic engagement contributed to breaking their acceptance of authoritarianism in social relations as a "natural" phenomenon. As one interviewee mentioned to me in 2000, since becoming involved in one of the organizations in 1992, she has become aware of the daily forms of authoritarianism in social relations. For example, she felt that her participation had an effect on her children's education: "Now I'm more open, I discuss problems with my children, and most important, my children's education at home has been deeply affected by my activism." Her children became more aware of authoritarian attitudes at school and reacted, for instance, when teachers overstepped their authority or abused their power (e.g., by making degrading remarks about a student or violating his privacy).[4] A longitudinal study of civic participants would be very useful for understanding which factors explain these types of attitudes and whether these dispositions are sustained over time.

Third, discriminatory attitudes were often present in group interactions in the form of verbal attacks or derogatory remarks about Jews, *negros* (the "dark-skinned"), *villeros* (shantytown inhabitants), and the poor in general. The evidence indicates that civic engagement did not help to reduce such attitudes and behaviors; on the contrary, the frustration sometimes associated with participation in a hostile environment fed intolerance among some members. Tolerance of criminals and the police did not grow either. A number of participants believed that common criminals could not be seen as defenseless or innocent victims and therefore argued that criminals did not have the same rights as noncriminals (as public opinion surveys in the 1990s showed, this belief could also be found in the broader society).[5] Members of one group only agreed to defend victims that they deemed to be "innocent"—that is, they refused to promote the rights of presumed perpetrators. Others had a similar attitude with respect to the police, explicitly accepting that "killing a police officer is not such a bad thing." On occasion, some of the participants said that they did not want to deal with the rights of minorities. During a meeting in which one of these groups was discussing another organization's proposal to collaborate in a grassroots conference on human rights, the agenda touched upon the rights of squatters. One group member emphatically refused to treat the issue as a "human rights" problem and stated that she did not like "blacks"— she used the derogatory term *negros*.[6] "I am not ashamed of revealing that I'm a racist," she said. Her remarks were not challenged by any other member of the group. This attitude reflected patterns of racism and xenophobia in Argentine society, as described in Chapter 3.[7]

Finally, civic participation in the cluster of groups did not produce generalized trust, namely, social trust beyond one's immediate circle of family, friends, and coparticipants. The idea of social capital as a resource that creates broad networks of reciprocity in society is based on the assumption that people learn to cast their trust net as widely as possible. However, among the groups in my sample, I found that civic engagement promoted relatively intense social interactions, but they were limited to the specific organization and did not extend to those who did not belong to the group. In other words, trust produced within groups (particularized trust) made participants less trusting of nonmembers.[8] This finding affirms the patterns observed in Weimar Germany and the United States. In fact, time and again organizations and networks of association tend to develop particularized trust under contextual conditions that threaten, in one way or another, their identity and cohesion as a group.

In the ethnographic study, I sought to distinguish, more specifically, levels of trust in participants—which involved coding their semistructured responses on a scale (low-high) of trust in others. I found that social trust among participants was not evenly distributed across socioeconomic status. Although participants in the cluster of groups belonged mostly to the middle class, a finer analysis of their socioeconomic status revealed that those with fewer socioeconomic resources (in the form of income, education, and contact networks) were likely to espouse lower levels of generalized trust than those with more resources.[9] As Foley and Edwards (1999) have observed, social capital is "context dependent" because the resources and access required to produce such capital are not evenly distributed across society (pp. 152, 168).

The general pattern of trust found among participants has two major implications. First, if we assume that a preference to cooperate with others is cost-sensitive, we can argue that the sociohistorical context in which associational activity takes place increases or decreases the costs of cooperation over time.[10] What we observe in Argentina is that, for the most part, cooperation among participants was confined to those individuals "whose dispositions and character [were] individually known to one another"—that is, small, homogeneous groups that relied on particularized trust (Williams 1988: 6, 8).[11] Second, contrary to the expectation of the neo-Tocquevillean thesis, the observed trend was that organizational activity engendered for one purpose (e.g., the demand for justice in cases of police violence) did not necessarily generate social capital readily available for other purposes (e.g., the promotion of civil rights across society) (see Coleman 1988: 108). Under conditions such as those described in Chapter 3, the "cost threshold" for cooperation increased considerably in the hostile context of Argentina, decreasing the chances for generalized trust to emerge, and also making social capital less accessible to those with fewer resources

TABLE 4.1

Logistic Regression of Social Trust Predictors

| Variable | B | S.E. | Wald | df | Sig. | R | Exp (B) |
|---|---|---|---|---|---|---|---|
| Group membership | .0112 | .0184 | .3754 | 1 | .5401 | .0000 | 1.0113 |
| Gender | -.1852 | .1828 | 1.0259 | 1 | .3111 | .0000 | .8309 |
| Age | .0009 | .0060 | .0239 | 1 | .8770 | .0000 | 1.0009 |
| Education | .0419 | .0307 | 1.8639 | 1 | .1722 | .0000 | 1.0428 |
| Income | .0929 | .0528 | 3.0987 | 1 | .0784 | .0384 | 1.0974 |
| Constant | -1.4834 | .4999 | 8.8048 | 1 | .0030 | | |
| Dependent variable | Social trust | | | | | | |

SOURCE: World Values Surveys (Argentina, 1991).

(Williams 1988: 6; Foley and Edwards 1999: 166). The weakness of the law "as institutionalized cultural values, norms, rules, and rights" intensified the negative aspects of this process (quotation from Cohen 1999: 66; see also Chapter 1).

Interestingly, the pattern found in the ethnographic study was confirmed by survey data in Argentina. Indeed, an analysis of public opinion data collected in the second wave (1991) of the World Values Surveys revealed that civic participation in Argentina (measured as membership in voluntary associations) did not breed social trust in participants. First, I examined the relationship between levels of participation in groups (the number of different organizations to which individuals belong) and social trust (trust in most people).[12] I found no statistically significant difference in participation between those who trusted others and those who did not (ANOVA test).[13] Also, the association between participation and trust was nonsignificant in the sample (Pearson's correlation). In brief, these data showed no connection between the level of involvement and social trust.

In turn, I modeled social trust with group membership and demographic and socioeconomic variables (gender, age, education, and income) as predictors.[14] As Table 4.1 shows, the logistic regression analysis reveals that the effect of group membership on social trust is not statistically significant—that is, participation in formal groups is not a significant predictor of trust.[15] This finding offers additional evidence (in this case, with a focus on group membership) that the social capital hypothesis as stated by neo-Tocquevilleans (civic participation promotes social trust) does not work in the Argentine case.

## Group Links

The analysis now shifts from the individual to the group level. It focuses on the kinds of interactions that the civic organizations in my cohort established within civil society and with the state. Before discussing my findings, let me introduce the conceptual framework that I employ as a basis for the analysis. The categories that structure the horizontal and vertical dimensions are summarized in Tables 4.2 and 4.3. I illustrate this discussion with examples from my research.

The horizontal dimension refers to the relations within civil society that help to "interweave the weft and warp of civil society and give it a more variegated, more resistant fabric" (Stepan 1989: xii). Studies of the voluntary sector have emphasized the importance of networks in which associations participate, stressing the need of explaining the role of civic organizations according to the structure of their *external connections* (Chalmers 1997: 6; Hadenius and Uggla 1996: 1627–35). "The impact of organized interests on the type of democracy," Schmitter (1992) has argued, "cannot be assessed by merely adding together the associations present in a given polity but must also take into account the properties that emerge from their competitive and cooperative interaction" (p. 439). Table 4.2 presents the most significant horizontal links within civil society, which are arranged according to modal patterns. These links can be characterized by fragmentation or coalescence.

First, as Table 4.2 depicts, the interaction among groups in a pattern of fragmentation is characterized by friction, so mutual hostility and conflict tend to dominate these relationships. In my sample of organizations, confrontation between groups involved competition for members, different opinions about cases, access to specific government agencies, or disagreement over sectoral agendas (e.g., a plan of action in response to a case of police brutality). Second, when organizations, as a result of their strategic priorities, are unable or unwilling to support sectoral interests (or even cross-sectoral interests), they tend to isolate themselves from the rest of civil society. This has happened, for in-

TABLE 4.2

Horizontal Links within Civil Society

| Link | Pattern | |
|---|---|---|
| | Fragmentation | Coalescence |
| Interaction | Conflict prevails | Potential for consensus |
| Strategic priorities | Group interests | Alliances |
| Social networks | Within cleavages | Across cleavages |

stance, when a group promoted an agenda without much support in society (e.g., the rights of prisoners) and lacked the capacity or willingness to integrate that agenda into a broader rights-oriented movement. Third, in a pattern of fragmentation, groups tend to establish connections exclusively within class, gender, or other cleavages. These groups cater to members of a particular socioeconomic sector and perceive other groups as unlikely partners, even when they share similar goals. In my cohort, upper- and middle-class organizations with access to international sources of funding were often reluctant to establish links with groups of lower-income activists.

When civil society organizations find space for consensual action, they are able to overcome, for instance, personal interests of leaders and internal group norms. This pattern of interaction, coalescence, was illustrated in my study by groups that collaborated, with successful results, in the presentation of cases before an international court—when all attempts to obtain justice in Argentina had been exhausted. When groups agree on strategic priorities, they are likely to establish alliances (not necessarily permanent) with groups advancing similar or related goals. After the city of Buenos Aires gained political autonomy, organizations were able to work together to lobby for the elimination of police prerogatives that allowed police officers to make arrests *even* for noncriminal behavior (such as "hanging around" on a street corner). Finally, when groups develop social networks that cut across social cleavages, they not only increase their broader influence but also strengthen the fabric of civil society (see Stepan 1985, particularly his analysis of the role of civil society in the Brazilian transition to democracy). In Argentina, organizations working in different areas—such as human

TABLE 4.3
Vertical Links with the State

| Link | Pattern | |
| --- | --- | --- |
| | Confrontation | Collaboration |
| Interaction | Zero-sum conflict | Mutual empower-ment |
| Strategic priorities | Mutually exclusive goals | Collaborative agenda |
| Perception | Monolithic state | Heterogeneous state |

rights, civil rights, women's rights, development, and environment—and catering to different social groups, have not been able to create effective networks to advance common objectives (see Thompson 1996).

Table 4.3 summarizes the most significant dimensions in the relationship between civil society and the state.[16] First, in a pattern of confrontation, the civil society–state relationship tends to be reduced to a zero-sum conflict.[17] For some groups, human rights could only be promoted in opposition to the state. In their view, the state was only capable of violating such rights. Second, in setting their strategic priorities, civic groups consider their objectives to be inherently opposite to those of the state and thus assume no common ground for cooperation. For instance, some organizations in my study employed polar categories (democratic/authoritarian) to define themselves in relation to a specific state agency (e.g., the Interior Ministry) and rejected any possible (formal or informal) links with that agency. Third, the perception of the state held by participants in civil society organizations is important because it shapes the type of relationship that a group seeks with state agencies. Several organizations in my study depicted the state as inherently authoritarian and corrupt, perceiving the state apparatus as a monolithic entity, which convinced them that it was in their best interest not to cooperate with government officials.

The interaction between civic groups and the state in a pattern of collaboration may be one of mutual empowerment (see Migdal 1994: 4; Chazan 1994: 279; Rothchild and Lawson 1994: 256). A request by the organization Poder Ciudadano (Citizen Power) that political candidates disclose their assets before elections increased the legitimacy of both Poder Ciudadano and the candidates who agreed to participate. Furthermore, the invitation served as a basis for future cooperation between the group and those candidates elected to public office. Second, the belief that it is possible to define an agenda in collaboration with a segment of the state led a few groups in my sample to work on specific bills (e.g., on victims' rights) with legislators at the national and provincial levels. In these cases, strategic priorities of groups were not defined on the basis of "temperamental" decisions (animosity toward a certain public official, for instance), but as a result of cultivating a relationship and offering their experience and expertise. Last, a perception of the state apparatus as an aggregate of heterogeneous agencies is likely to result in effective interactions with specific segments of the state. This perception leads to a more flexible approach to government institutions, which allows some groups to seek supportive niches within the state. As I found in my research, this approach was likely to modify the state, strengthening areas that could operate as spaces for mutually beneficial exchange with civil society. This type of link was not common among the groups in my study, though. One of the few exceptions was an organization in Mendoza (Relatives of Defenseless Victims of Mendoza, FAVIM) that had a multilayered view of the state and operated using different strategies of negotiation with different segments of the state hierarchy.

## Horizontal Links

The slice of civil society examined in my study showed that, even among groups that were most likely to coalesce, horizontal links were few, weak, and generally ineffective. Most of the groups in the cluster lacked the capacity, motivation, and willingness to cooperate, which diminished their impact on institutions. Not only did the evidence reveal a high degree of fragmentation among these groups, but their coalescence with the rest of civil society was very low. This lack of horizontal links was, to a great extent, a function of the high cost threshold for cooperation imposed by the broader political and social context in Argentina.

Two of the groups in the sample, which worked on cases of state repression and seemed to have a similar approach (strongly confrontational) toward government officials, did not converge because their restrictive membership practices determined their stance toward each other (one had to be a lawyer to join one organization and the child of a "disappeared" to join the other). They perceived each other as essentially different organizations in spite of their obvious similarities. In the end, interaction between these two groups was limited to signing statements repudiating acts of police violence or endorsing public demonstrations. These groups had a strong appeal among young sectors of the population; thus, a potential nexus of cooperation could have been the organization of campaigns focused on the rights of young people. In addition, the groups could have joined forces to approach sympathetic government officials (particularly in the Justice Ministry) who had previously worked in the NGO sector.

Even though trust was produced within groups, it was not translated into broader circles of cooperation. Paradoxically, among organizations that confronted a state accused of human and civil rights offenses, the level of hostility between the groups themselves (e.g., because of different approaches to pursuing a case of police violence) sometimes appeared to be more intense than their animosity toward the state. Over time, relations between some groups deteriorated to the point that, for instance, one organization sent memos to local radio stations announcing that a demonstration organized by another group had been canceled. As the president of the NGO organizing the event told me, they saw the incident not only as a boycott of their activities by the other group, but also as an attempt to win over the other organizations that had supported the protest.

With a few exceptions (such as CELS and Poder Ciudadano), the new groups did not establish steady links with other organizations in the cluster. There were tensions, mutual accusations, and constant disagreement. Groups did not see other organizations in the same universe as potential allies: the degree of mutual respect and esteem was dramatically low by any standard. Some groups pursued decisively confrontational tactics, such as public attacks against the police (e.g., in demonstrations with significant police presence or in exchanges with the media), which were strongly opposed by other organizations. "They are not interested in reforming the institution [the police]," said one member, referring to another group in the cluster. "They are interested in confrontation, because confrontation gives them legitimacy before the marginal youth."

If cooperation among groups was low, when it occurred, its impact (on state practices, for instance) was usually weak. Indeed, the inability to find common and sustained strategies of cooperation led to more fragmentation among groups: when cooperation failed, mutual respect and trust inevitably decreased.

There were, as noted, some exemptions to this poor record of cooperation. These were generally found among groups with a strong professional background. CELS, for instance, collaborated with organizations of relatives of victims to present specific cases before the Inter-American Commission on Human Rights (CIDH). CELS provided legal advice and facilitated international contacts (especially in the United States) with these groups. Another organization, Poder Ciudadano, sought to establish cross-sectoral alliances with NGOs working with minorities (the handicapped, indigenous people, women, and immigrants) in order to strengthen the role of citizens in promoting the accountability of public officials. This was part of a foreign-funded project designed to identify and publicize all the legal mechanisms available to citizens for the enforcement of accountability.

Interviewees sometimes referred to a sense of isolation from other organizations in civil society and society in general. A rabbi who had a prominent role in an organization of relatives of victims told me: "When I'm at the square demanding justice every Monday, I want to know who's with me, what kind of support there is from civil society. But they have left us alone. Society and our own [Jewish] organizations have deserted us."[18] This was a common complaint among victims, relatives of victims, and other participants in these groups: when they organized to make demands—to denounce injustice—they were usually ostracized, not only by society at large, but also by the civic organizations (religious, neighborhood, cultural) that had provided them with a sense of community before they started their rights-oriented activism.

## Vertical Links

The relationship between the groups in my study and government agencies is a microcosm that illustrates some aspects of conflict between civil society and the state in Argentina. During the 1990s, for several organizations in the area of human and civil rights, the state meant a cohesive, impermeable structure marked by corrupt and authoritarian practices. They perceived the state as an enemy and thus rejected any possibility of dialogue with government authorities. Some groups even promoted an antistate message with violent overtones. In this type of discourse, the police institution was described as a device for social control in a system perceived as essentially exploitative and undemocratic. "The ruling class needs this type of police apparatus, because it's a central component of the repressive system in Argentina," one lawyer active in a watchdog group told me. Therefore some activists believed that the police had to be confronted with violence. An expression often heard in some festivals (e.g., music festivals "against repression and 'trigger-happy' police") and demonstrations to protest police abuse was, "Let's kill the police and those who control them!"[19]

Among the groups that did not have a confrontational attitude toward government authorities, several claimed that cooperation with the state could damage their legitimacy in the eyes of the public. This dilemma convinced many participants that the potential losses of approaching the state would outweigh the potential benefits. As a member explained to me, their group had devoted significant resources to gaining public legitimacy, and therefore "the problem is that the social legitimacy that we have attained in the last few years could be lost if we cooperate with an agency of the state."

Two groups in my study (CELS and Poder Ciudadano) were able to communicate—though only occasionally—and sometimes cooperate with segments of the state without relinquishing their autonomy. CELS, for example, engaged in dialogue and collaborated with the Subsecretariat for Human Rights, the Federal Police, the Justice Ministry, the Office of the Ombudsman in Buenos Aires, and the armed forces in several provinces. According to the organization's former executive director, the outcome of these interactions was mixed. Bureaucratic limitations and intra- and interagency conflicts often hindered the development of wide-ranging programs on issues such as citizen security. For CELS, a closer link with state agencies gave them increased legitimacy with policymakers in general and with some other civil society organizations (though several groups perceived this approach as dangerous for the autonomy of the organization and criticized the idea of engaging the state in a nonconfrontational manner).

In my follow-up study in 2000, I observed that CELS had increased its contacts with state agencies, especially with the Federal Police and the Ministry of Justice. Reacting to public opinion's concern over police abuse, increasing levels of crime, and poor performance of the courts in the late 1990s, government agencies approached CELS for technical advice on specific issues (e.g., police reform programs). Indeed, some state agencies sought the assistance of organizations with legal and technical expertise. This suggests that civil society's expertise could be turned into a key asset to engage the state in a mutually beneficial relationship. Rather than working with a model in which civil society *replaces* the state (as the state shrinks, for example), it appears to be much more feasible and effective to engage civil society in areas of state action in which the state's expertise is deficient. Several groups in my sample had some know-how or experience that could be of great use to the state—from expertise in criminal law and forensics to insight into the psychological effects of violent death in the household.

The link between the state and the NGOs surveyed in this study was deeply affected by their mutual perceptions. Several of the government officials interviewed for my study believed that civil society groups did not have the professional capacity to play a meaningful role in promoting transparency and accountability in state institutions. Likewise, civil society activists perceived government officials as unlikely partners. Reflecting general beliefs in society, one NGO member said, "politicians will do nothing for the people, they only take care of their personal interests." Thus the possibility of cooperation was greatly reduced when both sides agreed that the other party was incapable of meaningful actions and acceptable performance.

What happens when the state seeks to build bridges with civil society? In the 1990s the Argentine government tried to "strengthen" civil society through programs in the provinces centered on civic education. Even though these programs did not engage my cluster of groups specifically, it is useful to look at them briefly. Primarily, the government focused on low-income communities, identified community leaders, and trained them in organizational and problem-solving skills. The objective was to reinforce existing associations as a means of increasing social capital among the poor. In addition, the federal government launched a program to train public officials at the provincial and municipal levels in order to improve the articulation between local authorities and civic organizations. This government-sponsored program was guided by the idea that effective governance relies on strengthening the power of citizens to participate. As the national coordinator for the program explained to me, the project advanced a conception of "good governance" centered on transparency, accountability, and popular input as building blocks of an effective administration. In the words of this government official: "Traditionally, the conception has been to undercut the power of the citizen. But if I give the citizen more education, more leadership, a more inclusive space, I become a better leader." The program was a sound step in the promotion of leadership skills at the local level, but the lack of resources in these communities was a major obstacle to the development of concrete solutions to their day-to-day problems (e.g., employment, child care, health services, education).[20]

Even though it is not known whether this effort improved civil society's capacity to affect policy outcomes (because follow-up studies were not part of the program), ethnographic evidence collected in Argentina in the late 1990s showed that the attempt (including the above-mentioned programs) to promote more democratic links between community organizations and local government (i.e., links that were not based on dominance and subordination) tended to be obstructed by poverty, social exclusion, and strong networks of clientelism, among other factors. In greater Buenos Aires, for example, solutions to the poor's problems primarily pivoted around networks of political brokers (Peronist Party bosses known as *punteros* or *referentes*), who served as intermediaries in the exchange of goods and services for political support and votes at the municipal level (Auyero 2000: 67; 2001: 90–91). This type of interaction left little space for autonomous grassroots organizations to have a real voice in local matters.

The existing system of socioeconomic stratification shaped the kinds of social links found in contexts of poverty and social exclusion. As studies in poor areas in Buenos Aires province have shown (e.g., Auyero 2001), in this context, clientelism is often "the sole mechanism providing protection" to those whose rights are not protected otherwise (Rossetti 1994: 100). Solutions to the poor's problems are controlled by a network of brokers, who serve as "*gatekeepers*, as go-betweens directing the goods and services coming from the executive branch of the municipal government (the mayor) to the individuals (the clients) who are to receive them" (Auyero 2001: 96). The attempts to build civic capacity in settings marked by material deprivation, chronic unemployment, violence, and harsh economic constraints were largely futile. Javier Auyero (2000) has shown that the "solutions, services, and protection" supplied by clientelistic networks in poor areas were not construed by the clients as embedded in a system of unequal power (p. 73). On the contrary, clients viewed these exchanges with party bosses who acted as intermediaries in clientelistic networks as nurturing "trust, solidarity, reciprocity, caring, and hope." As Carlo Rossetti (1994) has explained in reference to another setting: "If the protection of generalized rights is weak or absent, protest and political demands tend to find a niche within the clientelistic order, regulated by particularistic and illegal exchange, because clientelism is the sole mechanism providing protection." As a result, "clientelistic exchange, as an organizing principle of the polity, may involve far more than dyadic relations and favoritism; it may also affect the ground rules for the structuring of social relationships" (pp. 100–101). In brief, this analysis suggests that state-sponsored programs to build social capital cannot disregard the conditions that sustain structural inequality and social exclusion at the local level.[21]

Government-sponsored programs to promote civic engagement may represent a "second-best" option, especially for disadvantaged sectors of society, unless they incorporate actual measures to increase the prospect for citizens to influence policy decisions directly. When participation does not influence the decision-making process, it "might actually be counter-productive in raising expectations that are not then met" (Wilson 1999: 253, quotation on 250). This is especially true among traditionally excluded social groups. The impact of failed expectations on public support for political institutions may outweigh the results of civil society–building programs. Failed expectations can be especially damaging when the legitimacy of institutions is already very low, as in the case of Argentina (this is relevant for other countries in Latin America too; see Lagos 1997; 2001).

## A Combined Model

What happens when we combine the patterns at the horizontal and vertical levels in a single model and employ it to assess the practices of the organizations in my sample? The horizontal and vertical connections among organizations reveal the general characteristics of this cluster of associations. I sorted organizations according to their modal pattern of horizontal and vertical links, by which I mean a predominant mode of engagement, following the categories outlined in Tables 4.2 and 4.3. This analysis assumes that the behavior of an organization can follow a certain pattern, but does not necessarily mean that the organization has a unique, unidimensional profile.

The classificatory scheme is based on an index consisting of three variables. I employ the index to assign values to the organizations on the horizontal and vertical dimensions. The horizontal indicators measure the degree of conflict versus common interests, the group's strategic priorities in relation to other actors and its capacity to reach an understanding with other groups, and the nature of the group's embedment in social networks. At the vertical level, the indicators focus on the degree of collaboration and compromise with state agencies, the strategic priorities of groups in addressing government interests and agendas, and the group's aggregate perception of the state apparatus as monolithic or diverse.[22]

Coding entailed placing all groups within my classification scheme. In coding the qualitative evidence, I took into account data collected through interviews, archival research, and participant observation. In evaluating an organization, I made a judgment about key attributes of the group, taking into account the evidence as a whole. I paid attention to the extent to which coding reflected a single conceptual scheme or a trend among competing views within the group. Both discourse and practices were taken into consideration in the analysis.[23]

In general, the groups in my study showed a significant degree of homogeneity in the dispositions of their members. This homogeneity, however, was not always the result of a consensus in the group. In fact, it often concealed a phenomenon inimical to the creation of political pluralism and democratic attitudes in the realm of association: members were likely to choose the exit option when they disagreed with the leadership or a majority in the group. This pattern reflected a "bias against voice," because participants were likely to perceive those members who spoke up "as *introducing* a conflict and thus threatening the solidarity, mission, or purpose of the group" (Warren 2001: 103–8, quotation on 104). In the cluster of groups I examined in Argentina, exit was likely to create disengagement and disillusionment among individuals, despite the availability of alternative groups.[24]

Table 4.4 shows the distribution of my sample of organizations according to the classificatory scheme.[25] A group that fell into the northwest (NW) cell (fragmentation, confrontation) tends to perceive the state as a monolithic, antagonistic institution and to find no common interests with other groups. An organization in the northeast (NE) cell tends to be hostile toward the state, but has multiple interactions with other groups in civil society, especially in the area of human and civil rights. A group in the southwest (SW) cell gives priority to the interaction with the state at the expense of its links with other groups. This type of group does not participate in horizontal alliances or maintain sustained interactions with other organizations. Finally, an organization in the southeast (SE) cell tends to find potential for consensus and col-

TABLE 4.4

Empirical Relationship between Horizontal and Vertical Links:
Human and Civil Rights NGOs in Argentina (percent)

| Vertical Link (with the State) | Horizontal Link (within Civil Society) | |
| --- | --- | --- |
| | Fragmentation | Coalescence |
| Confrontation | 40 | 13 |
| Collaboration | 20 | 27 |

NOTE: Percentages are based on three-item series (for each dimension). $N = 15$.

laboration both within civil society and with the state. This type of group has repeated interactions with state agencies, participates in horizontal networks, and develops links with other civic organizations.

As Table 4.4 shows, nearly three-fourths of the civic organizations in my study fell outside the SE cell. This cell approximates the neo-Tocquevillean idea that civic organizations are likely to promote cooperation and collaboration with other groups in civil society and to engage in an interaction of mutual empowerment with the state. Forty percent of the organizations fell into the NW cell. These groups displayed a profile of confrontation with the state—often expressed in their inability or unwillingness to find spaces of cooperation with government agencies. They often approached the state—whether at the "commanding heights," in the "trenches," or at any other level of the hierarchy—as an enemy.[26] These civic groups were unlikely to cooperate with organizations advocating similar or complementary objectives. They were also unlikely to develop networks across social cleavages.

## International and Transnational Links

I have paid attention to the horizontal and vertical links of human and civil rights organizations at the domestic level. However, a reference to their connections with international actors and transnational networks is also warranted. Indeed, the two most "civic" organizations in the sample, CELS and Poder Ciudadano, were also among the most transnational ones. CELS has had long-standing links to international actors since the military regime of 1976–83 held power. As part of the domestic human rights movement that denounced the military's rights violations, members of CELS and other groups "traveled frequently to the United States and Europe, where they met with human rights organizations, talked to the press, and met with parliamentarians and government officials" (Keck and Sikkink 1998: 105). In order to effectively denounce human rights violations by the military government, these organizations "sought foreign contacts to publicize the human rights situation, to fund their activities, and to help themselves from further repression by their government, and they provided evidence to U.S. and European policymakers" (pp. 105–6). Financial support from U.S.-based and European foundations to Argentine human rights groups was key to the development of transnational links.[27]

The long-standing relationship between CELS and the Ford Foundation dates back to this period. After the transition to democracy, CELS continued to receive funding from Ford and other international organizations to support its activities.[28] In addition, CELS became part of several transnational networks for the promotion of justice and government transparency, and carried out joint projects with the Inter-American Institute of Human Rights (IIDH) in Costa Rica, the Center for Justice and International Law (CEJIL), and universities in the United States and Chile. Most of the members of CELS—especially those in leadership positions—are cosmopolitan and have fluid links with colleagues in similar organizations in the Americas and Europe. International funding and insertion in transnational networks helped CELS to sustain its everyday work, to maintain international visibility, and sometimes to legitimate its demands on the Argentine state during the 1990s.[29] However, reduced international interest in Argentina after the establishment of democracy made it difficult for CELS and other groups to secure financial support, to count on sustained international solidarity, or to expect international actors to help denounce such problems as police violence and exert pressure on government authorities, thus putting in motion the "boomerang process" that was so efficient in the late 1970s and 1980s (on this earlier process, see Keck and Sikkink 1998: 107). Attention to Argentina's democracy waned in the late 1980s when a candidate from the opposition party was elected to office and the country was perceived as having entered its democratic "consolidation" phase, and as international concern in the field of rights and democratization shifted to areas other than Latin America.

Poder Ciudadano emerged after the transition to democracy, but its pattern of international and transnational links has been very similar to that of CELS. In fact, Poder Ciudadano has successfully secured funding from international sources (including the U.S. Agency for International Development and several European and U.S.-based foundations) and domestic groups and businesses as well. This organization created an inter-American network for the promotion of democracy in 1995 and a year later became the Argentine chapter for Transparency International. As in the case of CELS, most of the leadership of Poder Ciudadano received advanced education abroad and regularly participate in international forums on democracy-building.

Whereas the direct impact of international actors has been generally positive, it is important to note some of the limitations imposed by international sponsors and some of the problems associated with maintaining transnational links while coping with a difficult domestic environment. Three issues in particular deserve attention. First, organizations with more international and transnational links have fewer connections to the rank and file. This pattern is especially evident in the case of Poder Ciudadano. According to my observations, this group did not establish solid and sustained relations with grassroots organizations working directly with underprivileged sectors. Indeed, the interaction that Poder Ciudadano established with less privileged groups was mostly hierarchical and tied to short-term issues (often funded from abroad).[30] In fact, a number of the association's decisions during my period of research suggested a propensity to favor international over domestic contacts.

Second, changes in international support for these groups had a significant impact on their activities and agenda. Having assumed that the advent of democracy itself would bring about a positive and mutually reinforcing interaction with civil society, many international organizations cut back their funding in new democracies such as Argentina. The combination of reduced support and a focus on short-term projects restricted the capacity of domestic groups to develop long-term programs dealing with such complex issues as access to justice and government accountability. Alternative sources of funding at the domestic level have not been able to replace the critical international support.

Third, the ability to project the issues raised by domestic groups onto an international stage depends on what kinds of issues are relevant to transnational publics. The relative political and economic stability enjoyed by Argentina in the 1990s (after the hyperinflation crisis) and decreasing international concern for the military abuses of the past pushed the country to the sidelines in the eyes of the international rights community. Deficiencies in the protection of individual rights and weak controls over police violence were not seen as serious threats to the stability of democracy. This new context closed many of the former avenues available to rights organizations to enlist international support for their activities. It is important to mention that Argentina received international attention in the early 1990s for reasons other than democracy or rights: it became a showcase of economic success for the international financial community; even the *Wall Street Journal* hailed the "Argentine miracle" on its front page (September 11, 1992).

Although international attention decreased in the areas of "traditional" human rights, the emergence of new issues in the international arena helped to advance the demands of some groups. For example, lacking support from the rest of Argentina's civil society, the incipient gay rights organization Homosexual Community of Argentina (CHA) turned instead to international support for its efforts to reverse the official decision to deny formal legal recognition to the association. Indeed, the government agency responsible for granting legal status to nonprofit organizations dismissed CHA's petition for recognition, claiming that the group's purposes were against the "common good" and, specifically, contrary to the family and the nation's moral order. CHA appealed the decision and the case eventually made it to the Supreme Court of Justice, which ruled against the group (Kornblit, Pecheny, and Vujosevich 1998: 26–27). The Supreme Court judges justified its decision with Roman Catholic doctrine and moral arguments, as well as arguments about protecting the family and the common good and the impossibility of sanctioning a condition that has negative effects on society as a whole.[31] Responding to CHA's calls for assistance, European and U.S.-based gay organizations organized public protests against then-president Menem during his visits to Europe and the United States in the early 1990s, in which he sought to attract investment in a stable and democratic "First World" Argentina. These protests prompted Menem to use his discretionary powers to change the ruling and give CHA legal recognition (pp. 127–28). This political decision was motivated by the president's desire to eliminate obstacles to his agenda, rather than by a sincere attempt to redress a succession of homophobic rulings. In this respect, the outcome of this case did not imply a legal victory for the gay organization because formal recognition was not granted as a result of a debate over constitutional arguments.[32]

## Controlling State Coercive Power

The question of whether civic groups have the capacity to control and impose limits on the coercive power of the state centers on the effect of civil society organizations at the institutional level. Indeed, most empirical studies of the civil society–democracy link have been focused on political culture effects, saying little about the capacity of voluntary associations to exert a direct impact on the state. So, how does civil society influence the state's coercive side? My analysis is focused on civil society's contribution to control and reform the police force—the effort to make the police accountable to the law.[33] The study consists of two parts. The first centers on the democratizing potential of organizations through the judicial system. The second examines the influence of civil society via the legislative process.

First, I focus on the role of organizations in securing indictments and convictions of police officers involved in acts of brutality (mostly arbitrary killings of civilians by police agents). When police officers torture or kill a civilian (in a case that constitutes abuse of force), it is extremely difficult for victims or relatives to seek justice in Argentina (see Chapter 3, Table 3.3). This fact was also confirmed in dozens of interviews with relatives of victims of police violence. Unless the relatives had large socioeconomic resources, they could not expect a proper legal resolution of their case (and even if they had the resources, the likelihood of a fair trial was slim) (see Brinks 2002: 44–49). The case was likely to be rapidly dismissed because of insufficient evidence (witnesses were often intimidated by the police, forensic reports were falsified or distorted) or because the police investigation "showed" that the victim represented a threat (this was usually done by planting a weapon or altering evidence at the crime scene).

If relatives successfully demanded an investigation, they had to obtain a private criminal lawyer and one or more forensic experts. As a study on the rule of law in Argentina has explained, "the length and complexity of the criminal process" in this country makes private legal defense "prohibitively expensive for the majority of the population" (Ungar 2002: 203). This is especially significant when we consider that most cases of police violence involved victims from lower-income sectors.[34] In addition to the financial burden of this process, the psychological toll on relatives of victims accusing the police was also very high, especially because of threats and harassment by the police themselves.

As a result, the pursuit of justice in cases of police abuse without any organizational help was likely to fail rapidly. Therefore voluntary organizations concerned with police violence played a fundamental role in this process. These groups often provided legal representation, expertise, and personal support to relatives of victims. It is thus important to examine the performance of these organizations in the realm of legal defense. My empirical question is, what was the success rate of the civic organizations that pursued criminal cases of police brutality in the 1990s? A high rate of indictments and convictions of police officers for acts of brutality may, over time, lead to reforms in the police institution and to increased protection of the rights of citizens. Even though we cannot assume that such a success will lead to sustainable, comprehensive police reform, an analysis of the outcome of these cases can provide a measure of the effectiveness of civil society groups in promoting accountability.

In the second part of my study, I examine the influence of civil society on congressional activity to democratize the police. As other studies have shown (e.g., Bermeo and Nord 2000), the connection between civil society and the legislature has vital implications for the construction of democratic polities (see Chapter 1). For example, the experience of Europe in the nineteenth century showed that "the internalized link between the citizenry and the formal arenas of representation" played a crucial role "in determining whether groups would be supportive of democracy or not." Weak links between citizens and parliaments had a negative impact on the prospects of building strong democracies: "The greater the mass of groups that felt disconnected from allegedly 'representative' institutions, the weaker the foundations of representative government itself." In Europe, the "sense of connectedness" between organized citizens and parliament came not only from political parties, which linked sectors of the citizenry to representative institutions, but also from the specific public policies generated by those institutions. Nineteenth-century Europe revealed that the level of connection between civil society and democratic institutions was a decisive element in the movement toward democracy (Bermeo 2000: 252, quotations on 244). In contemporary democracies, the influence of social actors at the law-making level is a key area of civil society's potential to affect the institutional sphere (Avritzer 2002a: 49).

If we want to assess the ability of civil society to influence the establishment of limits on the coercive side of the state, it is important to examine the impact of civic groups and networks on legislation designed to democratize the police. This is especially relevant in new democracies, where the police force often expresses strong authoritarian tendencies, resulting from years of military rule and lack of democratic controls. In order to explore this question, my analysis centers, first, on the cluster of human and civil rights organizations and their impact on legislation. I then investigate the connection between civil society in general and congressional activity in the area of police reform for the period 1983–96.

## Legal Effectiveness

It is extremely difficult to gather reliable data on the outcome of cases of police violence in Argentina and to determine the role played by human and civil rights organizations in these cases. One of the associations included in my ethnographic study, CORREPI (Coalition against Police and Institutional Repression), compiled an inventory of cases of victims of police violence dating back to 1983. Data are available for 327 individual cases of killings of civilians by the police in circumstances that showed an arbitrary use of force (some of these cases also included torture). These cases received attention in the media and support from organizations in the area of human and civil rights. The files recorded the legal outcome of each case as of 1998, classified by region (federal capital, Buenos Aires province, and the rest of the country).[35]

Table 4.5 shows the status of these cases by 1998. In 23.2 percent of the cases, police officers were detained and indicted for the killings, and in one out of four cases, police officers were convicted for the crime. One must note, however, that sometimes officers condemned for killing a civilian received light sentences—two or three years at the most. In one case, a police officer who killed an unarmed person after a soccer match was sentenced to nine years in prison and, following an appeal, the sentence was reduced to two and a half years. There were no major regional differences in indictments and convictions: the percentage of indictments in the city of Buenos Aires (the federal capital) was slightly lower than in the rest of the country, while the rate of convictions in the interior provinces was higher than in the federal capital and Buenos Aires province.

What was the actual effectiveness of civic organizations in the legal arena? The figures in Table 4.5 suggest some trends. First, the percentage of convictions (24.5) did not lag far behind the percentage of cases that did not result in a sentence (33.7).[36] This means that, in spite of the

TABLE 4.5

Legal Outcomes in Cases of Police Violence (percent)

|  | Federal Capital | Buenos Aires Province | Provinces | Total |
|---|---|---|---|---|
| Cases set aside | 30.8 | 13.2 | 13.5 | 14.7 |
| Cases not pursued | 3.8 | 0.7 | 7.8 | 4.3 |
| Cases reopened | — | 4.1 | 0.6 | 2.1 |
| In process | — | 4.1 | 1.9 | 2.7 |
| Cases being investigated | 11.6 | 13.1 | 14.7 | 13.8 |
| Detentions and indictments | 19.2 | 23.4 | 23.7 | 23.2 |
| Sentences | 23.1 | 22.8 | 26.3 | 24.5 |
| Acquittals or cases dismissed | 11.5 | 13.8 | 7.7 | 10.7 |
| Lesser charges / wrong indictees | — | 4.8 | 3.8 | 4.0 |
| Total | 100 | 100 | 100 | 100 |
| N | 26 | 145 | 156 | 327 |

SOURCE: CORREPI, "Archivo de casos, 1983–1998: Recopilación de muertes de personas a manos de las fuerzas de seguridad en Argentina," available at http://www.dere-chos.org/correpi/muertes.html.

hostile context in which these cases were pursued, the rate of success was quite encouraging. However, most of the cases under investigation or in process as of 1998—which constituted 16.5 percent of the total— should probably be considered discontinued because they had had that status for five, six, or even ten years. If this percentage is added to the cases with no convictions, then the rate of success is not as reassuring as it initially seemed.

Also, when the broader context of police violence is taken into account—that is, both the number of killings and the fact that most cases of police violence are swiftly dismissed without proper investigation— then the rate of success of civic groups in curbing impunity is more modest than it looks in the table.[37] Indeed, according to data on the total number of arbitrary killings of civilians by the police in the federal capital and greater Buenos Aires ($N$ = 1785; there are no systematic data for the rest of Buenos Aires province), the cases of police violence included in the inventory (only for these areas) represent around 10 percent of the total number of civilians killed by the police since the first years of democracy.[38]

## The Legislative Arena: Organizations and Reform

The cluster of human and civil rights organizations in my study had very few connections with the legislature. There were a few exceptions, however. As the following examples show, when state and civil society actors come together, the results can be encouraging. Indeed, civil society organizations can provide solid expertise—the result of years of experience in the trenches—that can be of significant use for legislators committed to reforming institutions.

The sustained work conducted by CELS on police violence had a substantial influence on a bill introduced in 1996 to reform personnel regulations in the Federal Police.[39] The core of the bill was to allow police officers to carry their weapons only while on duty. Indeed, several studies conducted by CELS showed that, in the city of Buenos Aires, nearly 50 percent of civilians killed by the police in shoot-outs involved off-duty police officers (CELS / Human Rights Watch 1998: 89; see also CELS 1996 and 1997). The research revealed that, in many cases, innocent civilians were victims of the police's excessive and indiscriminate use of firepower. Thus the rationale of the bill was to limit these occurrences by restricting the use of weapons by police officers under conditions in which the safety of civilians could be placed in jeopardy.[40] Although the bill was not passed, this example illustrates how the information produced by a civic organization could be employed by legislators to present a concrete solution that would probably have lowered the number of civilian victims in Buenos Aires.

A group of relatives of victims of police violence in the province of Mendoza (FAVIM) promoted a bill to reform a section of the province's penal process code (Article 89) that limited the rights of victims and their relatives in criminal proceedings: the victim or relatives could not have access to the results of preliminary investigations if no one had been indicted in the case. In the late 1980s and 1990s, Mendoza had a more serious police abuse problem than most provinces. There were numerous cases of police brutality involving executions, disappearances, and torture in this province.[41] Thus this bill represented an important step in the promotion of the rule of law in Mendoza.

Under increasing public concern with this situation, the provincial legislature approved the bill in 1993. The new article guaranteed the victim of any criminal act or his/her direct relatives (1) the right to be treated in a respectful manner by judicial authorities, (2) the right to be morally and physically protected during the criminal process, and (3) the right to be informed of the legal proceedings related to the case, including the status of the process and the indictments made. The article stated that victims and their relatives must be informed of all the legal possibilities available to them to affect the criminal proceedings, including the right to become a civil plaintiff in the case. By becoming a civil plaintiff, a victim or victim's relative could gain access to information relevant to the case, which could be used to push for further investigations and faster justice. This bill was the direct result of the experience of relatives of victims and their lawyers in cases of police violence in Mendoza. FAVIM played a central role in crafting the bill and lobbying for its sanction. In fact, the personal narratives of relatives of civilians killed by the police in this province had a strong impact on the legislature's decision to pass this reform quickly.

While the provincial media supported FAVIM's efforts to reform the penal process code, the very same media worked to black out news of the activities of FAVIM and other human and civil rights groups in Mendoza. This change was due primarily to government pressures. Indeed, in a context of corruption, co-optation, and weak legal guarantees, the media did not support in a sustained manner the prodemocratic role of groups such as FAVIM. In turn, FAVIM's greater willingness to cooperate with government institutions—partly in response to its legislative success—caused distrust and conflict with other rights organizations in the province. This pattern concurs with the findings in Buenos Aires, where, as noted, the interaction among groups was largely marked by mutual hostility and conflict. Also, it shows the difficulty of breaking a vicious circle of noncooperation within civil society and between civil society groups and the state nourished by a deeply embedded distrust of the government and a heightened competition for resources.

## A Broader Look

These illustrations show that cooperation between civic groups and the legislature (in these cases, at the national and provincial levels) can have democratizing effects. It is possible, however, to run a much more comprehensive test of the relationship between civil society and congressional activity in Argentina. The influence of civil society on the legislature can be examined from a broader perspective by measuring the connection between civil society activity and congressional debate on the reform of the police institution since Argentina's return to democracy in 1983. To do so, I collected data on legislative proposals that dealt with some reform aspect of the police institution. This information served as a basis for an initial dataset consisting of 120 bills for the period 1983–96 (96 bills originated in the Chamber of Deputies, 16 in the Senate, and 8 in the executive branch).

I categorized these bills according to two criteria: (1) their "democratizing" value, and (2) their level of importance. First, the content of each bill was codified according to a set of standards designed to place it along a continuum from "strongly democratic" to "strongly undemocratic" (a seven-point scale) (see below for details on the standards and rationale employed in this categorization).[42] In turn, the relevance of the law (important, somewhat important, low importance) was determined by the breadth of the bill, its potential impact on the police institution as a whole, and (when applicable) the number and magnitude of modifications to existing laws. For instance, a proposal that regulated the police's authority to detain citizens was considered an important bill; a proposal that reformed a specific feature of police officers' working conditions was classified as a somewhat important bill; and a proposal to cancel a certain monetary debt of the police institution with the state was coded as a bill with a low level of democratic relevance (see Molinelli, Palanza, and Sin 1999: 94 n. 71).

The central assumption underlying my criteria for democratic quality was that "human rights violations perpetrated by police officers are one of the major problems of Argentina's democracy" (CELS / Human Rights Watch 1998: 11). Therefore, the overarching criterion was to consider a bill democratic when it eliminated or restricted the police's power to violate human rights, individual rights, and constitutional guarantees. Specifically, a bill was classified as more democratic when (1) it corrected, modified, or eliminated authoritarian, corrupt, or negligent practices and procedures, (2) it restricted or eliminated police powers that were unnecessary for the effective deployment of security and protection, and (3) it corrected one of the following problems: (a) structural deficiencies in the decision-making system that hindered horizontal accountability (e.g., lack of external controls to police work), (b) informal rules embedded in the institution's culture that promoted violence, authoritarianism, or excessive use of force, (c) poor instruction and police training (which often resulted in recruitment of second-rate candidates), (d) substandard working conditions (which often led to corrupt practices), and (e) deficient internal organization (e.g., highly centralized leadership, arbitrary system of promotions, and overlapping responsibilities).[43]

The most challenging problem in this empirical analysis was to trace the presence of civil society input in the bills dealing with the police. I found a solution to this problem that tried to maximize the information available in the congressional material. The analysis was focused on the section of each bill (*Fundamentos*) in which the legislator(s) explained the basic principles that sustained the proposal and provided background to the bill. Adopting a broad definition of civil society—which included the various social networks, associations, and publics through which individuals interact and become involved in public life—I recorded all references to civil society in each legislative proposal. References to civil society included the following: (1) public opinion (general references to public concerns with police abuse, citizen security, and other issues); (2) media (direct references to the local media and to specific cases that attracted public attention, such as the Bulacio case,[44] police repression at sports events and rock concerts, and the kidnapping of businessmen); (3) organized citizen action (such as mobilizations of concerned citizens in reaction to specific incidents of police repression); and (4) organizations of civil society (specific references to NGOs, foundations, think tanks, professional associations, student organizations, committees of parents, and other civic associations).[45] In general, civil society organizations provided technical advice for the bills or voiced their concern to legislators on recurring problems concerning police action.

The analysis of the congressional data would not be complete without considering what led to the legislative activity. Therefore I included a measure of police violence in the analysis. The goal was to establish the extent to which legislation responded to variations in the levels of

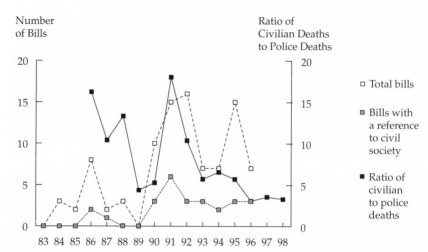

FIGURE 4.1    Congressional Response to Police Violence, 1983–1998
SOURCE: Congressional data, Argentina, 1983–1996; CELS data, 1986–1998.

police abuse. In order to express the degree of police violence over time, I calculated (using data collected by CELS) the yearly rate of civilians killed by the police relative to the number of police officers killed that same year. This measure was based on the rationale that, in a time series analysis, an increase in the number of civilians killed by the police *relative* to the number of police deaths expressed a rise in the arbitrary use of force by the police (e.g., "trigger-happy" occurrences).[46]

Figure 4.1 includes all bills rated as "democratic" (*N* = 95) according to the coding criteria explained above.[47] The figure shows a pattern of reactive congressional activity to variations in the level of police violence. The number of bills introduced in Congress followed almost identically the variations in the measure of police violence (with only one major difference in 1995). This pattern suggests that congressional activity to democratize the police was a response to police violence, especially because an increase in the level of police violence resonated in the media and thus influenced public opinion. If legislators submitted bills as an immediate response to peaks of police violence, it follows that most legislative proposals were geared to appease public opinion and probably resulted from a superficial analysis of the problems of law enforcement and citizen security. Few legislators could attest to having a consistent and informed approach to police reform and the problem of citizen security. As interviews with congressional aides and civil so-

TABLE 4.6

Congressional Activity Related to Police Reform, 1983–1996 (percent)

|  | Democratic Bills | Undemocratic Bills | Total |
|---|---|---|---|
| Bills including references to civil society | 27.4 | 12.0 | 24.2 |
| Bills including democratic language | 52.6 | 40.0 | 50.0 |
| No reference to civil society or democratic language | 20.0 | 48.0 | 25.8 |
| Total | 100 | 100 | 100 |
| N | 95 | 25 | 120 |

SOURCE: Congressional data, Argentina, 1983–1996.

ciety activists revealed, congressional commissions seldom sought the expertise of civil society groups, and there were no formal channels for introducing input from civil society. Indeed, input from some sectors of civil society was incorporated into the legislative debate only in selected cases that received a high level of media attention. As civic activists told me, the reactive nature of congressional activity made it virtually impossible for them to establish sustained, effective cooperation with legislators in matters of police reform. The interest of Congress in the question of police brutality was limited to responses to specific crises—as the data in Figure 4.1 show.

The bills with some reference to civil society followed closely the variations in police violence. These bills represented 27.4 percent of all the "democratic" proposals introduced in the period 1983–96 (see Table 4.6). A majority of the bills that included a reference to civil society had the potential to substantially affect police activity (73.1 percent).[48] Even though the presence of civil society in democratic bills was modest, the input from civil society was concentrated on important bills. Also, as the total number of democratic bills increased in the 1990s (there was an average of 3.6 bills per year in the period 1984–89 and 11.0 in 1990–96), the number of democratic bills with a reference to civil society followed a similar pattern (with an average of 0.6 bills per year in 1984–89 and 3.3 in 1990–96).[49] However, in more than thirteen years, only 7.7 percent of the bills to democratize the police with a reference to civil society were passed by Congress[50]—and only 8.4 percent of all democratic proposals were turned into laws.[51]

So far, these data reveal a modest presence of civil society in bills to democratize the police, a concentration of input from civil society on bills of significant relevance, and an increase in the link between civil society and Congress in the 1990s. There is yet another dimension of the link between civil society and the legislature that deserves attention. As explained in Chapter 1, informal and formal networks of association have the potential to create spaces for debate in the public sphere that can enter the realm of institutions (Ryan 2001: 242; Cohen 1999: 58–59; Young 1999: 157). In order to track this type of civil society influence on congressional activity, we can look for specific "democratic" elements of the legislative discourse. Indeed, when we trace the presence of a rights-oriented discourse in the legislative proposals to reform the police, we find that 52.6 percent of the democratic bills in the sample contain language that asserts notions of constitutionalism, individual rights, human rights, accountability, rule of law, and limits to state power (Table 4.6). Moreover, the presence of democratic discourse increased in the 1990s—from 2.4 bills per year with this type of discourse in 1984–89 to 5.4 bills per year in 1990–96.

If we place this last finding in the context of human rights activity in contemporary Argentina, we observe that the new human and civil rights movement may have inherited the democratizing role assumed by the old-line human rights movement that emerged in response to state terrorism in the 1970s. The presence of a democratic discourse with emphasis not only on human rights, but also on the rights of citizenship (with direct reference to the rule of law) may be a result of the new wave of associational activity that converged in the 1990s around issues whose referent was not an authoritarian past but the deficiencies of a democratic present. In this respect, this segment of civil society might have influenced public sphere debates by engaging in the production and circulation of information on police violence, lack of institutional accountability, and judicial ineffectiveness (see Chapter 1). Debates in the public sphere, in turn, entered the arena of legislative activity through bills intended to create a more democratic police in Argentina.

There is an important caveat to this analysis, though. As congressional data have shown in Argentina (and other countries), legislators often introduce many bills with little or no chance of becoming law. Indeed, these bills are only introduced to please voters and special interest groups (Molinelli, Palanza, and Sin 1999: 97, 435, table 2.207). This fact raises an important question: Was the presence of a democratic discourse in legislative production purely rhetorical? As the example of the infamous Federal Police's edicts (*edictos*) shows, when Congress faced the challenge to privilege constitutionalism and the rights of citizens over police prerogatives, it chose not to follow the path of commitment to democratic values. And as was already explained, the executive played a significant role in the legislative process because of the presidency's political and institutional power, used amply by Menem in the 1990s.

The edicts, which allowed police officers to detain and arrest people for noncriminal behavior (using criteria such as their physical appearance) were the focus of heated debate following Argentina's return to democracy. As Ungar (2002) put it: "Edicts allow police to punish people for who they are rather than what they have done, without being burdened by judicial processes and protections" (p. 92). After the federal capital gained political autonomy in 1995 and with the support of a broad network of civil society organizations, the newly constituted legislature eliminated the edicts and replaced them with a much more democratic code in 1998, which, among other provisions, established precise rules about detention procedures.[52] This decision, which represented an important step toward the democratization of the Federal Police, was soon contested by the police institution itself (which resorted to other mechanisms to preserve its old powers) and by middle-class neighborhood organizations (which protested the new code as permissive of criminal, offensive, scandalous behavior, and as a concession to marginal groups) (Ungar 2002: 95–96).

In 1999, President Menem took action on the matter and issued a decree that virtually reinstated many of the police prerogatives under the old edicts (Ungar 2002: 89–96; CELS 1998: 164–78). Two years after Menem's decree, the national Congress passed a law that increased the powers of the Federal Police to interrogate and conduct searches—new powers that, according to legal scholars and civic organizations, violated basic constitutional guarantees such as the right to privacy and the freedom of movement. The law passed in June 2001 gave the police new prerogatives, including the authority to demand information from a suspect on the site of the arrest and the power to make a search without witnesses. The law was contested by civil rights organizations. Indeed, before it was passed, CELS distributed a report to all legislators, alerting them to the serious constitutional violations contained in the legislation. Notwithstanding this warning, the bill was swiftly passed with almost no debate (Videla 2001). Subsequent legislation, including eventful modifications to the penal process code, carried new limitations on individual rights.[53]

## Conclusion

The contrasting trends among human and civil rights organizations in Argentina cannot be attributed solely to the features of these associations; one has to explain them in reference to the broader context in which civic engagement takes place. These trends cannot be understood without attention to the overall weakness of the rule of law in this country, as described in Chapter 3. Given the high cost threshold for cooperation in society, it has not been surprising to find few horizontal links among civil society groups and low levels of social trust among participants. In turn, the maze of obstacles that lies between a civic group and the achievement of justice—for instance, when an agent of the state commits a serious offense against one or more citizens—is so daunting that it is likely that civic participation will lead to distrust in institutions and cynicism about formal channels of participation.

Is there a positive link between civil society and democracy in Argentina, at least according to the universe discussed here? The analysis presented in this chapter shows that the connection between civil society and democracy is manifested through different types of effects. The findings of the ethnographic study revealed that individual groups often failed to promote democratic dispositions among their members. This cohort of groups did not develop strong horizontal networks; on the contrary, tensions between groups were common. Also, they had few connections with groups in other areas of civil society. Links between these groups and the state were weak. Their influence on the police forces and on the executive, legislative, and judicial branches of government was very limited.

In the legal arena, the data produced mixed results. If we consider the rate of success in convictions of police officers in cases of abuse and brutality, the results reveal a positive role for human and civil rights groups. However, when we consider the broader scenario—that is, the cases that have been under investigation for many years without any progress and the general problem of police violence in Argentina—then the level of effectiveness is more modest.

If we consider the direct and indirect impact of civil society on legislation to democratize the police, including that of NGOs dealing with police violence, the actual influence was only moderate. Legislative and ethnographic data suggest that human and civil rights organizations had much more impact on the public sphere than on state institutions. This wave of civic activism (organizations, movements, and the media) continued, and probably expanded, the rights-oriented discourse introduced by the earlier human rights movement, placing the question of individual rights and respect for the law on the public agenda. However, the institutional impact of this new wave of civic engagement has been very modest.[54] The serious weakness of the rule of law at the institutional level and a generalized problem of social cohesion—clearly mirrored in the associational realm—remain serious deficiencies of Argentina's democracy. These patterns attain relevance in light of the severe political crisis that the country experienced in 2001–2.

More specifically, the contribution of the new human and civil rights sector of civil society to democratization in Argentina during the 1990s may be assessed at three levels: (1) the dispersion of power, (2) the strengthening of political participation, and (3) the promotion of a more democratic political culture.[55] First, rights-oriented organizations and other social networks did not facilitate the strengthening of civil society as a whole, and their influence over the legislature to limit the coercive power of the state was limited. However, these groups contributed to the dispersion of power by supporting the judiciary through their involvement in the courts. The attempt to improve institutional mechanisms by pursuing judicial cases has been a positive contribution of some of these organizations.

Second, this sector of civil society did not show a definite contribution to political participation because of low levels of engagement with state agencies and only a modest degree of connectedness with the legislature. The ethnographic evidence revealed that civic participation often intensified cynicism toward and disengagement from the political system, failing to add legitimacy to the institutions of democracy. Still, the repeated calls of groups and various publics for respect of human and civil rights and their efforts to denounce abuses of state power entailed a positive contribution at the public sphere level. An open question is whether cynicism toward existing institutions will intensify citizen withdrawal from the political realm and reinforce a role for civil society as an alternative to political participation (see the analysis of Weimar Germany in Chapter 2).

Third, involvement in human and civil rights groups did not promote a more democratic political culture at the individual level. Most members of organizations did not demonstrate high levels of tolerance or a willingness to compromise. Civic activity contributed to developing organizational and leadership skills among participants, though the development of these skills does not necessarily imply the formation of a civic culture, as the example of the prison gangs in Texas illustrated (see Chapter 1). In turn, both qualitative and quantitative data showed no positive connection between civic engagement and social trust in Argentina. Finally, a troubling trend among participants was that the rejection of the state and the political arena was sometimes more important than proactive ideas. This finding drawn from a small number of civic groups became visible in the broader society after 2001, as thousands of average citizens took to the streets in December of that year to express their contempt for and rejection of government authorities and the "political class."[56]

I have shown the complex, changing, and often contradictory links between civic engagement and democratization in the context of a third-wave democracy. Next I explore, simultaneously, the relative impact of different variables—participation in formal organizations, political engagement, social trust, socioeconomic cleavages, national wealth, and education—on the quality of democratic institutions. The analysis in Chapter 5 shifts from the case-study approach to the use of quantitative data in a cross-national study.

CHAPTER 5

# A Cross-National Analysis

THIS CHAPTER shifts gears into a different kind of empirical analysis. Employing quantitative data drawn from several sources, I test the theories of civil society and social capital advanced by the neo-Tocquevillean literature across a set of old and new democracies around the world. In turn, I test some of the alternative claims advanced in this study, specifically the need to frame the discussion on social capital in contextual terms and the importance of accounting for the question of inequalities in society when studying the connection between social capital and democracy. Let me review some of the ideas set forth in Chapter 1 in order to link them to the plan of this chapter.

First, neo-Tocquevilleans agree that social, or interpersonal, trust is at the core of social capital and that a high stock of social capital is related to democracies that "work." This claim raises two questions. One is how to create social capital. For Putnam and others, civic participation produces social trust. The second question is whether civic engagement and social trust actually lead to better democracies. For neo-Tocquevilleans, civic participation improves the quality of government institutions through the production of broad networks of trust.

Second, I have argued, in contrast to the a-contextual claims of neo-Tocquevilleans, that structural conditions affect the production of social capital. I explore this alternative approach cross-nationally. As explained in Chapter 1, it is necessary to bring the question of inequality to the debate on social capital and democracy. Whereas the study's previous empirical chapters focused on the impact of various forms of inequality (e.g., racism and other forms of discrimination) on associational life and social capital, the analysis in this chapter looks in particular at the role of income inequality in the production of trust.

Finally, in the theoretical analysis I argued that dominant patterns of interaction within society play a fundamental role in the construction of the rule of law. Particularly important are relations of domination and subordination, which are often linked to economic disparities. In this chapter I focus on the connection between the rule of law (at the institutional level) and economic inequality.

## Civil Society, Social Capital, and Institutional Quality

One of the most interesting dimensions of the debate about civil society and democracy concerns the link between microsocial and macropolitical levels—namely, the degree and mechanisms by which values, habits, and practices shaped in the realm of associational life are transferred to the broader sphere of governance. As explained earlier, proponents of civil society–building as a path to deepening democracy across the world have argued that associational life facilitates norms of cooperation and reciprocity among individuals and that this process in turn influences the democratic quality of institutions. The case studies demonstrate that citizen involvement in associational life can lead, under certain conditions, to social conflict and to cynicism toward democracy. Furthermore, as the case of Weimar Germany reveals, dense and vital associational networks may not strengthen the quality of democracy; on the contrary, in Germany they disseminated antisystem attitudes and Nazi ideas, which contributed to the collapse of democratic politics in that country.

I test the neo-Tocquevillean hypothesis that voluntary associations and social networks contribute to promoting a form of community interaction that produces trust and cooperation between citizens, facilitating broader social articulation and generating the conditions for good and effective democratic governance (see Newton 2001: 201). As I will show, this hypothesis fails when tested across a sample of twenty-eight nations, including well-established democracies (the first and second waves) and new democratic regimes (the third wave).[1] After showing that the civil society thesis does not explain institutional quality—specifically when we try to predict the effectiveness of the rule of law at the institutional level—I test an alternative hypothesis: economic inequality, a key structural condition, accounts for the production of social capital and in turn explains the quality of democratic institutions across nations.

The discussion is organized around the three ideas outlined earlier. First, I investigate the relationship among civic engagement, social capital, and institutional quality, focusing on the institutional effects of civil society and social capital in actual democracies. I test the connection that runs from civic engagement and social trust (a core component of social capital) to institutions with a more comprehensive conception of democracy than the one employed by Putnam (1993) and others (e.g., Inglehart 1997). This test explores, in particular, the potential of associational life to generate institutional changes. My findings show that participation in voluntary organizations does not predict institutional quality, and social trust does emerge as a strong predictor of democratic institutions that work effectively. But, as further analysis reveals, trust is dependent upon socioeconomic conditions that work adequately for some and not for others (Foley and Edwards 1999: 161–62).

Second, I treat social capital as a dependent variable, directing the emphasis toward the role of context in order to investigate the cross-national impact of socioeconomic structures on collective levels of trust. I test whether social capital is context-dependent, modeling trust with civic engagement and social cleavages as predictors. The results show that civil society participation (measured as membership in voluntary groups and political engagement) is not a determinant of trust. In contrast, GDP per capita and income distribution emerge as predictors of social trust. The finding that economic inequality plays a key role in social trust formation provides evidence that the "everyday" production of social capital cannot be detached from the specific socioeconomic conditions under which people interact with each other (Rao and Walton 2002; see Newton 1999; Foley and Edwards 1999; Bourdieu 1986). This result affirms what we have learned with a different methodology in the case studies. Furthermore, whereas a context-dependent approach to social capital at the national level tells us that the production of trust is shaped by broader structural conditions, an analysis of social trust formation that takes into account "winners" and "losers" at the subnational level confirms the idea that an individual's relative position in society affects his trust in others. The data show that trust at the subnational level is unevenly distributed across cleavages of class and education. Interestingly, this pattern is consistent across well-established and new democracies.

Third, I direct the attention to a key dimension of institutional quality: the rule of law. Finding that trust depended on economic equality, I wanted to investigate the role that these two variables play in predicting the effectiveness of the rule of law (which I treat as a dependent variable here). In particular, I am interested in exploring the relationship between income distribution and the rule of law; that is, the relationship between contextual variables. The analysis reveals that inequality in the distribution of income is negatively related to the strength of the rule of law across old and new democracies.

## Data

Measuring democratic institutional performance in a way that allows for cross-country comparison is a difficult task. Not only is it arduous to obtain reliable measures given the vast contextual differences across nations, but it is also difficult to construct indicators that measure "democratic" governance. Studies such as that of Putnam (1993) were questioned because of their approach to measuring democracy—Putnam's measure focused on such policy "outputs" as cabinet stability, day care centers, and agricultural spending capacity (pp. 65–73).[2] For Putnam, democracy equals policy performance. His concern with effectiveness of service delivery (e.g., promptness, innovation, and bureaucratic capacity) is not related to democratic practices. Indeed, what is problematic about Putnam's operational conception of democracy is that his focus on performance does not discriminate between democratic and undemocratic politics (Tarrow 1996: 395–96). For instance, Putnam's conception of democracy does not take into account the effectiveness of the rule of law or the ways in which the state protects (or does not protect) the rights of individuals. Therefore, if our goal is to explain how *democracy* works, it is necessary to find indicators that capture the inherent dimensions of actual democracies in the world today.

Other studies have examined the link between civil society and democratic *stability* and *quality* with measures that capture defining attributes of democracy—but in a limited way. Inglehart (1997), for example, has argued that associational life is strongly linked to democratic stability and to the quality of democracy. His analysis provides cross-national evidence to support the neo-Tocquevillean thesis of a positive link between civil society and democracy, but his measures are not as comprehensive as one would like, given the complexity of such concepts as civil society and democracy. His only measure of civil society is membership in voluntary associations (see below for a discussion of this issue) and his indicator of democratic quality is drawn from a single source—Freedom House's ratings for political rights and civil liberties (Inglehart 1997: 188–205).

## Institutional Quality

Recently, a team of World Bank economists developed a set of indicators that measure key dimensions of institutional performance in democracies (Kaufmann, Kraay, and Zoido-Lobatón 1999b). Their database on democratic governance includes over 300 measures of institutional quality collected from a wide variety of sources. Measuring the quality of governance (understood as "the traditions and institutions by which authority in a country is exercised"), these data are drawn from "polls of experts, which reflect country ratings produced by commercial risk rating agencies and other organizations, and cross-country surveys of residents carried out by international organizations and other non-governmental organizations" (p. 1).[3]

In the analysis, I employ four composite governance indicators developed by Kaufmann and colleagues: voice, government effectiveness, control of corruption, and rule of law. The composite governance indicators are based on 1997–98 data.[4] They are measured in units ranging from -2.5 to 2.5. Higher values correspond to higher-quality outcomes. The measures employed in the construction of the voice indicator included aggregate levels of political rights, civil liberties, and government responsiveness. For government effectiveness, Kaufmann and colleagues employed measures of the provision of public services, performance of bureaucracy, competence and independence of the civil service, and government credibility. The measures utilized to create the index on control of corruption ranged from the impact of graft on business transactions to the frequency of bribery in state-citizen interactions. Finally, the indicator for the rule of law included measures of the independence and effectiveness of the judiciary, enforceability of contracts, quality of policing, and the incidence of crime (Kaufmann, Kraay, and Zoido-Lobatón 1999b: 7–8).

These indicators represent an improvement in our ability to test the hypothesized link between civil society and democracy employing quantitative data because they allow us to explore much more than policy performance. Of special significance is the index measuring the rule of law at the institutional level. As noted, the rule of law is a variable achievement in any country (see Örkény and Scheppele 1999: 57, 73; O'Donnell 1999b: 321). If the effectiveness of the rule of law is incomplete even in well-established democracies, then it is particularly interesting to test whether the levels of civic engagement and social capital in a given society are associated with the variations in the effectiveness of the rule of law.[5]

## Civic Engagement and Social Capital

Quantitative studies of civil society tend to operationalize associational activity as membership in voluntary organizations. This measure of civic engagement—particularly if taken as an indicator of the vitality or strength of civil society—is limited, both conceptually and empirically. Indeed, it conveys a narrow representation of the vast networks and forms of association (formal and informal) contained in the idea of civil society.[6] Still, there are few alternatives to the measure of membership when it comes to cross-national studies using quantitative data. Thus I employ membership in formal groups as one, but not the only, measure of civic engagement in my analysis.[7] Following Stephen Knack and Philip Keefer (1997), my aggregate measure of civic engagement is the average number of associations mentioned per respondent in each nation (p. 1272). As they have acknowledged, this indicator does not account for intensity of civic participation; that is, it does not tell us about multiple membership patterns. It does not inform us on the degree of personal involvement in voluntary groups either. The other measure of civic involvement is an index of citizens' political engagement, which addresses the dimension of social movement mobilization. This index is constructed on the basis of people's involvement in signing a petition, joining in boycotts, and attending lawful demonstrations. In other words, this index seeks to capture participation linked to both formal and informal social networks.[8]

The social trust variable employed in the analysis is an item with two response categories ("most people can be trusted" and "you can't be too careful in dealing with people").[9] One must acknowledge that this measure of trust is ambiguous at best, because the idea of "trusting most people" has different meanings in different nations, cultures, and socioeconomic groups. However, there is enough conceptual agreement—and empirical support—to argue that this measure helps to distinguish generalized trust (confidence in all sorts of people, with special emphasis on strangers or those different from ourselves) from particularized trust (confidence in people we know, particularly family and friends) (Uslaner 1997: 2–3, 16). As explained in Chapter 1, generalized trust is associated with positive predictability in interactions beyond our immediate social circles (Janoski 1998: 87). Thus the measure of social trust that I employ seeks to capture the kind of "bridging" or "inclusive" social capital that Putnam (2000) has highlighted as vital for the development of cross-cutting cooperative relationships in society.

It is important to acknowledge an important limitation contained in indicators such as social trust. As in the case of other data based on aggregate national assessments by country experts or mean values at the national level, this measure assumes uniform distributions across socioeconomic lines within countries, which does not occur in actual democracies. As Foley and Edwards (1999) have argued:

Cross-national research relying on mean scores at the national level on variables such as social trust, civic norms, or trust in government ignore[s] the significance of varying distributions that may lie behind identical statistical profiles. In this respect, work like that of Ronald Inglehart on "political culture" and Putnam's on the "civic culture" in Italy is vulnerable to the same criticism that has been applied in the development literature against the use of per capita GNP as a measure of "development." In both cases, the underlying distributions may reflect wildly varying national or regional patterns. (p. 151)

At the same time, Foley and Edwards (1999) have suggested that researchers exploring the role of civil society and social capital may include data on economic distribution (such as the Gini coefficient) in order to estimate the role of this type of economic variable in explaining outcomes (p. 170 n. 8). In agreement with this suggestion, my statistical analysis employs data on income distribution in order to explore the role of the socioeconomic context in social capital formation in first-, second-, and third-wave democracies. It also examines differences in social trust at the individual level, across social cleavages within nations.

## Socioeconomic Cleavages

I employ two indicators to explore the impact of socioeconomic cleavages on institutional quality and the production of social capital: income inequality and ethnic fragmentation. Inequality in the distribution of income is measured with data on Gini coefficients drawn from Klaus Deininger and Lyn Squire (1996), who assembled a dataset containing an average of six high-quality observations for each nation.[10] As a result of the number and quality of observations, their data represent a substantial improvement in quality over other data on income inequality. Divisions along ethnic lines are measured with an index of ethnolinguistic fragmentation (Knack and Keefer 1997). My assumption is that higher levels of this type of fragmentation result in too diverse and often antagonizing interests, which makes consensus and self-enforcing agreements much more difficult to reach than in homogeneous societies (Inter-American Development Bank 2000: 188; Knack and Keefer 1997: 1278–79).[11] In the different models, I control for education and GDP per capita.[12]

The income inequality variable is particularly relevant for my analysis because it allows me to measure the incidence of structural conditions on the production of social capital and the institutional quality of democracy, in particular, the dimension of the rule of law. A concern with income inequality can provide empirical evidence to show that the production of networks of trust and reciprocity is dependent upon the socioeconomic resources available to individual and collective actors in specific contexts. If such evidence does exist cross-nationally (it emerged in Argentina's microstudy, for instance), then it can challenge the idea of social capital as a purely cultural construct and support a notion of social capital as largely determined by structural factors (Foley and Edwards 1999: 153, 166–68). In turn, as noted, it is important to examine the link between economic inequality (which texturizes interactions within society) and the rule of law at the level of the state. There is ample evidence that, in highly stratified societies, the poor and underprivileged generally lack access to justice and enjoy few actual rights (see, e.g., Méndez, O'Donnell, and Pinheiro 1999).

## The Institutional Effect of Civil Society and Social Capital

The development of a dense network of social relations based on reciprocity and solidarity has been viewed as vital for the strengthening of institutional performance (Putnam 1993; 2000). A central hypothesis of proponents of civil–society building states that associational life generates changes in social relations, which are aggregated to the broader level of institutions. Taking participants in voluntary organizations as the unit of analysis, this approach posits that associational life socializes

ABLE 5.1

redicting Institutional Quality

| | Voice | | Government Effectiveness | | Control of Corruption | | Rule of Law | |
|---|---|---|---|---|---|---|---|---|
| | Eq. 1 | Eq. 2 | Eq. 3 | Eq. 4 | Eq. 5 | Eq. 6 | Eq. 7 | Eq. 8 |
| GDP per capita | .315 | .413 | .229 | .346 | .324 | .362 | .524* | .535* |
| Primary school | .255 | .246 | .262 | .238 | .100 | .080 | .051 | .049 |
| Secondary school | .029 | -.016 | .005 | -.042 | -.025 | -.036 | .039 | .035 |
| Social trust | .473* | .521* | .522* | .579* | .455* | .464* | .414* | .429* |
| Group membership | .083 | | .121 | | .170 | | -.093 | |
| "Olson" groups | | -.116 | | -.120 | | .052 | | -.084 |
| "Putnam" groups | | .139 | | .136 | | .097 | | -.058 |
| $R^2$ | .685 | .697 | .645 | .652 | .650 | .642 | .721 | .723 |
| N | 26 | 26 | 26 | 26 | 26 | 26 | 26 | 26 |

OURCES: Governance Research Indicators 1997–98 (Kaufmann, Kraay, and Zoido-Lobatón); Eu-
omonitor International 1999–2000; Barro-Lee Schooling Data (years 1970 and 1980); Knack and
.eefer 1997.
IOTE: Table reports standardized beta coefficients.
* $p \leq .05$.

individuals into cooperative behavior. The mechanism that links societal patterns at the micro level to institutional outcomes is the production of social trust. Trust, for neo-Tocquevilleans, is *the* fundamental in-
gredient in social capital. In brief, they posit a causal connection that
runs from civic engagement to social capital to institutional quality. It is
thus important to test this hypothesis in both old and new democracies.
I employ four variables of democratic quality, including the effectiveness of the rule of law. Therefore, in this test, I reverse the causal direction posited in earlier chapters in order to explore whether the neo-Tocquevillean hypothesis of the impact of group membership and trust on
institutional success holds true.

Table 5.1 displays the results of the OLS regression analysis. First, it shows the effect of social trust on the four composite indicators of institutional quality, controlling for GDP per capita (1997–98) and percentage of population with completed primary (1970) and secondary school (1980). The results show a statistically significant relationship between social trust and all dimensions of institutional quality. Second, the table shows the effect of civic engagement (measured as membership in voluntary organizations) on the indicators of institutional quality. As equations 1, 3, 5, and 7 indicate, group membership is not significant in any of these indicators.[13] In other words, trust matters when it comes to the quality of governance. In contrast, involvement in associations is not relevant. I also ran the model without including social trust, that is, solely with group membership and the other variables as predictors. The results (not shown) revealed that group membership was still insignificant in all the regressions.

Some studies have argued that different types of groups have different effects on their members and the broader society (see, e.g., Stolle and Rochon 1998). Therefore it might be necessary to distinguish among types of groups when assessing their impact on democratic quality. Knack and Keefer distinguished between groups most likely to function as "distributional coalitions" producing rent-seeking behavior—"Olsonian" associations—and groups most likely to produce horizontal networks of trust and cooperation—"Putnamesque" associations (see Olson 1982; Putnam 1993).[14] Thinking along these terms, we may ask: Does the detrimental influence of "Olsonian" groups—which could be counteracting any positive effects by "Putnamesque" groups—explain the lack of impact of the group membership variable? (Knack and Keefer 1997: 1272–74). As equations 2, 4, 6, and 8 of Table 5.1 show, this is not the case. Distinguishing between types of groups does not produce any different results. Interestingly, both "Olsonian" and "Putnamesque" groups are negatively correlated with the rule of law, though their impact is nil.[15]

If participation measured as membership in formal groups is not a significant determinant of institutional quality (even after discriminating between types of groups), what happens when we employ the index of political engagement based on measures of political mobilization? In fact, an emphasis on people's decision to sign a petition, join in boycotts, and attend demonstrations avoids the problem of focusing exclusively on membership in formal groups and thus might capture the concept of civic engagement more precisely and directly than the other variable. However, when political engagement replaces group membership in the multiple regression, the results reveal that this alternative variable is not a significant determinant of institutional quality in three of the four dimensions tested. Political engagement has a statistically significant impact only on the dimension of voice, showing an impact of this type of civic participation on government responsiveness and political rights and civil liberties (beta = .356, $p \leq .05$; results not shown). This impact suggests that citizen mobilization can have an effect on some aspects of democratic governance, as studies on social movements have demonstrated.

The findings shown in Table 5.1 thus support the notion that the stock of social trust held by a nation is strongly associated with the quality of its institutions. In contrast, the density of associational life (specifically group membership) does not predict effective and democratic governance. Conceptually, these findings correct the claim by Putnam and others that social capital is dependent upon the existence of a dense network of associations. As the data have shown, social capital as a determinant of institutional quality is driven by the power of social trust, not of associational life. At the aggregate level, then, social trust has a positive institutional effect across old and new democracies alike.[16]

## Determinants of Social Trust

If social trust is linked to positive democratic outcomes, perhaps the production of trust in new democracies can be a path to good institutions. Thus it is important to explore the sources of social trust. First, we need to explore whether civic engagement creates trust. As Kornhauser, Almond, Verba, Putnam, and others have told us, citizen involvement in voluntary associations instills trust and tolerance in individuals because these groups offer people a chance to work together and share their different experiences, values, and ideas (Newton 2001: 206). In order to test this assertion, we can look at the relationship between civic involvement (operationalized as group membership and political engagement) and social trust. Changing social trust into the dependent variable, we can test the claims of Kornhauser, Putnam, and others. This is a relevant test in light of what we have seen in the case of Argentina, where both ethnographic evidence and individual-level survey data showed no inherent association between civic participation and interpersonal trust. The qualitative study suggested that associational ex-

TABLE 5.2
Predicting Social Trust I

|  | Social Trust | |
| --- | --- | --- |
|  | Equation 1 | Equation 2 |
| GDP per capita | .829** | .937** |
| Primary school | -.266 | -.321* |
| Secondary school | -.127 | .009 |
| Group membership | .079 | |
| Political engagement | | .113 |
| $R^2$ | .603 | .642 |
| N | 26 | 27 |

SOURCES: World Values Surveys 1990–93; 1995–97; Euromonitor International 1999–2000; Barro-Lee Schooling Data (years 1970 and 1980).
NOTE: Table reports standardized beta coefficients.
\* $p \leq .05$; \*\* $p \leq .001$.

perience was likely to reinforce preexisting attitudes and values in participants—even when they were at odds with a civic culture—and sometimes strengthened distrust in others. Other studies (e.g., Newton 1997; 1999) have shown similar findings for other countries. In brief, what happens when we test the impact of civic engagement on social trust cross-nationally?

As Table 5.2 shows, civic engagement measured as membership in voluntary organizations (equation 1) is not a significant predictor of social trust (OLS regression). Even when distinguishing between "Olsonian" and "Putnamesque" groups in the regression analysis (results not shown), the impact of group membership on trust is not statistically significant. Furthermore, employing the measure of political engagement shows no different result (equation 2): civic engagement measured in this way is not a determinant of trust either. This means that social trust is not readily manipulable by promoting citizen participation (Uslaner 2000–2001: 575–76; Newton 2001: 204).[17] Social trust, however, is strongly determined by national wealth. Both equations in Table 5.2 show that per capita GDP is a strong predictor of trust.

Whereas a number of studies have examined trust as an a-contextual

TABLE 5.3
Predicting Social Trust II

| | Social Trust | |
|---|---|---|
| | Equation 1 | Equation 2 |
| GDP per capita | .680*** | .904*** |
| Primary school | -.424** | -.318* |
| Secondary school | -.159 | -.123 |
| Income inequality | -.440** | |
| Ethnic homogeneity | | -.007 |
| $R^2$ | .703 | .599 |
| $N$ | 27 | 28 |

SOURCES: World Values Surveys 1990–93; 1995–97; Euromonitor International 1999–2000; Barro-Lee Schooling Data (years 1970 and 1980); Knack and Keefer 1997; Deininger and Squire 1996.
NOTE: Table reports standardized beta coefficients.
  $* p \leq .05; ** p \leq .01; *** p \leq .001.$

phenomenon, I have argued that it is necessary to reconnect social trust with its specific socioeconomic setting. Thus the next step in the analysis is to explore the relationship of social trust to contextual factors. I employ two variables to assess the effect of socioeconomic factors on social trust: income inequality and ethnic fragmentation. Equation 1 of Table 5.3 regresses social trust on income inequality (Gini), controlling for per capita GDP and education.[18] As the equation shows, income inequality is a significant determinant of trust (beta = -.440); these variables are inversely related (economic inequality is not a fertile ground for the production of trust). In contrast, as equation 2 reveals, ethnic homogeneity is not a significant predictor of social trust.[19] It is interesting to mention that the $R^2$ for equation 1 is higher than that for equation 2, which means that the model with income inequality has a stronger explanatory power.

These results show that the more egalitarian a country is, the higher its aggregate level of trust (see Uslaner 2000–2001: 589, for a similar finding). The Scandinavian countries, for instance, have a very egalitarian distribution—the bottom 20 percent of the population receives

TABLE 5.4

Predicting Social Trust III

| | Social Trust | |
| --- | --- | --- |
| | Equation 1 | Equation 2 |
| GDP per capita | .595* | .741** |
| Primary school | -.371 | -.419** |
| Secondary school | -.186 | -.080 |
| Income inequality | -.418* | -.391* |
| Ethnic homogeneity | -.018 | -.080 |
| Group membership | .115 | |
| Political engagement | | -.052 |
| $R^2$ | .687 | .719 |
| $N$ | 25 | 26 |

SOURCES: World Values Surveys 1990–93; 1995–97; Euromonitor International 1999–2000; Barro-Lee Schooling Data (years 1970 and 1980); Knack and Keefer 1997; Deininger and Squire 1996.
NOTE: Table reports standardized beta coefficients.
  * $p \leq .05$; ** $p \leq .01$.

around 10 percent of the national income while the top 20 percent receives about 35 percent—and, as expected, the four nations display
very high levels of trust (for example, Norway's average social trust
score is 64.8). At the other extreme, Brazil shows an extremely inegalitarian economic distribution: the bottom 20 percent receives 2.5 percent
of the national income while the top 20 percent of the population receives 64.2 percent, and its aggregate-level social trust score is extremely low (2.8).[20]

The preceding two models have explored, independently, the effect
of civic engagement and socioeconomic cleavages (income inequality
and ethnic fragmentation) on social trust. To complete this analysis,
Table 5.4 presents a single model with both civic engagement and cleavages as predictors of social trust. The OLS multiple regression confirms
that civic participation, whether expressed as membership in voluntary
associations or as a form of politically oriented citizen involvement,
does not account for the production of social trust. In contrast, this

model affirms that economic inequality hinders social trust formation (and that national wealth and high levels of social trust go together).

The impact of economic inequality on social trust shows that generalized trust, and therefore cooperation and reciprocity, are largely dependent upon the egalitarian nature of society. Stated differently, inegalitarian societies do not foster the conditions that sustain expectations of reciprocity in social relations. The case studies only affirm this claim. Most individuals are "conditional cooperators" because they "act cooperatively only when they have high expectations that others will reciprocate" (Knack and Keefer 1997: 1258, citing Hardin 1982). Indeed, people do not show distrust in every interaction, but their trust in others is a result of hard experience (Peel 1998: 333). It is difficult to create broader networks of trust in societies where there is a tradition of social exclusion based on economic inequality, among other factors. "You can't build trust," Uslaner (2000–2001) has argued "when some groups feel left out of the society and believe that others control the resources" (p. 580). Building bridges across social groups—that is, creating a common culture, a shared identity, broad radii of trust, or whatever term we use for this goal—is not an easy project in highly unequal societies. But this finding does not apply only to this kind of society. This pattern is also relevant for more egalitarian—and generally wealthier—nations. Indeed, there is a well-established relationship between GDP and reductions in inequality, but even in wealthy countries, economic inequality has a negative effect on social capital over time, as recent studies have shown. For example, a recent study of the United States found that a steady increase in income inequality from the 1960s through the 1990s led to lower levels of social trust (Uslaner 2000–2001: 587–89).

## Who Trusts?

Neo-Tocquevillean approaches to social capital tend to be ahistorical: they neglect the role of inequality, social exclusion, discrimination, racism, and other contextual factors. In contrast, I argue that the structural position of individuals in society is fundamental to understanding the question of social trust (see Edwards and Foley 2001: 230). Indeed, the placement of individuals in the social structure matters for their willingness to trust others. In order to explore the question of who trusts at the individual level, I follow an analytical approach posed by Kenneth Newton (1999: 182, table 8.7). I examine individual-level data for the set of twenty-eight nations: the analysis focuses on social trust across income and education. I am interested in comparing trust within countries. The figures in Table 5.5 indicate the percentage differences across education (lower and upper educational attainment) and income (lower and upper income levels) for those respondents who said that most people can be trusted.[21] Negative figures show lower levels of trust among less-educated and lower-income respondents. For example, take the case of the United States at the bottom of the group of first- and second-wave democracies. The first figure shows that individuals with lower levels of education are 22 percent less trusting than those with higher educational attainment. In turn, the second figure shows that individuals with lower incomes are 12 percent less trusting than those with higher incomes.

As these results show, access to social capital is not evenly distributed within nations—at least according to differences of education and income (which are related). Canada's aggregate level of trust is about twice that of Argentina, but as Table 5.5 shows, the percentage difference in levels of social trust between upper- and lower-income respondents is very close in both countries. This means that a political culture variable such as trust cannot be dissociated from socioeconomic disparities (see Foley and Edwards 1999: 162).[22] These results complement the findings in the case studies: the lesson is that building social trust among individuals who have reasons to distrust each other (because of disparities in wealth but also as a result of discrimination, social exclusion, restricted access to goods and services, and so on) is difficult in all societies (though more difficult in some than in others) (Uslaner 2000–2001: 580). As the qualitative evidence has shown, cleavages other than income and education matter for social capital formation as well. Consider the United States, where vast differences in trust emerge also when we focus on the cleavage of race. For the period 1972–96, 46 percent of whites—and only 17 percent of blacks—said that most people can be trusted (p. 580). This is not surprising given the exclusionary trends in U.S. society, as the analysis in Chapter 2 illustrated.

The survey data summarized in Table 5.5 suggest that people who possess fewer resources have strong experiential reasons to distrust. Therefore they are "careful and economical in their allocation of trust" (Peel 1998: 333). These people feel more vulnerable in their social interactions than they perceive other private actors to be (on this point, see Putnam 2000: 138).[23] Social trust, Newton (1999) has argued, is "the prerogative of the winners in the world" (p. 185). "It is more frequently ex-

TABLE 5.5

Social Trust by Education and Income in First-, Second-, and Third-wave Democracies

| | Difference in Trust between Less- and More-Educated Populations (%) | Difference in Trust between Lower- and Higher-Income Populations (%) |
|---|---|---|
| *First- and second-wave democracies* | | |
| Australia | n.a. | n.a. |
| Austria | -15 | -12 |
| Belgium | -20 | -11 |
| Britain | -24 | -10 |
| Canada | -26 | -17 |
| Denmark | -23 | -18 |
| Finland | -18 | -6 |
| France | -18 | -20 |
| Germany | -17 | -12 |
| Iceland | -18 | n.a. |
| Ireland | -19 | -19 |
| Italy | -14 | -20 |
| Japan | -28 | -20 |
| Netherlands | -22 | -19 |
| Norway | -30 | -20 |
| Sweden | -26 | -8 |
| Switzerland | -33 | -7 |
| United States | -22 | -12 |
| *Third-wave democracies* | | |
| Argentina | -11 | -14 |
| Brazil | -3 | -2 |
| Chile | -9 | -7 |
| India | -5 | -2 |
| Mexico | 1 | -2 |
| Portugal | -12 | 0 |
| South Africa | -8 | 0 |
| South Korea | -15 | -5 |
| Spain | -17 | -16 |
| Turkey | -12 | -2 |

SOURCE: Inglehart, Basañez, and Moreno 1998.
NOTE: Figures are percentage differences across education and income for interviewees who said "most people can be trusted" (see Newton 1999: 182, table 8.7).
n.a. = not available.

pressed by the 'winners' in society, rather than the 'losers'" (Newton 2001: 204). Who are these losers? They are "the minorities, blacks, unemployed, working class, poor, poorly educated, low socio-economic status, low income" (Newton 1999: 180–81). Indeed, the stock of social capital held by different social groups is not dependent on their participation in associations, but on their position in the socioeconomic structure.

Survey data explain only part of the link between social trust and differences in income, education, and social status (Newton 2001: 204). Indeed, the micro-level ethnographic data for Argentina indicate that socioeconomic cleavages may account for differences in trust; but there are other factors (among them, impunity and systematic humiliation at the hands of state and private actors) which show that, under certain conditions, one may be a middle-class, educated, white person and still suffer high levels of abuse at the hands of the police and other state agents. In this type of situation, traditional social and economic variables are generally not useful in accounting for the vulnerability of these individuals (though they explain different *degrees* of vulnerability).

## Inequality and the Rule of Law

Is there more than a "political culture" explanation (i.e., one based on social trust formation) to good democratic governance? Do structural variables have a direct impact on the quality of democratic institutions? Analyzing regime change in 135 countries over forty years, Adam Przeworski and colleagues (1997) found that wealth, economic growth, and income equality played a critical role in sustaining political democracy (theirs is a strictly electoral conception of democracy).[24] Prosperity, they argue, is a path to democratic stability. However, national wealth is not the only road to stability. Even in the poorest countries, they claim, democracy has a chance to survive if it produces economic growth *and* if it distributes the profits so as to reduce economic inequality (Przeworski et al. 1997: 306; Rockman 1997: 18–19).

On the basis of the Przeworski study one would expect that the less skewed the income distribution is, the longer democracy will endure—and more important for my analysis, the better the quality of its institutions will be. A possible explanation for this relationship is that high levels of economic inequality tend to increase distributional pressures, leading to heightened political conflict (Muller and Seligson 1994: 635–52). This is what happened, for example, in El Salvador, Guatemala, and Nicaragua during the 1970s and 1980s. Beyond the threat of internal conflict, it has been shown that deep inequality has a negative effect on democratic practices (see, e.g., Caldeira 1996; Leeds 1996). Respect for the law is undermined in conditions that reinforce social exclusion, discrimination, and other forms of subordination, particularly those linked to vast economic distances. In many new democracies, for example, inequality sustains power relations that remain largely authoritarian in spite of democratic changes at the national institutional level. In fact, new laws, codes, and other legal devices designed to democratize social relations may have a limited impact in highly stratified societies, where "the huge social distances entailed by deep inequality foster manifold patterns of authoritarian relations in various encounters between the privileged and the others" (O'Donnell 1999b: 322–23).

High levels of inequality (economic and other types), coupled with a weak rule of law at the institutional level, often sustain what O'Donnell (2001) has called "fractional legality," that is, a system in which those at the top of the socioeconomic hierarchy often position themselves above the law, those in the middle are expected to function within the boundaries of the law (but have to do so in a largely arbitrary and corrupt system), and those at the bottom encounter the state-as-law largely through relations of domination and repression. In this type of setting, judicial systems and police forces tend to answer more rapidly and effectively to the demands of the privileged than to the needs of the lower and more vulnerable sectors of society (O'Donnell 1999b: 312). The result is a highly irregular distribution of civil rights even when political rights are universally available. In Brazil, for example, public opinion polls have shown that most of the population in this highly unequal country believe that there are vast disparities in the distribution of justice. In a survey conducted in 1999 by the Brazilian Institute of Public Opinion and Statistics (IBOPE), only 17 percent of respondents said that the justice system treated rich and poor in the same way.[25] Studies of police violence, for instance, have provided clear evidence of this pattern (Mitchell and Wood 1999; Brinks 2002)

Around the world, the challenge of creating an effective rule of law in new democracies has become prominent in recent years. Even proponents of market reform as a precondition for the strengthening of democracy have acknowledged that markets cannot function adequately under a weak rule of law. If the rule of law is a necessary condition for democracy, it is important to explore the relationship between economic inequality and institutions that sustain the rule of law across countries. On the basis of my previous assertions, I argue that economic inequality is inversely related to an effective rule of law.

I ran a partial regression plot indicating the relationship between income inequality and the rule-of-law index, controlling for GDP per capita and primary and secondary school.[26] Figure 5.1 clearly depicts this relationship in the sample. Societies with an equal distribution of wealth go hand in hand with a robust rule of law.[27] In other words, controlling for the effect of per capita GDP and education, we obtain conclusive evidence of the relationship between economic distribution and the effectiveness of the rule of law at the institutional level.[28] This cross-national evidence affirms the central claim of recent studies in comparative democratization, which have advanced the hypothesis of a strong connection between an egalitarian socioeconomic structure and a generalized rule of law (O'Donnell 1999b: 322).

## Conclusion

The findings point to three issues that deserve particular attention. First, civic engagement, by itself, has no significant impact on the quality of democratic institutions; nor is associational life a source of social trust. These findings challenge the hypothesis of a positive and universal connection between civil society and democracy. If we want to find the sources of good institutions, we need to look someplace else.

The second point begins to solve this problem. A nation's stock of social capital is associated with institutional quality in a democracy. While building civil society does not seem to consistently benefit institutional quality, increasing the stock of social capital does. It is important to qualify this finding in two respects. First, while the cross-national analysis shows that the more people who trust widely the better institutions are likely to be, the case studies (particularly the U.S. case) revealed that, in specific groups within a country, social capital can be employed for democratic and undemocratic objectives (e.g., to restrict the rights of others). In brief, the picture is more complex than expected. Second, as the quantitative data have shown, trust (a core component of social capital) does not emerge from associational activity. Rather, it is dependent on socioeconomic conditions. This shows the influence of structural conditions on the production of social capital. At the systemic level, a more egalitarian context creates the conditions for

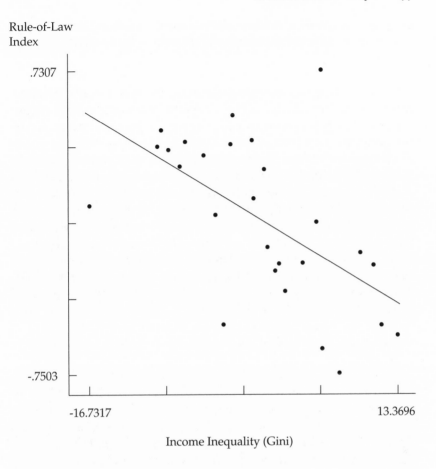

FIGURE 5.1    Income Inequality and the Rule of Law
Partial regression plot controlling for GDP per capita, primary school, and secondary school.
SOURCES: Governance Research Indicators 1997–98 (Kaufmann, Kraay, and Zoido-Lobatón); Deininger and Squire 1996; Euromonitor International 1999–2000; Barro-Lee Schooling Data (years 1970 and 1980).

higher levels of trust in society. At the individual level, trust appears to be a function of the placement of the individual in the social structure. Generally speaking, "losers" (e.g., people with low levels of education and income) are more likely to express lower levels of social trust than "winners" in society. Thus trust seems to be a function of people's hard experience. "Losers" are less likely to enjoy the life chances that merit a widening of their social trust (Rao and Walton 2002: 27; Foley and Edwards 1999: 153, 166–68).

If we combine what we learned from the case studies and the cross-national study, we can conclude that access to socioeconomic resources helps to create social capital, but sometimes this capital can strengthen the power of groups with better access to political influence and resources to advance undemocratic goals (e.g., to resist the expansion of civil rights for African Americans in the U.S. case) and even to insist that the state oppose demands for democratic reform (Richard and Booth 2000: 246). Furthermore, as ethnographic case studies have shown, social capital may reinforce inequality (see, e.g., Ndegwa 1996), particularly "by preserving differential access to networks," which limit the chances of underprivileged individuals "to access and mobilize resources" and serve the privileged to expand—or preserve—their socioeconomic advantages (Rao and Walton 2002: 9–10; Young 1999: 156–58). Thus social, economic, and legal equality not only breeds social trust (and consequently social capital) but produces *generalized* trust (and thereby social capital that *bridges* different groups in society) by reducing the likelihood of social conflict, subordination, and power abuse.

Finally, it is important to discuss the impact of economic inequality on the rule of law. A number of studies have shown that, in highly stratified societies, the poor and underprivileged lack access to justice and enjoy few actual rights (see, e.g., Méndez, O'Donnell, and Pinheiro 1999). In these settings, legal-formal rules tend to be replaced by informal rules, dependent upon networks of influence and the arbitrary decisions of authorities (da Matta 1987: 320; Jelin 1996: 108). When the rule of law is weak, those who lack access to networks of influential personal relations are the most vulnerable to violence, exclusion, and humiliation at the hands of state agents, whether high state officials or street-level bureaucrats (Rao and Walton 2002: 18). The discussion of police violence in Argentina illustrates the abuse that the underprivileged suffer at the hands of the police and, often, judicial authorities. This abuse ranges from corruption to assassination.

It is important to mention that the results of the quantitative analysis have some important implications for policy. Highly inegalitarian societies do not breed social trust, and high levels of socioeconomic stratification constrain the democratic potential of state institutions, thus hindering a nation's democratic quality. Thus one of the main deficits of current investment in social capital by international and multinational organizations is that not enough attention has been given to the problem of socioeconomic inequality. Accordingly, redistributive efforts to reduce the vulnerability of specific social sectors appear to be a sound investment in social capital formation, with the potential return of better democracies that work more evenly for all citizens (see Chapter 6).

Conceptually, these findings affirm my argument that underlying social conditions are central to the question of social capital. This form of capital is dependent on the resources available to individuals and groups. Therefore, in order to study the production of social capital we need to consider both the broader national conditions and the location of individuals within the socioeconomic structure at the subnational level.

In turn, the cross-national findings confirm an important point made earlier in the theoretical analysis. While state institutions shape the creation of a culture of legality in society, social conditions also influence the strength of public legality. The quantitative data affirm the need to consider the role of economic inequality in the robustness of the rule of law. Viewed in combination with the evidence in the case studies, which capture additional forms of inequality, this finding provides empirical support to the thesis that an unequal socioeconomic structure is a major obstacle to a strong rule of law. Inequality produces large social distances, which in turn breed various forms of authoritarian relations between state agents and citizens and among citizens themselves. These authoritarian relations restrict the attainment of the rights of citizenship (primarily civil rights) for vast sectors of the population (O'-Donnell 1999b: 322–23). By connecting the problem of inequality to the rule of law, this approach suggests a theoretical and empirical perspective on democracy that departs from what I view as limited conceptions of democracy—namely, minimalist approaches (in the Schumpeterian tradition) that consider the process of selecting elites through electoral competition to be the defining element of democratic rule or approaches exclusively focused on policy performance (e.g., Putnam's) that do not allow us to capture what is democratic about a regime.

# CHAPTER 6

# Conclusion

THE CASE STUDIES and the quantitative cross-national analysis have shown that the thesis of a positive and universal link between civil society and democracy, as conceived by neo-Tocquevilleans, is nonrobust; that is, its generalizations are limited. Having explored this link in very different historical contexts, in new and well-established democracies, and most important, having examined civil society in its broad range of expressions (avoiding an exclusive focus on any one form of association) and assessed outcomes with attention to features *specific* to democracy, thus going beyond Putnam's restrictive concern with policy performance, I believe that the evidence is overwhelming.

Unobjectionable civic groups such as sports clubs, choral societies, and veterans organizations contributed to the propagation of Nazi ideology in Weimar Germany. A broad movement of working- and middle-class citizens with strong networks of quotidian sociability mobilized to defend exclusionary practices in U.S. society; and some of the best examples of associationism in the United States (such as the Rotary Club, Lions, and the American Legion) provided fundamental social connections, resources, and members to the infamous Citizens' Councils in the South. In Argentina, grassroots organizations created for the specific goal of controlling the state and defending the rights of citizens did not further broader networks of trust or tolerance among participants and helped reinforce the fragmentation of civil society. In turn, survey and other contemporary data from twenty-eight nations showed that civil society participation did not account for the production of social trust or explain the presence of institutions that sustain the rule of law.

In addition to challenging the idea of a positive link between civil society and democracy, this study has advanced an alternative set of hypotheses oriented to rethinking the role of association in democratic settings. Focused on the impact of institutions, the various types of social inequalities, and the effectiveness of the rule of law in the sphere of the state and society, these hypotheses offer a theoretical framework for understanding the role of institutional and societal factors and processes in the associational sphere, indicating the most significant ways in which the sociohistorical context influences civic engagement.

Before reviewing these theoretical ideas and my empirical findings, I provide two additional examples that point in the same direction as the evidence presented in this study. These illustrate that there are other circumstances that challenge the thesis of a positive and universal connection between civil society and democracy. A particularly intriguing case involves the role of civil society in the 1994 genocide in Rwanda.

## The "Serpent's Egg" in Africa

In the 1980s, Rwanda was heralded by many in the international development community as a model for the promise of civil society. A World Bank report stressed in 1987 that "social life in the rural areas is intense and numerous forms of association give concrete shape to mutual solidarity and community actions." The report presented a glowing account of the marvels of civil society in this country: "The widespread presence of cooperative, associative and risk-sharing groups, which is considered to be one of the distinguishing features of the Rwandese countryside, is largely responsible for the vitality of local communities" (World Bank 1987: 28, as quoted in Uvin 1998: 163). In 1992 the U.S. Agency for International Development (USAID) argued that civil society in Rwanda had a prodemocratic role to play by promoting civic education, political advocacy, and the circulation of information in society (USAID 1992, as quoted in Uvin 1998: 175). International organizations argued that a growing human rights movement in Rwanda was one of several encouraging signs of democratization (de Waal 2000: 53).

The analysis of the World Bank, USAID, and other international donor agencies suggested that the strength of civil society could be translated into democratic governance. The assumption was that a vital associational life would increase cooperation and develop networks of reciprocity in society, which in turn would improve institutional performance and democratic politics. A seemingly vital civil society, however, did not prevent catastrophe. In 1994, Rwanda descended into the abyss of genocide. Between 500,000 and 800,000 people were killed in just three months.

Perhaps, one may argue, domestic civil society was unable to counteract other, more powerful social and political forces that drove Rwanda toward this extreme outcome. However, though more systematic research is still needed, evidence has shown that various sectors of civil society supported the values underlying the genocide, including a willingness to employ violence against specific social groups, undemocratic attitudes, and tolerance for human rights abuses. Under conditions of deep inequality, social exclusion, and long-standing societal rifts introduced by the colonial power—which bred resentment and reduced moral constraints on the use of violence—these values existed not only among state actors, but among civil society organizations as well (Uvin 1998: 54). Indeed, "adherence to an undemocratic and genocidal ideology and willingness to use violence and human rights abuses in the quest for power" were prevalent among ruling elites *and* civil society activists (p. 235).

The example of Rwanda shows how, as in pre-Nazi Germany, civil society organizations can pave the way to the most grave of outcomes. "The genocide was not simply a state project," as Mahmood Mamdani (2001) has explained: "Had the killing been the work of state functionaries and those bribed by them, it would have translated into no more than a string of massacres perpetrated by death squads. Without massacres by machete-wielding civilian mobs, in the hundreds and thousands, there would have been no genocide" (p. 225). The participation of teachers, relief workers, doctors, nurses, members of religious orders, and even human rights activists in the mass killing shows that civil society was not extraneous to the genocide (Mamdani 2001: 226–28; de Waal 2000: 55). Perpetrators viewed themselves as "the people" and defined their victims as the "public enemy." This process stressed the *political* character of violence and thereby legitimated the popular involvement in the massacres (Mamdani 2001: 223, 228). The propagation of hatred was facilitated by the tenuous boundaries between state and civil society. These links served the purpose of political violence (de Waal 2000: 52).[1]

One of the organizations most actively involved in the killings, the informal militia *Interahamwe* (which means "those who stand together") had been originally created as a youth organization in 1990. Soon it became a vigilante group, and finally it turned into "a death squad whose members led the house-to-house search for identifying and killing Tutsi in 1994" (quotation from Mamdani 2001: 212; Sharlach 2002: 117). The Interahamwe and other groups were not created for the purpose of political violence, but to pursue such goals as civil defense and the expansion of political participation (Mamdani 2001: 217). Their function mutated as a result of Rwanda's civil war and a series of changes in the political arena. Indeed, as I argued earlier in the study, the orientations of civil society organizations cannot be predicted merely on the basis of the groups' features and professed goals.

As an illustration of civil society's "dark side," Rwanda is interesting because it highlights another issue examined in my study, namely, the impact of societal divisions on civil society's dispositions. In particular, Rwanda serves as an example of how international forces contributed to the creation of a fragmented society. The Belgian colonial state created deep societal divisions in Rwanda by establishing a social stratification with profound political implications. Colonial policies (administrative procedures, education, and taxation) transformed the Tutsi-Hutu divide from "a transethnic distinction of local significance" into a cleavage of race, in which the Hutu were constructed as indigenous and the Tutsi as outsiders (Mamdani 2001: 101, 229). On the basis of physical characteristics (associating Caucasian features with "civilization"), the Belgians adopted a "scientific" classification of the various social groups (initially implemented through an official census in 1933–34), which conferred on Tutsis a superior social and political status over Hutus (Barnett 2002: 49–60; Mamdani 2001: 98–100). This "reality" cemented deep lines of societal fragmentation over the following decades. In fact, the racialization of politics in Rwanda determined a highly stratified mode of incorporation of different groups into the structure of colonial power. This process would eventually deem the presence of the privileged Tutsi in the political arena as illegitimate and define the struggle for power as a conflict between indigenous and alien races (Mamdani 1996: 15; 2001: 101–2, 233; de Waal 2000: 45–46, 48).

The same region provides other examples of civil society's dark side. Privileged groups with access to political and economic resources may sometimes use association to expand—or preserve—their socioeconomic advantages in highly stratified settings (Young 1999: 156–58). In

Kenya's transitional democracy in the early 1990s, dominant class and sectoral interests successfully employed association to preserve existing distributions of power in state and society.[2] Major civic organizations in this country were shaped by a form of "personal rule" in which established elites assumed leadership roles in influential NGOs and shaped the agenda of these organizations. As Stephen Ndegwa (1996) has explained, these associations were NGOs in the area of development, which received substantial foreign aid. They tended to be controlled by elites with distinctive ethnic interests and served privileged sectors as a source of societal and political influence. An important feature of the pivotal role of personal rule in Kenya's civil society was the fact that key civic groups displayed authoritarian or democratic orientations not on the basis of a principled standpoint, but according to the relative power of their leaders to adopt positions of authority or influence.[3] In brief, important sectors of associational life in Kenya served as a vehicle for maintaining highly unequal power structures in this country.

## The "Bright Side" of Civil Society

Although I have focused on cases that illustrate dimensions of civil society's dark side—including those in which it helped to the erosion of democracy, as in Weimar Germany—civil society can also contribute to deepening democratic politics, as some recent research in Latin America illustrates. Leonardo Avritzer (2002a; 2002b), for example, has described how civil society groups successfully helped shape local government budgets in Brazil. This novel experiment consists in "the transfer of budgetary powers from the state to social actors." "Participatory budgeting" incorporates civil society participants "in a process of negotiation and deliberation" that connects new cultural practices developed in civil society to the political arena (Avritzer 2002a: 135–42, 145–48, 151–55). Starting in 1989 in Porto Alegre, this phenomenon expanded to over a hundred cities across Brazil. Under an innovative institutional framework that bridged local participation and the political system, civil society helped make government more responsible, increased political and administrative accountability, and discouraged clientelistic practices (pp. 136–42).

Another instance of what Avritzer calls "participatory publics" was the emergence of an electoral organization in Mexico based on new political practices developed in civil society.[4] The Federal Electoral Institute (IFE) undertook a "process through which citizens took charge of the organization of elections and in which the high deliberative rankings of the institution were occupied by citizen councilors" (Avritzer 2002a: 142–45, 157–62, quotation on 142). While in Brazil civil society participation contributed to the creation of a new institutional mechanism that diluted long-standing practices of clientelism by political elites, civic participation in Mexico played an important role in curtailing electoral fraud (p. 145). The coalition of prodemocratic civil society groups (Civic Alliance) that led the grassroots campaign for clean elections helped promote the 1996 electoral reform; however, it was less successful at influencing the government's political agenda (especially its economic policies) and making the authorities more accountable to public opinion (particularly concerning the budget and civil service) (Olvera Rivera 2002). In both Brazil and Mexico the state played a critical role (at the municipal and national levels, respectively) in the creation of institutional channels that allowed for participatory publics to enter the policy-making arena (Avritzer 2002a: 163).

There are numerous other examples in Latin America and other regions of democratic forms of collective action in civil society. But for every "successful" link between civil society and democracy, one can identify a "mixed" or "failed" link too. Civil society can lead to democratic and undemocratic outcomes because what matters are not the kinds of groups, movements, or networks, but the context in which people associate. In Brazil and Mexico, factors in the political, economic, and international arenas were central to the success of the experiments. These factors included the establishment of innovative institutions. In addition, the role of political parties in both countries,[5] and in Mexico domestic pressure, primarily from the business sector, and international pressure, mainly from the United States, were fundamental factors in shaping the outcome of these experiences.

As shown in a comparative study of participatory budgeting in Porto Alegre and other decentralization experiences in South Africa and the Indian state of Kerala, political and institutional variables are critical to understand how civil society's democratic impulses lead to different outcomes (Heller 2001). The study argues that, though the South African experience was not successful, "grassroots democratic impulses in Kerala and Porto Alegre were given life and successfully scaled up only because they were underwritten by a political project and were given state support" (p. 158). In turn, the transformation of grassroots interests into actual democratic impulses was owed to the progressive development of mobilization capacities in a context of "high-density citizenship (both in terms of basic individual capabilities as well as the overall strength of rational-legal authority)" and political and organizational pluralism. Also, the role of political parties with the capacity to mobilize grassroots participation was vital for the success of these experiments (pp. 149–57).

As these cases confirm, while societal conditions in which people organize are important in explaining their capacity for prodemocratic collective action, experiences of civil society participation are also shaped by "the ways in which states create and structure channels, opportunities, and incentives (or disincentives) for collective action" (Heller 2001: 148). In fact, the role of "politically orchestrated action from above" was pivotal for the amalgamation of "the institutional capacities of the state and the associational resources of civil society" (p. 158). The expansion of the scope of democracy was, to an important extent, dependent on state implementation of "a host of new regulations and oversight structures to ensure transparency and accountability of local government," the creation of "institutional spaces for democratic participation," and the neutralization of groups opposed to democratization at the local level (such as political brokers running clientelistic networks) (pp. 141, 144, 149). In sum, these three cases point to the conclusion that the "bright side" of civil society is primarily dependent on conditions external to association itself.

## Conceptual Issues

In emphasizing the dark side of civil society, I have tried to show that organizations and movements that might seem compatible with democratic dispositions and orientations can multiply undemocratic beliefs and practices in society or contribute to undermining democracy. Putnam and other neo-Tocquevilleans have looked at civil society as an independent variable that promotes democratic outcomes independently from the specific context, and thus have "missed" the various, and often contradictory, associational effects observed in different settings. In contrast, I have shown various ways in which context shapes both the nature and outcomes of civic engagement. Let me summarize these ideas and findings.

I have advanced a framework to establish which factors external to civil society activity play a central role in shaping civic capacity and orientations. This effort is not just about "bringing the state back in," but demands an understanding of both state- and society-centered factors. Therefore, civic participation cannot be detached from the ways in which state institutions protect the effective rights of individuals and contribute to creating respect for the law in society; nor can it be dissociated from social and economic stratification, which ranges from income inequality and various forms of discrimination to patterns of domination and subordination in society (Edwards and Foley 2001: 228). As the empirical analysis confirmed, some of the most relevant considerations are state policy, economic inequality, racism and ethnic/ religious cleavages, and the effectiveness of the rule of law in both the institutional and societal spheres.

The importance of the rule of law in texturing relations at the level of the state, state-society interaction, and relations within society should not be underestimated. The rule of law is critical for the emergence of positive predictability, or the possibility to estimate sanctions for one's own and other people's actions. This kind of predictability vanishes in those contexts where state arbitrary and/or illegal actions and impunity are prevalent and where discrimination, patronage, and other related practices become organizing principles within society. The erosion of positive predictability generally corrodes social trust and confidence in political institutions.

I have shown different ways in which contextual factors and the activity of civil society interact. Among them, two patterns deserve particular attention. First, the articulation of political or economic developments (such as a court decision to desegregate or a series of economic crises) and underlying tensions in society (such as divisions of race, ethnicity, religion, or other forms of identity) lead to specific forms of organizing. This explains why microlevel interactions in civil society may cement antisystem beliefs and give legitimacy to undemocratic ideas and practices. As the three case studies illustrated, tensions and patterns of exclusion are reinforced in civil society, which in turn shapes social cleavages and processes of identity formation (see Berman 1997a: 427).

Second, the capacity of political institutions to process diverse demands and the overall effectiveness of the rule of law shape attitudes in society, such as levels of tolerance and acceptance of authoritarian and violent practices, which provide the setting in which individuals associate for various purposes. Accordingly, associations created for a democratic or purely social purpose may become the carriers of beliefs and attitudes that can weaken democracy, and even lead to extreme outcomes, as in Weimar Germany and Rwanda. As argued, the formulation and implementation of the law play a central role in defining contextual conditions. Respect for the law and individual rights is generally higher when the laws themselves are formed and applied in an adequately inclusive and balanced way. Key to this process is the overlooked problem of the rule of law within society, especially the development of a culture of legality. Also, the characteristics of the institutional and legal systems shape an important part of the context in which civil society groups and networks operate, namely, the possibility to connect with short- or long-term targets, which has implications for the kinds of contributions to democracy that can be expected from civil society.

Another important conceptual area is that of social capital. On the basis of my empirical findings, I have proposed a reformulation of the neo-Tocquevillean conception of social capital with particular attention to two aspects. First, social capital should not be conceived as an automatic result of civic participation, but as dependent on the ability of individuals to access social networks with the capacity to obtain, secure, and mobilize resources (Rao and Walton 2002: 9; see Bourdieu 1990: 162–99; see also Portes 1998; Portes and Landolt 2000). The most basic of these resources are those that allow individuals to offset the effects of "risks that fall on [them] in ways that are not mediated by their voluntary choice" (Arneson 2000: 336). Second, social capital can be employed for very different purposes. The orientations of social capital depend on such factors as underlying tensions in society and embedded patterns of social relations, the capacity of different groups to access and mobilize resources, the catalyst that triggers defensive postures in civil society, and the links between civil society groups and the state. As discussed in the U.S. case, social capital can contribute to the multiplication of inequalities—for example, via social connections built into social, cultural, or recreational organizations. Moreover, little attention has been given to the relationship between social capital and the use of coercion and violence. Again, as the U.S. case showed, powerful antidesegregation groups sometimes employed violence and also used coercion and intimidation, including economic retaliation against blacks and whites involved in prointegration efforts. Social capital provided a fundamental resource for this economic "lynching" and other coercive tactics. In the South, the use of violence and coercion was closely linked to the weak rule of law at the institutional and societal levels.

The emphasis given to domestic factors in my analysis should not be taken as a disregard for the significance of international factors in understanding civil society and its link to democracy. In particular, international forces may influence domestic political and economic conditions, and international actors may engage in efforts to support democratizing societies. Consider Germany, where political tensions and economic difficulties were triggered by the problem of war reparations and post–World War I feelings of national humiliation. And in the United States, the impact of global patterns of trade and Cold War imperatives on the U.S. industrial sector in the post–World War II years resulted in large economic and social dislocations—for example, the substantial contraction of the labor market in areas as diverse as auto production, textiles, and electronics. The loss of these jobs affected whites and, especially, the newest wave of unskilled black migrants to urban centers, thus creating conditions that intensified underlying racial problems and class differentiations. In Argentina, the dramatic increase in foreign debt and the structural reform of the state (influenced by an international concern with increasing financial openness and deregulation, and a heightened preoccupation with low inflation), were among the factors that contributed to major changes in the country's socioeconomic structure and the fast growth of the informal sector. In all three cases, international and global factors indirectly affected civil society by influencing the domestic context.

The impact of international actors can also be clearly observed in newly established democracies, where changes in international support for and attention to these nations had major consequences for civil society activity. Assuming that the transition to democracy itself creates a positive and mutually reinforcing interaction with civil society, many international organizations cut back their activities and funding in democratizing countries, neglecting socioeconomic problems, the weakness of the rule of law, and other challenges after the transition from authoritarianism. The mistaken assumption that international assistance centered on building or bolstering civil society in these countries would lead to strong and high-quality democracies affirms the argument advanced in this study. In addition, external assistance can weaken local civil society in a number of ways, for example, by creating intergroup competition and dependency on outside donors. Thus international efforts can contribute to fragmentation within civil society and to the strengthening of "donor-driven" NGO communities in new democracies (see Mendelson and Glenn 2002).

## Empirical Findings

The case studies tell us that the dark side of civil society is not exclusive to newly democratized nations. Civil society in both new and well-established democracies can reinforce existing institutional weaknesses and societal conflicts, making them more vulnerable to antisystem forces (as in Germany), eroding the legitimacy of political institutions (as in Argentina), or reinforcing exclusionary aspects of society (as in the United States). In Weimar Germany and Argentina—both new democracies—the "vitality" of civil society was not necessarily linked to democratic outcomes. Civil society in Germany legitimated antidemocratic discourses and ideas and thus contributed to the destabilization of democracy; in Argentina, organizations dedicated to defending human and civil rights produced cynicism and distrust among their members and deepened patterns of societal fragmentation while failing to have a wholly positive impact on government structures. In turn, in the United States—a well-established but exclusionary democracy—civically active white groups placed important obstacles in the way of expanding civil rights for African Americans.

The case studies and the cross-national tests yielded several findings on the interaction between contextual factors and civic engagement, and on the outcomes of civil society activity. First, the case of Germany showed that weak political institutions (which, for example, were perceived as unaccountable and proved incapable of processing broader interests and demands) and a highly fragmented party system nurtured associations that intensified the alienation of citizens from their political representatives. As an alternative to politics, the realm of association legitimated antisystem ideas, thus eroding people's confidence in the institutions of government. The negative role of this institutional scenario was reinforced by the economic crisis, which affected the construction of collective identities and social boundaries, especially as most middle-class citizens experienced a decline in their standard of living (yet the economic crisis and government responses to the crisis did not have a homogeneous effect throughout the middle class). This was the framework in which the dark side of civic engagement emerged. Dense social networks and ostensibly inoffensive civic groups reinforced antipoliticism in society, eroded respect for democratic mechanisms of governance, and gave legitimacy to Nazi ideology. Indeed, Weimar's broad associational life was effectively exploited by the Nazis, particularly after 1929, when the political parties (both the established ones and the new one-issue splinter parties) had completely failed to integrate the disparate interests of the middle classes. Civil society contributed, unwittingly, to hatching the "serpent's egg" of totalitarianism.

Second, the case of the United States showed that deep socioeconomic and political dislocations (major transformations in the productive sector, vast migration to urban centers, and critical legal decisions affecting race relations) were played out in civil society, which became the locus of an intense contestation over the definition and allocation of civil rights. Under these conditions, large groups of citizens decided to employ their organizational capacity to restrict public debate and oppose the expansion of rights for other, less-privileged sectors. For many, civic engagement became a vehicle for asserting their rights by negating the rights of others. This case also illustrated that states do not act uniformly or "pull in single directions" (Migdal 1994: 8). Indeed, some federal agencies (e.g., the FHA) and local courts and authorities reinforced patterns of domination and subordination in society through policies and decisions that served the interests of white groups. In contrast, other government agencies and courts attempted to dismantle racial barriers, especially through the law. These efforts were met with strong resistance by large sectors of civil society.[6]

Third, in Argentina, a weak rule of law (in a context of increasing inequality) was instrumental in shaping a civil society divided against itself, which echoed many of the broader society's undemocratic norms and values (e.g., low levels of respect for the law and formal rules, and pervasive discrimination). A paradoxical finding was that unresponsive and confrontational state institutions intensified disengagement and social fragmentation even among those civic groups seeking to democratize the state. Indeed, in an institutional context marked by serious deficiencies in controlling state coercive power (e.g., the police forces), addressing impunity, and guaranteeing access to justice for all citizens, the potentially democratizing role of civil society was often frustrated by state forces. As a result, civil society groups manifested low levels of engagement with the state (e.g., limited connectedness with the legislature), and they tended to reinforce cynicism toward politics, politicians, and institutions. The examination of the ambivalent relationship between civic engagement and democracy in Argentina seemed to anticipate, in several respects, the intricacies of the wave of middle- and working-class mobilization that shook the country in 2001–2. Moreover, the main characteristics of middle-class associations in the 1990s have been intensified by the general political and socioeconomic crisis of the early 2000s. Some of these patterns (e.g., fragmentation, particularism, confrontation with the state) raise doubts about civil society's potential contribution to solving the country's extensive crisis. On a positive note, the promotion of a discourse centered on citizenship rights and the rule of law, as shown in Chapter 4, seems to play a prodemocratic role in the public sphere with the potential to permeate state institutions.

Finally, the quantitative findings confirmed, at the cross-national level, the important role of structural variables in the production of social capital (measured as social trust) (see Chapter 5). The analysis of old and new democracies also showed that social trust matters when it comes to institutional quality. However, it revealed that one form of inequality—income disparity—not only shaped the production of trust but also had a direct impact on the presence of institutions committed to the rule of law. The tests also made clear that the impact of civil society in both the production of social trust and democratic governance is inconsequential. At the individual level, social trust is dependent upon the specific conditions that shape the socioeconomic context of individuals. Those who have access to resources via income, level of education, or other assets are more willing to trust widely than those who lack this kind of access. Overall, the cross-national analysis showed that we should look at structural conditions (e.g., income inequality) and not at civil society participation to explain the quality of democratic institutions across different nations.

## Lessons for New Democracies

The presence of voluntary organizations cannot be taken simply as evidence that citizens are cooperating with each other, learning to become more tolerant and trusting, limiting and controlling state power effectively, or even endorsing—directly or indirectly—a democratic system of rule. The case studies provide ample evidence that we cannot take civil society's democratizing potential for granted. This problem is not, as Putnam (2000) seems to imply, a matter of discovering which organizations are good and which are bad, or who will walk away from a voluntary association a better citizen and who will not (pp. 341, 358). Civil society in general—not just formal groups—tends to potentiate dominant features in the broader sociohistorical context. This finding carries an important policy lesson: if civil society is not a determinant of either institutional quality or social trust—and if it has the potential, under certain conditions, to channel or generate undemocratic orientations—then an exclusive emphasis on civil–society building may be futile or even counterproductive for democracy. Building civil society—by expanding the number of civic organizations, for example—does not guarantee democratic outcomes. It follows that the international movement that has advocated civil society as a path to democratic success in developing nations has largely based its efforts on false premises. Extensive investment in building civil society in third-wave democracies—without rigorous and systematic testing—indicates that policy has been running ahead of research.

It appears to me that many international organizations assumed that civil societies which displayed a balanced combination of different associational forms and activities (a "democratic ecology of associations") would provide an "optimal mix of democratic effects" in any given setting (Warren 2001: 12–13). Although this approach seems reasonable in theory, my study has shown that a well-balanced ecology of groups does not necessarily lead to democratic outcomes. The case of Weimar Germany provides an excellent rebuttal to the assumption of a positive relationship between a best associational ecology and democratic results. German civil society contained a majority of "Putnamesque" groups (those most likely to produce horizontal networks of trust and cooperation), which provided citizens the possibility to engage in face-to-face interactions, discuss political affairs, and participate in public debates. However, the eventual outcome was the collapse of democracy—and German civil society participants contributed to it.

The aggregate-level cross-national analysis discussed in Chapter 5 shows that social trust is a determinant of institutional quality, but trust can be mobilized for undemocratic purposes too. Is it then time to abandon the idea of social capital as a democracy-building approach? I believe not. As the cross-national findings demonstrate, one of the main deficits of current investment in social capital is insufficient attention to the problem of economic inequality. The evidence shows that inegalitarian societies do not breed social trust and that high levels of stratification constrain the democratic potential of civil society and institutions. In other words, economic disparities hinder the construction of democratic societies. Accordingly, redistributive efforts to reduce the vulnerability of specific social sectors can represent a sound investment in social capital formation across social cleavages. This approach is likely to increase the possibilities for the emergence of social networks, organizations, and movements that can serve as a source of innovation, counteragendas, and new collective projects (see Foley and Edwards 1999: 166; Cohen 1999: 58). Interestingly, this strategy has been recently proposed by some analysts as a way to revitalize community life in the United States (Warren 2001: 225; Uslaner 2000–2001: 589–90).

Of course, the state can play a fundamental role in this respect, because it has the capacity to address problems of inequality by investing in social needs and education, providing adequate infrastructure, and protecting environmental conditions for everyone, among other potential support to vulnerable social sectors (Young 1999: 159). These policies can contribute to the emergence of more cohesive societies and a stronger social fabric that will support institutions committed to the rule of law. There are also more direct ways in which state-enforced legality may lessen the pernicious effects of intense social stratification—for example, by widening access to justice, controlling the exercise of coercion, facilitating citizen access to the parliamentary sphere, and promoting effective mechanisms for interagency accountability.[7]

The problem of inequality should not be reduced to the economic dimension. Among the factors influencing civil society activity in new democracies are social exclusion and systematic humiliation of the most vulnerable. The epigraph that opens the Introduction—"If the police catch those criminals, they should execute them" (a statement by a human rights activist in Argentina)—cannot be properly understood without taking into account the country's situation of structural violence, in which pervasive impunity and social exclusion and degradation play a core role. This situation affects individuals to different degrees according to their position in society (see Uvin 1998: 103–8; Leeds 1996: 49). As the case of Argentina illustrates, civic participation does not appear to lessen tolerance for violence and aggressive attitudes toward certain groups (e.g., the poor, the police, minorities). These attitudes are fed by contexts in which the rule of law is weak, socioeconomic stratification sustains authoritarian patterns in social interactions, and vast sectors of the population lack effective access to civil and social rights. This perspective suggests that policies and legislation to improve the situation of the most vulnerable need to be accompanied by measures to increase access to social, political, and cultural resources for the underprivileged by gradually dismantling exclusionary patterns (Robinson 1996: 55, 57–58). Policies to increase access should be accompanied by a frontal attack on racial, ethnic, and other forms of discrimination and exclusion (e.g., dismantling embedded patterns of discrimination in the formulation and implementation of state policy). Patterns of discrimination and exclusion (such as the perpetuation of a racial stigma) restrict the choices of individuals and reinforce intolerance and rifts in society (Rao and Walton 2002: 4).

As the framework of the rule of law presented in Chapter 1 makes clear, the democratization of the state is critical for creating conditions that can empower civil society to influence the policy-making realm. An important dimension of this process is the challenge to make government agencies more accountable and transparent. Argentina's deficiencies in the public sector illustrate the areas that are in dire need of reform. Particularly important is the task of building accountability and transparency capacities in both the central government and local and regional governments.[8]

Many of the obstacles that can prevent a synergy between state and civil society were evident in Argentina. From the top down, state agencies failed to create and institutionalize channels, incentives, and chances for civil society involvement. From the bottom up, the patterns of interaction, strategic priorities, and perceptions that structured the action of civic organizations consistently blocked opportunities to develop a partnership with the state. The interaction (or lack thereof) between state and civil society did not expand the scope of democracy. In fact, negotiations between state agencies and civil society groups often closed new spaces and impulses for collaboration because conflict was treated as a zero-sum interest negotiation; there was very little institutional learning on either side, there was a sustained inability to connect the state's capacity for authoritative decisions with civil society's access to information about social needs and interests, and actors' concerns pivoted around questions of short-term legitimation and payoffs rather than the search for innovation and compromise (Heller 2001: 158).

Because the "state" is not a homogeneous and cohesive entity, linking state and societal actors may depend on strengthening government organizations with more democratizing potential than others. It would then be important to explore the democratizing potential of segments that connect the state with civil society (see Chalmers, Martin, and

Piester 1997). This approach may help break self-defeating cycles that have prevented the deepening of democratic governance and practices in many nations. In Argentina, some executive agencies raised the possibility of democratic cooperation with civil society. The development of links between these government agencies and organizations of civil society might enhance the effectiveness of the rule of law in this country.

The possibility of integrating state and civil society components opens, in turn, a new set of questions. One well-established democracy, Norway, illustrates this point. Under a very close relationship between the state and civil society in this country, the "third sector" receives economic support from the government and actively participates in critical areas of policy-making (such as ecological modernization). However, government promotion of associational activity and integrating it with the state has been seen by some analysts as counterproductive for democracy, because, they argue, it can result in a serious contraction of the public sphere as an autonomous arena for organization, communication, and the production of criticality (Dryzek, Hernes, and Schlosberg 2001: 9–10). The state's demand for third-sector involvement in the implementation of public policies has increased the need for professionals and has centralized power within the voluntary sector (see Chapter 1). As a result, this sector has become less democratic in its practices and structure (centralization, less pluralism, and decrease of volunteerism's role) for the sake of efficiency.[9]

This example raises important questions about the relationship between civil society and the state. What are the implications for civil society when a civic group acts with the state? To what extent does attempting to democratize the state from within weaken the democratic potential of civil society? (Dryzek 1996: 482, 485). It is necessary to assess the tradeoff between "inclusion in the life of the state" and "relatively unrestricted democratic interplay in the oppositional public sphere" when we look at the potential involvement of civil society groups in the policy-making process (p. 480). This question has implications for new democracies, especially in regions such as Latin America, where the rejection of traditional party politics has resulted in broad calls for civil society to offer solutions to deep and generalized crises.

## Questions for Future Research

In this study I have focused on some of the issues that lie at the core of the complex relationship between civil society and democracy. This analysis (especially the discussion of civil society's dark side) raises, in turn, a number of questions that have implications for future research. Here I refer to some of these questions that are especially relevant for the study of new democracies.

First, recent studies of democratization have paid increasing attention to agency, and in particular to inequalities of agency (see, e.g., O'-Donnell 1999c; Rao and Walton 2002). This approach acknowledges that, without autonomy and the capacity to choose from a reasonable set of options, individuals cannot be constituted as citizens, that is, as legal subjects with effective rights and responsibilities (O'Donnell 1999c: 15, 18–19, 24–25). This is a fundamental improvement in the study of democracy; however, we have given only passing attention to the fact that any transformations in the structure of agency entail a challenge to existing inequalities in power and are therefore likely to intensify social conflict (Rao and Walton 2002: 21). Studies on civil society should examine the ways in which social contestation takes place in this realm.

Sometimes challenges to inequalities of agency are overt and violent; at other times they need to be traced by uncovering gradual processes in which underprivileged sectors introduce demands for citizenship rights as public issues. Conflicts over inequalities in agency are thus connected to the problem of violence (see Ungar, Bermanzohn, and Worcester 2002). More specifically, future research needs to connect the question of association and citizenship rights to both societal and state forms of violence. The question of collective violence in society, mainly common crime, is particularly relevant in Latin America, where the homicide rate made the region the most violent in the world in the late 1990s.[10] Given the vast economic and social transformations brought about by globalization, it is particularly important to examine new forms in which people employ violence to make claims on the state and ways in which they utilize social capital to make violent demands that concern their citizenship rights (Holston and Appadurai 1999: 16). It is also important to examine in more detail the conditions under which civil society organizations and networks take up violence, split over the use of violence, or encourage the state to carry out violence.

A second question involves the important role of informal ties in associational life, especially the relationship between socialization processes and social networks. As Chapter 2 describes, grassroots networks of "quotidian sociability" carried undemocratic values and beliefs. Indeed, informal networks channeled Nazi ideas in Weimar Germany, and local social connections in the United States gave impulse to white resistance to integration and linked antidesegregation activists to government officials in several states. This dimension of associational life is indispensable for understanding contemporary phenomena that cannot be examined solely on the basis of formal group membership. One example is the networks that sustain terrorist volunteerism in the Palestinian Islamist groups that sponsor suicide bombings in Israel.[11]

Third, the question of the relationship between civil society and political society is important, particularly for new democracies. I refer to political society as distinct from the state. Political society is the "arena in which the polity specifically arranges itself for political contestation to gain control over public power and the state apparatus" (Stepan 1988: 4; see Linz and Stepan 1996: 8–10). Weimar Germany and Argentina are fine examples of the need to understand how civil and political society interpenetrate and connect with each other. In other words, it is important to understand the nature of and changes in the organic links between civil and political society. In pre-Nazi Germany, associational life was an alternative to political society. In post-2001 Argentina, the massive rejection of "politics as usual" and the "political class" raises the crucial question of the capacity of civil society to generate new political leaders and political organizations. The cases of Weimar Germany and Argentina show that civil society cannot replace programmatically-based political parties.

A fourth area for future research involves the impact of international forces on civic organizations and social networks.[12] Changes in international attention to and support for civil society groups in democratizing regions have a profound impact on internal relations within civil society and with the state. Recent attention to the negative impact of international influence in light of societal catastrophes (such as that in Rwanda) has raised new questions about the role of international actors (see, e.g., Kuperman 2001). I have addressed only briefly how international action has helped or undermined domestic civil society organizations, but this question deserves careful examination. It is also important to explore how the withdrawal or lessening of international support, coupled with domestic political developments, can give rise to or encourage civil society organizations that advocate violence or utilize nationalistic sentiments to advance an antidemocratic agenda.

Finally, the study of a fundamental dimension of civil society, the public sphere, cannot be isolated from the effects of economic and cultural globalization. The contribution of global economic processes to the gap between rich and poor, the introduction of consumption standards from the postindustrial West into noncentral societies, and the impact of transnational publics are crucial elements for the formation of national public spheres. It is important to understand how state and social forces are shaped by global trends that traverse geographic, cultural, and political boundaries—and the ways in which these forces shape the public sphere (Portes 1997: 4). For example, the role of "long-distance nationalism"—the sustained links that immigrants establish with their home countries—is an important factor in the creation of publics and the formulation and communication of issues in the public sphere (Anderson 1994: 326–27; see also Sassen 1999).

## Creating a Different Link

Challenging the conceptual and empirical edifice built by neo-Tocquevilleans leaves us with many unanswered questions, as the previous list illustrates. Still, there is one question that remains central for the discussion advanced in this study: Should the debate triggered by the civil society boom be refocused on state institutions? I do not believe so. We need to consider not only the realm of the state but also the social sphere in the analysis of association and democracy. So, what does this analysis contribute to the design of a future research agenda for understanding democratization processes? I believe that our efforts should be redirected toward the development of an integrative model of democratization that can account for the complex interaction between institutional and societal forces (see Yashar 1999; McAdam, Tarrow, and Tilly 2001).

If it aims to correct some of the central flaws of recent democratization studies, this model should articulate "top-down" and "bottom-up" approaches to democracy, assess democratic systems for their positive attributes (and not for what they lack), and depart from the teleological approach of consolidation perspectives (see O'Donnell 1996a: 39; 1996b: 164; 1999b: 303–4; von Mettenheim and Malloy 1998b: 175; Holston and Caldeira 1998: 288; Yashar 1999: 97–99). To conclude, let me suggest some ideas that can help us envision this alternative framework. I will build on the conceptual framework that I introduced in Chapter 1 and later explored empirically in the qualitative and quantitative studies.

First, I propose a shift from the political regime to the question of citizenship rights. This model would advance a type of analysis that can account for variations in the distribution of rights within and across nations—variations that are fundamental to understanding democracy. The crux of the model is the differential access to rights for different sectors of the population (see O'Donnell 1999c).[13] I propose a new concept, "field of citizenship," which results from the articulation of the state (its administrative, coercive, and legal apparatus) and specific "relational settings" (which express patterns of social interaction involving the cultural, economic, political, and social spheres) (Somers 1993: 595).[14] The articulation between the state and social forces yields different fields of citizenship within a polity (pp. 595–96, 589).

The model of fields of citizenship, I argue, is relevant for all democracies because the distribution of rights is uneven in both well-established and new democracies. It is thus important to stress that "benchmark democracies," that is, the oldest and most stable democratic systems (such as the United States) should not be treated as a *type* of democracy that is inherently different from newly established ones. Though there are important variations of degree in their institutional quality, the effectiveness of the rule of law, and their political culture, old and new democracies share an essential feature that should affect the way we theorize them, namely, the irregular and disjunctive ways in which the rights of citizens are extended and institutionalized (Holston and Caldeira 1998; Varas 1998).

Rather than employing exclusively aggregate-level data, which are focused on the national regime, the task of identifying and mapping fields of citizenship will allow us to examine within-country variations in the distribution of rights and to compare nations by assessing their particular distribution of fields (see Foley and Edwards 1999: 151, 166–68). This approach redirects our analysis of democratization to investigate the structure of these fields, the conditions under which they are constituted, and the ways in which they are challenged, renegotiated, and redefined by societal and state actors.

Second, it is vital to bridge institutional and societal factors and processes by looking at micro-macro relations in a single model. From the top looking down, I propose to examine how the various levels of the state hierarchy reach specific relational settings. As already explained, by "traveling down the political and social hierarchies," it is possible to learn how separate parts of the state interact with society at different levels of aggregation and in different contexts (Migdal 1994: 8; quotation from Kohli 1994: 106). This involves an analysis that takes into account state-citizen interactions from the higher end of the state hierarchy (e.g., ministers, governors, mayors, and judges) to the trenches (e.g., police officers, teachers, tax collectors, and other street-level bureaucrats) (Rao and Walton 2002: 18; Migdal 1994: 16). From the bottom looking up, it is important to look at "actors' places in the multiple relationships in which they are embedded" (Somers 1993: 595). By assuming a "relational" approach, this perspective considers the various forms of capital available in a given setting—social, economic, human, and cultural—to be co-determined (Rao and Walton 2002: 11). These forms of capital are available to both individuals and groups: they shape the relative power of individuals to make choices and to achieve preferred outcomes, and the potential of groups to engage in collective action (Rao and Walton 2002: 12, quoting Sen 1985). By contrasting different relational settings, this approach allows us to determine the empirical conditions that shape, from the bottom up, the "meeting grounds" between society and the state (Somers 1993: 595; Migdal 1994: 23).

This approach might examine the extent to which universalistic laws become actual rights for different sectors of the population. This allows us to understand the conditions under which laws can be connected to cultural and social resources and thus be turned into actual "forms of empowerment" (Somers 1993: 611). From this perspective, it is possible to understand the phenomenon of association in a different light from that provided by traditional approaches. Consider the interaction between structural conditions in the United States, particularly socioeconomic stratification, with discriminatory practices by state and private actors, which reinforce patterns of racial segregation. Relational settings for blacks impose serious obstacles on their capacity to overcome embedded patterns of exclusion, and thus on the possibility of turning the law into a form of empowerment. Attempts to do so faced strong resistance from sectors of the state and civil society, as illustrated in Chapter 2.

The case studies presented in this volume offer many examples of how top-down and bottom-up processes are articulated to produce specific configurations of rights and, in general, certain organizing principles in society. Consider the case of Argentina. If we direct our attention to the articulation of the state / legal system with the social / cultural realm in this country, we can begin to understand the paradoxical aspects of democratization in this case. This entails considering, on one hand, the state's deficient oversight capacity, the ineffectual and biased system of justice, and the abuse of citizens' rights by agents across the state hierarchy, and on the other hand, relational settings characterized by a weak culture of legality, particularistic relations, and systems of meaning influenced by social stigmas. Only by examining this articulation, and the different ways in which it affects rights across the social spectrum, can we make sense of such problems as the weak link between political and civil societies, the widespread sense of impotence, alienation, and cynicism among citizens, little regard for moral restraint (which has led to the acceptance of abusive and violent practices), the high "cost threshold" for cooperation among groups and individuals in this nation, and the pattern of fragmentation in associational life.

Finally, the framework I propose may help us to account for the continuous transformations in state-society and intrasociety relations that take place in democratic settings. In other words, fields of citizenship are not static; they are constantly redefined by collective actors and the state. As the case studies illustrate, we can draw important lessons about the tensions and conflicts involved in democratization by studying how groups employ collective action to defend or challenge certain terms of citizenship and the resulting response (e.g., resistance) of other groups (and, of course, the state). This kind of analysis would benefit from a broader historical perspective that can integrate long-term processes of conflict and negotiation over the terms of citizenship for different social groups within and across nations. A related area for research is the relationship between fields of citizenship and the public sphere. Based on the evidence presented in the study, it is possible to assume that these fields play a key role in the formation of publics and affect the ways in which these publics dispute spaces within the public sphere (see Eley 1992: 325–26). Undoubtedly, an understanding of these issues will affect our understanding of democracies.

Is the democratic polity improved by participation and deliberation? This is a complicated question that demands careful scrutiny of the assumptions that have shaped the study of civil society, social capital, and democratization in the past decades. As my study has shown, this scrutiny leads to the revision of several of these assumptions. The task ahead involves a further revision of paradigmatic ideas that have structured this field of study. The questions and the model that I have posed here suggest some of the areas in which future research can further elucidate the uncertain relationship between civil society and democracy.

The challenge to build better democracies should not be limited by unidimensional approaches that ignore evidence from "crucial" cases, adopt restricted methodological strategies, or attempt to translate— without critical analysis—the paradigmatic experiences of some countries to others. Good *democratic* institutions and plural, tolerant, societies are intricately connected. The future challenge is to rearticulate what we now know into new understandings. Uncovering the uncertainties and paradoxes of civic engagement and democratization does not mean taking a step backward in what we thought we knew, but taking a new step in discerning the unsettled anatomy of democracy.

# Notes

1. In his study of civic engagement in the United States, Putnam (2000) acknowledges that "strengthening the social and political power of voluntary associations may well widen class differences" (p. 358). Still, he argues, there is a "mutually reinforcing" connection between association / social capital and equality. However, while demonstrating that high levels of civic participation in U.S. states are associated with better and more livable communities (better schools, lower crime rates, happier people, etc.), Putnam does not take into account racial divisions, income differentials, age distribution, rural population, and other variables (chaps. 16–22). See Wuthnow 2000. To be sure, Putnam concedes that it is important to define whose interests are advanced by social capital and whose are not. However, in his chapter on the problematic dimensions of the civil society–democracy thesis ("The Dark Side of Social Capital"), Putnam does not really explain how we should approach this issue. His answer focuses on the kinds of social capital ("bonding" versus "bridging") that communities should produce in order to deal with different types of problems (see pp. 22–24).

2. The phrase "bring the people back in" is drawn from Inglehart 1997: chap. 6.

3. I discuss social capital in Chapter 1.

4. Data on group membership are often collected through public opinion surveys. For an analysis of some of the problems of using survey data exclusively to study patterns of civic engagement, see Skocpol and Fiorina 1999b: 7–8.

5. Let me clarify that civil society, as Philip Nord (2000) explains, "is not coextensive with society as a whole but occupies a smaller swatch of territory" (p. xiv).

6. As Joseph Schumpeter (1942) argued, "The democratic method is that in-stitutional arrangement for arriving at political decisions in which individuals acquire the power to decide by means of a competitive struggle for the people's vote" (p. 269). This minimalist perspective offers a measure to identify the pres-ence or absence of *political* democracy at the nation-state level, placing the em-phasis on the *stability* of the democratic political system. As Ian Shapiro (1996) points out, "[one of the major problems] with Schumpeterian democratic the-ory is that the premium it places on stability is so high that it is often difficult, in the end, to see what is democratic about it" (p. 105).

7. As noted, I collected data in 1996 and 2000. The 1996 study consisted of one year of field research in the city of Buenos Aires, greater Buenos Aires, and the provinces of Mendoza and San Juan. In 2000, I conducted a follow-up study primarily focused on updating information on organizations and gathering data on attitudinal changes of selected participants over time. I collected data employing the following tools: (1) open-ended, in-depth interviews with lead-ers and members of civic groups, government officials, scholars, and journal-ists; (2) participant observation of groups' private meetings and various forms of collective action (from street protests to the lobbying of legislators); and (3) archival research in civic organizations, newspapers, government agencies, and Congress. See Chapter 3 for details on data collection and analysis.

CHAPTER 1

1. Indicators of social movement activity may be, for example, the number of events, their duration, and the number of participants. See Tarrow 1994: 110–11, 156–62.

2. As Warren (2001) argues, "The democratic functions of associations may differ from the motives and purposes of members" (p. 37). Therefore, "distin-guishing the purposes and goals of associations from their functions guards against the reductionist view that associations are good *only* if they have dem-ocratic goods and goals" (p. 38).

3. Coincidentally, only a few months after King and his partner were sen-tenced to death, a young member of a white-supremacist group in Indiana murdered an African-American teenager to gain the respect of his comrades (Berryhill 1999: 23).

4. Warren (2001) has developed an interesting typology of associational types and a description of how these types are likely to connect to democratic effects (pp. 134–205).

5. I employ the term "social trust" as synonymous with "interpersonal trust." See Chapter 5 for a discussion of measuring trust.

6. For an earlier analysis of social capital, see Coleman 1988; 1990.

7. Putnam (2000) notes that the concept of social capital is closely linked to that of civic virtue. They are different, though, because the idea of social capital emphasizes "the fact that civic virtue is most powerful when embedded in *a dense network of reciprocal social relations*" (italics added). Therefore, Putnam says,

"A society of many virtuous but isolated individuals is not necessarily rich in social capital" (p. 19).

8. Some studies (e.g., Brehm and Rahn 1997) have examined the reciprocal relationship between participation and trust.

9. Other measures of civic engagement may include voter turnout and various forms of contacting public officials (Foley and Edwards 1999: 148).

10. Even though Putnam's distinction between bridging and bonding forms of social capital is interesting, it is not addressed in detail in his study, as he acknowledges (2000: 24). See Foley and Edwards 1999: 148.

11. While some consider trust a prerequisite for democracy (e.g., Inglehart 1999: 88, 109–19), others view it as a source of economic growth. Social trust, Francis Fukuyama (1995) has argued, plays a major role in determining a country's industrial structure and thus its position in the global capitalist division of labor (p. 325). He posits the argument that a broad "radius of trust" decreases "the transaction costs associated with formal coordination mechanisms like contracts, hierarchies, bureaucratic rules, and the like" (Fukuyama 1999: 3). Trust also increases confidence in the market, thus contributing to the expansion of productive trade (Levi 1999: 20). In contrast, low levels of trust are seen as associated with economic failure (Gambetta 1988: 171). A narrowing of the radius of trust, Fukuyama (1999) argues, generates "a two-tier moral system, with good behavior reserved for family and personal friends, and a decidedly lower standard of behavior in the public sphere" (p. 4). According to this author, lack of wide networks of trust in a society has both economic and political consequences. The most clear *economic* manifestation of a narrow radius of trust is corruption and one of its most visible *political* expressions is a state that encroaches into the private life of individuals (pp. 3–4).

12. My results also show that social trust has an impact on institutional quality. However, while Inglehart measured democratic quality with Freedom House data on civil liberties and political rights, I also employ indicators of governmental responsiveness and effectiveness, control of corruption, and respect for the rule of law. See Chapter 5.

13. Generalized trust, Warren (1999) argues, "helps to build large-scale, complex, interdependent social networks and institutions and for this reason is a key disposition for developing social capital. Moreover, generalized trust is connected to a number of dispositions that underwrite democratic culture, including tolerance for pluralism and criticism" (p. 9). See the various points of view on trust advanced by the contributors in Warren 1999.

14. For Uslaner (1999), "Optimists believe that other people will be helpful, are tolerant of people from different backgrounds, and value both diversity and independent thinking; they have confidence in their own capacity to shape the world" (p. 138). In this analysis, optimists seem to be the icons of the American Dream: "If they take a chance and lose, their upbeat world view leads them to try again" (p. 138). In his most recent work, Uslaner shifted his attention to structural factors. In a study on the United States he found that economic equality is a key predictor of social trust (Uslaner 2000–2001).

15. For their analysis of the "context-dependent nature of social capital," Foley and Edwards draw from Bourdieu's (1986) social-structural analysis of social capital.

16. Putnam (2000) himself has noted that social capital is not always a positive force; that is, it "can be directed toward malevolent, antisocial purposes, just like any other form of capital" (p. 22). He acknowledges that social capital can be produced "*in opposition* to something or someone else" and that, in the 1950s, social capital was "often exclusionary along racial and gender and class lines" in the United States (pp. 358, 361). However, he does not incorporate this crucial dimension into his theoretical framework nor does he offer a systematic explanation of why this is the case.

17. Social capital can be linked to crime and violence. It has been shown that different types of crimes (e.g., petty and violent crime) and criminal networks (e.g., gangs) are connected to different degrees of social interaction and networks of (particularized) trust and reciprocity (e.g., Glaeser, Sacerdote, and Scheinkman 1996). Also, existing social networks can play an important role in shaping violent and criminal behavior, particularly among young people, in certain contexts; for instance, as a study of Boston has shown, in a tight labor market, youths who live in low-income neighborhoods where a substantial number of young people are involved in criminal activity are significantly more likely to be involved in crime than youths living in other neighborhoods (Case and Katz 1991).

18. As Almond and Verba (1963) put it, by means of voluntary associations, "the individual is able to relate himself effectively and meaningfully to the political system. These associations help him avoid the dilemma of being either a parochial, cut off from political influence, or an isolated and powerless individual, manipulated and mobilized by the mass institutions of politics and government" (p. 300).

19. Another key mass society theorist, Hannah Arendt, argued that the rise of mass movements in Europe was the outcome of a process of atomization triggered by the collapse of protective class boundaries (Arendt 1966: 315–17; Hagtvet 1980: 72–77).

20. From this point of view, civil society is a key component of a nation's "cultural health." It entails notions of "personal freedom," "camaraderie," "personal caring," "optimism," and "compassion" (Wuthnow 1991a: 4; 1991b: 302). On "communitarianism," see Etzioni 1996.

21. Using these criteria, Salamon and Anheier (1997) measure the third sector in thirteen countries, surveying voluntary associations in the United States, the United Kingdom, Germany, France, Italy, Sweden, Japan, India, Egypt, Brazil, Thailand, Ghana, and Hungary. See also CIVICUS 1997. In addition to counting the number of organizations, these studies classify voluntary associations according to their structure and operation, their relationship with beneficiaries, funding base, number of members / volunteers, and geographic distribution, among other criteria.

22. It is often difficult to assess the size and growth of the third sector be-

cause these sources provide incomplete, outdated, or unreliable information (Thompson 1995a: 48).

23. A cross-national analysis of 150 grassroots organizations found that membership structures cutting across socioeconomic cleavages (as well as informal, participatory forms of decision making) were positively associated with effectiveness in advancing group demands and monitoring state bureaucracies (Esman and Uphoff 1984: chap. 5).

24. Smulovitz and Peruzzotti (2000) refer to civic associations and NGOs as well as social movements and the media (p. 151). Interestingly, most of the literature on civil society in new democracies does not examine the potential of civil society to monitor the sphere of the market or "economic society" in detail. For an exception to this trend, see Linz and Stepan 1996: chap. 1.

25. For instance, as Cohen and Arato (1992) have argued, "Social movements constitute the *dynamic element* in processes that might realize the positive potentials of modern civil societies" (p. 492; italics added). "Among other things," they said, "movements bring new issues and values into the public sphere and contribute to reproducing the consensus that the elite/pluralist model of democracy presupposes but never bothers to account for" (p. 20). There is a direct relationship between social movements and formal groups in civil society. From a "linear model of development" perspective, "all social movements move from forms of noninstitutionalized, mass protest action to institutionalized, routine interest group or party politics" (Cohen and Arato 1992: 556). As a result of this process, "Formal organization replaces loose networks, membership roles and leaders emerge, and representation replaces direct forms of participation" (p. 556). On social movements and their effects, see Tarrow 1994: chap. 9.

26. While various expressions of civil society may work "as forms of organization of consent whose role is exclusively the stabilization of domination," as Antonio Gramsci claimed, they can also be utilized by subordinated social groups to create alternative formulas and actions that challenge such domination (Cohen and Arato 1992: 149; see also pp. 142–74).

27. According to Jürgen Habermas (1995), the public sphere influences political decisions when it "enters through parliamentary debates into legitimate lawmaking" (p. 371). In Chapter 4, I examine empirically how civil society penetrates the legislature in Argentina. Innovative institutional designs may transform informal publics into spaces for deliberation where social actors, rather than transferring "influence," become directly involved in the policy-making process (as in the case of Brazil, where civil society groups assumed budgetary powers at the municipal level) (Avritzer 2002a: 49–54, 138–42, 151–57). Thus, under favorable political conditions, the creation of specific institutional mechanisms introduce public-level deliberation into the political realm of decision-making, that is, these mechanisms "transfer the results of public discussion to the democratic [political] arena" (p. 53).

28. Political rights entail the rights that guarantee the freedom to participate in politics as constituent and officeholder. Civil rights refer to freedoms of

speech, thought, religion, and culture; equality before the law; and equal access to justice. Civil rights include cultural rights (e.g., the right of indigenous peoples to maintain their language and customs). Social rights entail a guaranteed minimum standard of living and equal access to public services. These rights refer to the minimum conditions that individuals need to make choices and to shape the immediate factors that influence their well-being (Rao and Walton 2002: 2). See Hasson and Ley 1997; Fainstein and Fainstein 1996.

29. Only *general, clear, stable, and nonretroactive* laws can effectively guarantee legal security and personal freedom (Raz 1979: 214–16).

30. As O'Donnell (1999b) puts it, "Whether state agents perpetrate unlawful acts on their own or *de facto* license private actors to do so, does not make much difference, either for the victims of such actions or for the (in)effectiveness of the rule of law" (p. 318).

31. In several cases, these demands represented important symbolic successes for social movements. See Yashar 1998; Brysk 2000a.

32. In his ethnographic study of state-society relations in working-class neighborhoods in Australia, Peel (1998) found evidence that a government which approaches citizens it believes are not trustworthy promotes distrust for institutions and lowers voluntary compliance with the law: "These citizens have good reasons for distrusting a government that, through its agents, so consistently manifests its distrust of them." Among residents in these poor suburbs in Australia, "distrust is a rational, critical response to their actual experiences of distrustful and even destructive governance" (p. 316). In this case, such a vicious circle of distrust takes place in the day-to-day delivery of public services and in other forms of community interaction with the state. A similar pattern can be found in several Latin American countries, usually not only in connection with the delivery of public goods and services but also with law enforcement, access to justice, and consumer protection. See Stillwaggon 1998; O'Donnell 1999b; Dandler 1999; Fry 1999; Garro 1999.

33. Citizens develop a culture of legality when they "internalize the legal rules, act according to them and use the court system to back up serious violations of expectations" (Örkény and Scheppele 1999: 70).

34. When referring to this political doctrine, one should note that some democracies do not have constitutions.

35. This principle establishes a possible threshold against which we can measure the "democratic" impact of civil society activity. For example, as I show in Chapter 4, we can examine the outcome of legal cases on police violence sponsored by human and civil rights groups.

36. Consider the extremely weak judicial guarantees for some sectors of the population or systematic exposure to arbitrary police violence in democratic systems that sustain fairly effective political rights at the national level. See Mitchell and Wood 1999.

37. Fraser (1993) notes that "unequally empowered social groups tend to develop unequally valued cultural styles. The result is the development of powerful informal pressures that marginalize the contributions of members of sub-

ordinated groups both in everyday life contexts and in official public spheres" (p. 11).

38. The rights and responsibilities ascribed to full membership in a democratic community are virtually meaningless for those who lack the necessary "autonomy and / or the availability of a reasonable range of choice" that constitute them as agents (O'Donnell 1999c: 15, 24–25). In his analysis of the "(un)rule" of law in Latin America, O'Donnell (1999b) refers to the connection that "runs from an inegalitarian socioeconomic structure to the weakness of political and, especially, civil rights" (pp. 322–23). See also p. 325 for a comment on the importance of creating "decent" societies "in which the institutions do not humiliate people" (quoting Margalit 1996: 1). A wide gap between rich and poor reinforces patterns of social interaction based on domination and subordination, which tend to remain impervious to democratic changes at the institutional level (O'Donnell 1999b: 322–23). See Tokman and O'Donnell 1998.

39. I thank Mark Ungar for this observation.

40. For illustrations of restricted access to justice for the underprivileged in Latin America, see Méndez, O'Donnell, and Pinheiro 1999.

41. In highly stratified societies, legal norms are not usually perceived as having originated in social habits or practices, acceptable to all parties involved (Isuani 1999: 34). In Argentina, for instance, it has been argued that this feature of society dates back to the origins of the Argentine nation-state, as ruling elites imposed a political and social model based on the exclusion (from effective citizenship rights) of indigenous people, immigrants, women, mestizos, and other subordinated groups (Isuani 1999: 47; Sidicaro 1982; Crahan 1982: 28–30).

42. Impunity can be manifested as legal impunity for the perpetrators of criminal acts and as a day-to-day impunity, when, for example, money and power influence judicial procedures and public officials abuse their power systematically against those who lack the "proper" social rank or relationships (Uvin 1999: 53; O'Donnell 1999b: 312–13).

43. In general, support came from the poorest neighborhoods, where residents did not have the means, such as private security, to protect themselves. Mark Ungar, personal communication, June 7, 2000.

44. Since 2001, the World Social Forum has gathered activists from various countries in an effort to oppose neoliberalism and to resist the "undemocratic" actions of multilateral organizations such as the International Monetary Fund.

45. For classical analyses of citizenship, see Marshall 1950 and Bendix 1977.

46. From the perspective of citizenship, a decline in some rights for a sector of the population (e.g., social rights) generally also reduces their capacity to exercise other rights (civil or political). See O'Donnell 1999c.

47. The idea of the reciprocal "taming" of state and society was suggested to me by David Nugent.

CHAPTER 2

1. Among recent work showing a positive link between civil society and de-mocratization in Latin America, see Abers 2000 and Avritzer 2002a.

2. As Larry Jones (1979) has argued, inflation should be seen within a long-term process of economic decay, that is, "as part of a continuum which also included World War I, the so-called stabilization from 1924 to 1929, and the depression of the early 1930s" (p. 144).

3. On the exclusion and marginalization of women, see Friedan 1963. For more on the 1950s as a "golden age" of civic engagement, see Putnam 1995a and 1995b.

4. Sexual fears also played an important role in the anxiety of whites over losing the identity sustained by an all-white community. In Chicago, for instance, notions of aggressive sexual behavior by blacks had an important place in the articulation of white fears. There was a strong concern among whites that residential transition areas would become breeding grounds for interracial marriage, sexual attacks, or moral decay (Hirsch 1983: 196).

5. The domestic link between race and inequality was also affected by global factors. The loss of industrial jobs in this period was especially hard on unskilled black migrants. Subsequently, low-skilled African Americans have been among those most hard-hit by new trends in globalization initiated in the mid-1970s.

6. Interestingly, sports clubs weighed "more prominently in the organizational background of Marburg National Socialists than in that of the sample of ordinary townspeople, especially in 1933–35" (Koshar 1986a: 218–19).

7. Nazi Party activists in Marburg were members of at least two associations. "The ratio of affiliations to individuals for these party members was 2.48" (Koshar 1986a: 212). On cross-affiliation patterns in Marburg, see pp. 202, 287–88, 292–97 (table A-1).

8. In this period, the town's vote for the Nazis multiplied thirty-five times (Allen 1984: 18–19, 142).

9. The *Stammtisch* consisted of "a group of men who ate lunch together on a specified day every week at the same restaurant around the same table," and the beer clubs were "regular meetings at some tavern for talk, beer, and possibly card playing" (Allen 1984: 18–19).

10. Surprisingly, the same strategy of organizing public events where people can meet and bond has been proposed by Putnam (2000) as a way to increase social capital in the United States (pp. 23, 362, 411).

11. As the former member explained: "There was no direct or obvious political indoctrination until later—after Hitler came to power. . . . I think most of the other boys joined for the same reason I did. They were looking for a place where they could get together with other boys in exciting activities" (Allen 1984: 76).

12. Allen (1984) provides a description of these local leaders: "They had the network of contacts (at least on the local level) to know where specialized

skills could be located, to deal with practical problems like renting a microphone or getting a poster designed and printed overnight. Their middle class background and business experience meant that they were already trained to punctuality, industriousness, disciplined task-solving, orderliness, and frugality" (p. 143).

13. See Foley and Edwards 1999 for a conceptual analysis of this dimension (pp. 166–68).

14. Koshar (1986a) employs the term *apoliticism*. I believe that *antipoliticism* is a better term to describe the hostility toward the party system and the "political class." Germans' disengagement from the political system did not mean that they lacked interest in politics.

15. Political parties failed to articulate and aggregate competing interests and demands. "The party system," as Bernt Hagtvet (1980) explained, "lacked crucial integrative capacities because it remained focalized on regional attachments and social groups which were already politically mobilized at the time of Bismarck." The parliament, in turn, did not function as an effective "bargaining arena with adjudicative capacities" (pp. 95, 67). See Fritzsche 1990: chaps. 10–11.

16. As in urban populations, this conversion process was influenced by the erosion of traditional partisan allegiances (Zofka 1986: 60).

17. Though created by a political party with a partisan purpose, these were civil society groups like many of those studied by Putnam (1993) in Italy—which, contrary to what he argued, were created by political parties to mobilize certain sectors of the population or were traditionally the result of Catholic Church activity (Wilson 1999: 255, citing Maraffi 1998; Sabetti 1996).

18. There was also a very strong left-wing component in Weimar's associational life. Some of it was democratic; some was communist and antidemocratic.

19. The pattern reversed following the Nazi takeover (Koshar 1986a: 298, table A-2).

20. Evidence that the Nazi Party was essentially a "successful party of protest" was that its number of voters decreased in late 1932. In the November 1932 elections—after political bargaining to elect Hitler as chancellor faltered and the Reichstag was dissolved—the NSDAP lost about 2 million votes (Childers 1986: 233, 253). As Childers has noted, "the NSDAP had reached the limits of its middle-class appeal and yet any serious attempt to broaden the party's constituency by more aggressive efforts to mobilise working-class voters ran the very substantial risk of alienating the NSDAP's essential core of middle-class support" (p. 253). Strategically, this situation highlighted the limitations of the Nazi Party organization to gain access to power via electoral means (Childers 1983: 264–65, 268–69).

21. According to Hagtvet (1980), "Like the working class subculture, the middle class unions and the guilds promoted a distinct way of life by founding their own organizations encompassing cultural and social activities as well. Thus they tried to preserve the distinctions between petty bourgeois and

proletarian lifestyles. These distinctions had less and less basis in income differentials but were for that very reason guarded more zealously than before" (p. 86).

22. As a reaction, some industrial and business sectors engaged in a zero-sum game of competition with other sectors of society, attacking the democratic rules of the game (Kolb 1988: 101–3). In a context of fierce class antagonism, powerful industrial interests actively followed a strategy of "class struggle from above" and pushed for an extrasystemic solution to the crisis (Kolb 1988: 158; Abraham 1981: 19, 36).

23. Bankruptcies affecting middle-class sectors continued well into the early 1930s. See Childers 1983: 144, 211–13, 216–18.

24. See, for example, Abraham 1981: chap. 5; Mommsen 1991: 18, 24, 26–27. Also see Noakes and Pridham 1983; Feldman 1993; Falter and Zintl 1998.

25. On the role of academics in the diffusion of Nazi ideas, see Gallin 1986.

26. A "*völkisch* pseudo-science" or as the Nazis put it, "a branch of medicine," "racial hygienics" served to legitimize attacks against the Jews. For instance, based on the principles of racial hygienics, the Nazis claimed that "the Jewish element figured negatively in any attempt to purify the 'Nordic' race." Jews were viewed as responsible for the country's moral decay. One of the arguments advanced by the Nazi Physicians' League was that Jews' support for sexual freedom was an important source of the crisis in Germany (Kater 1986: 162–64).

27. From 1933 to 1938, in response to the policies of the totalitarian regime, the league largely shifted its focus from feminist objectives to the defense and support of Jews and Jewish organizations (Kaplan 1984: 190).

28. The term "serpent's egg" comes from legends in which a monster (a dragon or a snake) was born from an egg laid by a rooster and hatched by a serpent. Its use here was inspired by Ingmar Bergman's film *The Serpent's Egg*, which depicts pre-Hitler Berlin in the 1920s. As I use the term in this chapter, the demon hatched from the serpent's egg in Weimar Germany was the collapse of democracy and the rise of Nazism; in the United States, the phrase denotes the wave of undemocratic reaction to the expansion of citizenship rights after World War II.

29. Most studies refer to these prosegregation organizations as "Citizens' Councils" and not "White Citizens' Councils." Benjamin Muse (1964), for instance, explained: "By far the most influential molders of the movement of resistance to desegregation were the organizations which sprang up in every Southern state and either coagulated in what became the 'Citizens' Councils of America, Incorporated' or allied themselves with that body. At first there were many 'White Citizens' Councils' and an 'Association of Citizens' Councils'; local groups also used such names initially as 'National Association for the Preservation of the White Race,' 'States' Rights League,' 'Hermitage Crusade,' 'Southern Gentlemen'—or 'Pond Hollow Segregation Club'" (p. 47). For a detailed list of studies on the Citizens' Councils and massive resistance to desegregation in the South, see Bartley 1969: 372–73; 1995: 481–82. In addition to the

works cited in this chapter, see the following journalistic accounts of the council movement: Martin 1957; Carter 1959; and Cook 1962.

30. Organized resistance to desegregation was, from the outset of the *Brown* ruling, a theme of regional politics on the municipal and state level, encompassing sheriffs and ad hoc vigilante actions, Ku Klux Klan chapters, white clergy, media, politicians who vowed resistance to school desegregation, and other opinion molders.

31. In his study of the Citizens' Councils, McMillen (1994) argued that they employed intimidation tactics but not violence: "Whatever may have been the theoretical relationship between the explosive atmosphere [they] so often created and the actual outbreak of violence, there is no tangible evidence which suggests that [they] engaged in, or even overtly encouraged, criminal acts. From time to time individual Council members were implicated in acts of vigilantism, including homicide and bombing, but the organization itself was never directly linked with these things" (p. 360).

32. Experts on the Citizens' Councils have stressed the difficulty of estimating the actual membership of the movement. According to council leaders, members were not always actively involved, but they maintained their loyalty and support to the movement: "In times of crisis, most official spokesmen professed to believe that all Councilors, whether dues-paying or otherwise, would stand united behind the Citizens' Councils of America and the defense of white supremacy" (McMillen 1994: 152–53).

33. On informal networks and "interpersonal solidarities," see Tarrow 1994: 57.

34. A Council leader described the situation in Clarksdale, Mississippi, following a NAACP petition: "The good folks there had said 'we don't need a Citizens' Council, our niggers are good niggers, they don't want to integrate, if we organize a Citizens' Council it'll agitate 'em.' But one bright morning they woke up with a school petition with three hundred three signers, including most of their good ones. So they organized a Council" (as quoted in McMillen 1994: 30–31).

35. Mississippi's Councils "campaigned for passage of a suffrage restriction amendment to the state constitution, which was approved by heavy majorities in November [1954], and then turned to support of the 'last resort' school closing amendment, which was ratified by a comfortable majority in December" (Bartley 1969: 86). See also McMillen 1994: 320.

36. The council movement also extended to Georgia. However, Georgia's prosegregation activity did not reach the intensity attained in the other Deep South states (McMillen 1994: 80–81).

37. Councils were also organized in Florida, but with less success and effectiveness. The segregationist movement expanded to Tennessee, Arkansas, Texas, North Carolina, and Virginia too. In some of these states (e.g., Tennessee, North Carolina, and Virginia), the antidesegregation movement consisted mainly of kindred groups. In Virginia, for example, the segregationists organized groups such as the "Defenders of State Sovereignty and Individual Liber-

ties," which exerted strong influence over state legislators and political leaders. Groups such as these emerged out of informal social networks that linked politicians and average citizens. The Defenders of State Sovereignty had informal links with the Citizens' Councils of America (Bartley 1969: 94–96, 89–101; 1995: 199; Muse 1964: 10; McMillen 1994: 105–7, 120–21, 310). See McMillen's chaps. 6 and 7. For more on the Defenders of State Sovereignty, see Smith 1965: chap. 6. For a discussion of the council's efforts to extend the movement to California, Maryland, and other states, see McMillen 1994: chap. 8.

38. The council movement was portrayed by its leaders as "the modern version of the old-time town meeting called to meet any crisis by expressing the will of the people" (a council promotional pamphlet, as quoted in Bartley 1995: 201).

39. When criticized for the promotion of blacklists of petitioners, the council leadership responded that employers were just resorting to their "freedom of choice" in making decisions that affected their businesses (Bartley 1995: 205).

40. On some occasions, African Americans were able to organize their own boycotts and fight back successfully, drawing upon their power as consumers. Also, the NAACP offered financial assistance to blacks who had suffered from white retaliation. The conflict imposed a heavy cost on both blacks and whites. However, it was not until the U.S. Congress and President Eisenhower denounced the use of economic intimidation that the councils withdrew their support for this practice (McMillen 1994: 211–14).

41. Questionnaires to screen candidates' attitudes were often used in Mississippi, Alabama, Louisiana, North Carolina, South Carolina, and Tennessee (McMillen 1994: 307).

42. On the general topic of networks of interactions between governmental and societal actors, see Sparrow 1992; Laumann and Knoke 1987.

43. It is interesting to observe, for example, that as authorities in the southern states abandoned their defiant position toward the federal government, the Citizens' Council movement rapidly lost its momentum in the fight against desegregation. As struggles within the state gave way to developments in the direction of democratization, the antidesegregation movement became gradually demoralized in the face of political changes (McMillen 1994: 362).

44. In late 1956 the council organized the "Education Fund of the Citizens' Councils," which was designed to function, in the council's view, "as a southern counterpoise to the NAACP's tax-exempt educational fund." The idea was that the fund would take over the costs of the council's publications and "seek access to the national information media, including the wire services, television, radio, national periodicals, and the motion picture industry" (McMillen 1994: 38).

45. Other sources of government support for the council's activities in Mississippi included the State Sovereignty Commission (McMillen 1994: 336).

46. On the origins of restrictive covenants and the real estate business, see Abrams 1955: chap. 13; Jones-Correa 2000–2001. Until 1950, the "Code of Ethics" of the National Association of Real Estate Boards said: "A realtor should

never be instrumental in introducing into a neighborhood a character of property or occupancy, members of any race or nationality, or any individual whose
presence will clearly be detrimental to property values in the neighborhood." In
1950 the canon was changed to: "A realtor should not be instrumental in introducing into a neighborhood a character of property or use which will clearly be
detrimental to property values in that neighborhood" (as quoted in Abrams
1955: 156, 157). Still, nationality and especially race continued to play an important role in the assessment of real estate values.

47. A number of these associations were originally created by real estate
agencies (Sugrue 1996: 212). In the 1940s the realtors' national organization
launched the idea of creating homeowners' associations in order to enforce
covenants and regulations. As Charles Abrams (1955) explained: "Some home-
builders had been practicing race restrictions for years. The others now found
the response of their customers encouraging too. Buyers liked the idea of being
accepted into an 'exclusive' neighborhood. To be discriminating, they were
told, you must be discriminatory." Until 1948 the restrictive covenant was an
important tool in the real estate business: "All the builder had to do was
covenant the land with restrictions banning various types of people and he or
his buyers could invoke the aid of the courts to enforce it against a violator"
(pp. 170–72). See Rosenblum 1998 (chap. 4), for an analysis of contemporary
homeowners' associations or Residential Community Associations (RCAs).
Rosenblum's analysis highlights the fact that the "voluntary" dimension of
these associations is restricted: "When buyers purchase property in a residential community governed by a homeowners' association they become members
as well as owners" (p. 112).

48. Many of these activists were members of labor organizations and
parochial groups. The homeowners' movement received support from labor
unions and churches.

49. The MIC, which was created in 1948, worked with a large group of religious and civil rights associations as part of the Coordinating Council on Human Relations (CCHR) (Sugrue 1996: 191).

50. For example, see Sugrue 1996: 151 (table 5.5) for data on the impact of
changes in the city's industrial base upon unemployment and joblessness
among blacks.

51. From its creation in 1937 until 1950, the FHA loan program contributed to
maintain racial discrimination practices in housing by encouraging, for instance, "the use and application of racially restrictive covenants as a means of
ensuring the security of neighborhoods" (Massey and Denton 1993: 52–55, quotation on 54). See also Gotham 2000.

52. The volunteer's quotation is from Wilkinson 1979: 138, as cited in Weisbrot 1990: 289. In Detroit, the Courville District Improvement Association told
its members: "Our boys fought to uphold freedom and safeguard our present
rights. Are you willing to pick up the torch and carry on? There is no freedom
without responsibility" (as quoted in Sugrue 1996: 219).

53. There are other important benefits associated with homeownership. As

Rosenblum (1998) explains: "The point of accrued equity (and potential appreciation of property value) is that as the mortgage is paid, owners can borrow against it for personal consumption, college tuition, retirement, and so on" (p. 122).

54. Communities like Trumbull Park "hardly rate as civil rights landmarks in the same sense as Montgomery, Selma, or Birmingham, but they are symbols, nonetheless," Hirsch (1995) has argued. "More than mere examples of the anti-Black animus, they exposed the political and ideological limits of the civil rights era" (p. 523).

55. Homeowners' associations also were instrumental in the movement that unified the antitax revolt, the antidensity campaign, and the antibusing protest (Davis 1990: 184).

56. The erection of barriers in lower-income neighborhoods fences these communities off from poorer people, thus replicating the phenomenon of spatial segregation found in middle- and upper-class gated communities (El Nasser 2002: A1).

57. In general, these associations enact numerous rules that regulate physical aspects of properties and in some cases even residents' behavior outside their own homes (Blakely and Snyder 1997: 20–22).

58. As Steven Taylor (1998) has explained: "Many of Boston's Irish Americans viewed busing as the latest of unwanted reforms being forced upon them by a political culture that had been hostile toward them. Hence the implementation of busing opened up very old wounds that had not yet completely healed" (p. 167).

59. In this context, the federal courts—and sometimes the federal government—played a pivotal role in advancing the rule of law.

60. For different roles in organizing along gender lines in Detroit, see Sugrue 1996: 250–52.

61. Koshar (1986b) found in Marburg that, by early 1933, "there had been at least one Nazi Party member in 104 local associations, or about one-quarter of all voluntary groups in the city. Opportunities for promoting the Nazi message were far more numerous in this 'underground' interpenetration of the Nazi Party and organisational life than in big demonstrations or protest marches" (pp. 28–29).

62. While political scientists have been engaged in a debate on the connection between civic engagement and democracy, many U.S. historians would probably reject the notion that civic engagement inevitably promotes democratic outcomes. Studies such as Morgan 1975 have argued that U.S. democracy developed together with slavery and racism. Along with studies of the Progressive era culminating in the early twentieth century, this scholarship questions the claim that white civic engagement has necessarily advanced black rights in the United States. I thank Robert Weisbrot for this observation.

CHAPTER 3

1. In 2001, after failing to lift Argentina out of a four-year recession that had eroded the country's fiscal base, and which had sent unemployment and poverty to record levels, the administration of Fernando de la Rúa seemed unable to avert a default on Argentina's multibillion-dollar foreign debt. The International Monetary Fund (IMF) refused to help Argentina repay its debt obligations due at the end of 2001. The belief that the Argentine peso would be devalued spread rapidly across society. In response to this confidence crisis, people rushed to the banks to convert their pesos to U.S. dollars at the one-to-one rate. Following massive withdrawals in November 2001, the De la Rúa administration announced restrictions on the amount of money people could withdraw from their bank accounts. This was a desperate device, known as the *corralito* or "playpen," to save the national banking system from a crisis that posed threats to the federal reserves and the parity between the peso and the dollar. The measure, in fact, accentuated the country's economic recession, which included an unemployment rate of around 20 percent, a high fiscal deficit, and the inability of the government to respond to the demands of a very dissatisfied middle class and the working class. In the days following the government's announcement of the restrictions, a general strike paralyzed the country, and shantytown residents began looting shops and supermarkets. In a context of great uncertainty and social tension, the government declared a state of siege in the week before Christmas. Immediately thereafter, thousands of citizens went into the streets to protest against the government. Protests turned violent in the form of rioting and looting. Police repression resulted in more than two dozen deaths. A very worn-out De la Rúa resigned on December 20 and a temporary president took over. In fact, four presidents followed De la Rúa in the two weeks after his resignation. The fourth, Peronist strongman Eduardo Duhalde, was appointed by Congress to serve until new elections in April 2003. Peronist candidate Néstor Kirchner was then elected president.

2. This movement promoted some significant changes in state practices and helped educate citizens about their rights—how citizens should demand and use their rights to exert control over state action (Jelin 1996: 113–14). See Brysk 1994, esp. chaps. 4–10, for an analysis of the movement's impact in the first decade of democracy.

3. As O'Donnell (1999a) put it, "there was not only a state and a government that were brutally despotic, but . . . there was also a society that during those years was much more authoritarian and repressive than ever before" (pp. 54–55).

4. Other groups in civil society—more traditionally supportive of authoritarian governments—were part of this effort too. These organizations included the Jockey Club, Círculo de Armas, and the Sociedad Rural (Bayer 2001).

5. Data from INDEC and Equis, as reported in Restivo 2002 and *Clarín.com* 2002a. On earlier impoverishment trends, see Minujin 1992; 1993. See also CELS 2000: chap. 3.

6. Greater Buenos Aires includes twenty-two suburban counties around the city of Buenos Aires.

7. Data from confidential interviews with federal government officials in 2000. Experts have indicated that most people do not report crimes to the police, particularly when they involve low levels of violence and result in property loss, because they do not trust the police.

8. Commissioner Pedro Klodczyc, *La Nación*, May 8, 1996, as quoted in Oliveira and Tiscornia 1997: 61.

9. The major associations of lawyers in Buenos Aires reacted against the president's plan, which they considered dangerous to the independence of the Supreme Court. The press denounced the plan as a stratagem to secure the executive's political influence on the judiciary. The court-packing plan was also vehemently resisted by the opposition Radical Party and a sector of the judiciary (Verbitsky 1993: 28, 33–51).

10. Corruption, as explained, was especially prevalent in the 1990s. As Menem's second term in office drew to a close, "well over 100 government officials and their relatives had been charged—and acquitted" in cases of corruption (Ungar 2002: 147).

11. On the IBM-Banco Nación and other scandals involving state agencies, see the 2001 report by the Chamber of Deputies' Special Investigating Committee on Money Laundering. For a synthesis of the commission's findings, see the report's executive summary, available at http://www.informelavado.com. The report shows, for instance, how state agencies such as the country's central bank—charged with the responsibility to control and regulate the financial system—failed to do so.

12. On post-1998 developments regarding the Office of the Ombudsman, see Ungar 2002: 202–3.

13. For a detailed description of the reform and its aftermath, including the reversal of key advances in the democratization of the Buenos Aires provincial police, see Palmieri, Filippini, and Thomas 2001: 6–31.

14. This description is based on an author's interview with Alicia Pierini, then head of the subsecretariat, Buenos Aires, May 9, 1996, as well as the agency's publications and interviews with members of civic organizations.

15. This account is based on an author's interview with María Julia Zarate, one of the bureau's lawyers, Buenos Aires, May 8, 1996, and interviews with members of civic groups.

16. Data from Gallup Argentina corresponding to surveys conducted in the city of Buenos Aires (the federal capital) and greater Buenos Aires in the period 1984–96. In addition to the trends concerning the judiciary, Congress, and political parties, trust in public officials, police, labor unions, big business, and the educational system also experienced a steady downfall since 1984. As of February 2002, according to a UN survey published in *La Nación*, 93 percent of Argentines distrusted politicians.

17. The sources for these data are the following: Survey conducted in the city of Buenos Aires and greater Buenos Aires by the APDH (1995); survey con-

ducted by the Public Opinion Department at Taller, Escuela, Agencia (TEA) in the city of Buenos Aires and greater Buenos Aires (July–August 1992), as reported in "La ley de la calle," *Quinto Poder* 1, no. 3 (September 1992): 14; and a 1996 poll by Gallup Argentina. Another sphere of state-citizen interaction in which the rule of law has been systematically violated is that of imprisonment. Conditions in federal prisons have been very precarious because of overcrowding, lack of personnel, human rights abuses, and inadequate facilities. In violation of the criminal code, the system of justice has acted with excessive slowness. Around 75 percent of the inmates in the Buenos Aires penitentiary system have been in prison for longer than two years without being tried, and more than 70 percent have not received a sentence. As a result of these conditions, there have been major prison revolts with deadly consequences—as in 1996, when nearly 13,000 prisoners in nineteen prisons across the country revolted in protest against inhuman conditions of detention (Ungar 2002: 44–46).

18. See Coordinadora contra la Represión Policial e Institucional (CORREPI), "Archivo de Casos, 1983–1998," available at http://www.derechos.org/correpi/muertes.html.

19. Access to legal defense has been a serious problem in Argentina, primarily for low-income sectors. Public defenders are few relative to prosecutors, and they lack the most basic resources to do their job. Legal clinics in universities have been largely ineffective because of a virtual absence of supervision, lack of infrastructure, and constant turnover (Ungar 2002: 203–5, 220–21).

20. The budget for the judiciary at the national level (including the Supreme Court of Justice) increased from a range of 0.14 to 0.18 percent of the country's GDP in the period 1984–90 to a range of 0.21 to 0.33 percent in the period 1991–97 (it was at its highest point from 1994 through 1997). See Molinelli, Palanza, and Sin 1999: 663, table 4.7.

21. For instance, in the early 1990s (World Values Surveys data), only 23 percent of respondents in Argentina said that "most people can be trusted" (less than half than in the United States).

22. In addition to high levels of mutual distrust among Argentines, Kirkpatrick (1971) also found high levels "of cynicism about government, and of lack of agreement about the desirable form of political organization" (p. 231). When responses to the first statement were compared with results in the five countries analyzed by Almond and Verba in *The Civic Culture* (1963), they showed that Argentina ranked lower than the United States (68 percent), Italy (73 percent), the United Kingdom (75 percent), and Germany (81 percent). Only Mexicans (94 percent) showed lower levels of mutual trust than Argentines (p. 120, table 6.2). Indeed, nearly four decades ago only 16 percent of Argentines believed that others would not take advantage of them.

23. This 1990 survey was reported in *Crónica*, "Significativas cifras sobre el uso de la tortura," January 23, 1991. The poll revealed that 30.2 percent of those interviewed considered that the use of torture "depended on the case" and 7.9 percent approved of it without reserve (Chevigny 1995: 195).

24. After a massacre of prisoners in São Paulo's largest penitentiary in 1992,

a poll revealed that 44 percent of interviewees approved of the military police's action. Furthermore, in São Paulo thousands "took to the streets to demonstrate in favor of the police and against human rights advocates who had criticized the prison massacre" (Caldeira 1996: 197–98).

25. This is a nonrepresentative sample (N = 244). The sociologists who conducted the survey, however, balanced the sample according to socioeconomic variables. For sample details, see Belvedere 1999: 279–81.

26. See also Thompson 1995a; Levy 1996; Inter-American Development Bank 1998; and data reported by the National Center for Community Organizations (CENOC).

27. The original list of types of voluntary organizations included: (1) social welfare services for elderly, handicapped, or deprived people; (2) religious or church organizations; (3) education, arts, music, or cultural activities; (4) trade unions; (5) political parties or groups; (6) local community action on issues like poverty, employment, housing, racial equality; (7) third world development or human rights; (8) conservation, the environment, ecology; (9) professional associations; (10) youth work (e.g., scouts, guides, youth clubs, etc.). In 1991 the survey was expanded to include: (11) sports or recreation; (12) women's groups; (13) peace movement; (14) animal rights; (15) voluntary organizations concerned with health; (16) other groups.

28. To do so, I created an overall measure of membership in formal associations that totals the number of different groups to which a respondent belongs. Respondents who did not mention any of the groups in the list were coded 0 (i.e., these were considered nonparticipants). Membership in only one type of group was coded 1 and in two types, 2. Because the number of respondents who belonged to more than three types of organizations was small, I aggregated them into a single category (3 or more) in order to avoid presenting misleading means. On this methodological aspect, see Young and Seligson 1997.

29. To a significant extent, the difference can be attributed to the inclusion of sports / recreation groups in the index.

30. Survey conducted by the Public Opinion Department at TEA in the city of Buenos Aires and greater Buenos Aires (May 1992), as reported in "¿El ocaso de la participación?" *Quinto Poder* 1, no. 3 (September 1992): 22–26.

31. The actual question was, "Have you ever been active in a political campaign? That is, have you ever participated in any political activity, such as contributing money, demonstrating, and so on?" (Kirkpatrick 1971: 243).

32. In addition, some *anti*–civil rights movements, usually temporary, emerged in some towns in Buenos Aires province and in the city of Buenos Aires, where middle-class groups mobilized to protest a rights-oriented Urban Coexistence Code and demanded more police power to clear their neighborhoods of "undesirables" (Ungar 2002: 95–96).

33. This bombing was the deadliest anti-Jewish terrorist act against a civilian population since World War II, killing eighty-six people. As in the Cabezas case, the police were implicated in the attack. An earlier anti-Jewish attack destroyed the Israeli embassy in Buenos Aires in March 1992, killing twenty-nine people.

The 1994 bombing of the Jewish community center led to many civil society activities, but not to any conclusive investigation or prosecution.

34. A well-known journalist called this effect *intoxicación informativa* (information intoxication). Meeting of the Argentina Working Group (the Argentina Project at the Woodrow Wilson Center), Buenos Aires, June 26, 2002.

35. The Center for Legal and Social Studies (CELS) was founded in the late 1970s, but underwent such a major organizational transformation in the 1990s that it could be included among the "new" human and civil rights groups. Among other activities, CELS developed an advocacy and research program on citizen security, pursued legal challenges to the constitutional status of certain laws, and monitored designations of judges and promotions of military officers in Congress.

36. The following are the organizations included in my study: Asociación por los Derechos Civiles; Asociación Travestis Argentinos; Comisión de Amigos y Vecinos de Ingeniero Budge (CAVIB); Centro de Estudios Legales y Sociales (CELS); Comisión de Familiares de Víctimas Indefensas de la Violencia Institucional (COFAVI); Conciencia; Coordinadora contra la Represión Policial e Institucional (CORREPI); CORREPI-Familiares; Familiares de Víctimas Indefensas de Mendoza (FAVIM); Foro del Sector Social; Gays por los Derechos Civiles; Hijos por la Identidad y la Justicia contra el Olvido y el Silencio (HIJOS); Memoria Activa; Movimiento contra la Discriminación; and Poder Ciudadano. My study did not include, for example, women's organizations, which promoted a strong gender-based agenda that led to political and legal reforms in the 1990s.

The primary data utilized in the examination of the Argentine case included conversational interviews with leaders and members of civic groups, as well as government officials, scholars, and journalists in Buenos Aires, Mendoza, and San Juan (sixty open-ended, in-depth interviews). I did not collect a random sample of activists. I employed a snowballing approach to generate a sample of participants as balanced and broad as possible. Most of the interviews were conducted in the city of Buenos Aires and greater Buenos Aires. Additional sources included documents from civic organizations and government agencies, and major Argentine newspapers (*Clarín*, *Página/12*, and *La Nación*). Participant observation was a fundamental component of my field research. I attended numerous public and private meetings of groups, demonstrations, festivals, and street protests and also observed how groups engaged in lobbying and other forms of advocacy with state agents. I gathered evidence from various sources in order to cross-check information and triangulate my data.

In the interviewing process, I employed the same semistructured questionnaire with all interviewees. After some preliminary field research, I decided against conducting a survey of participants in the groups. When I talked to grieving mothers whose children were killed by "trigger-happy" policemen, underpaid lawyers who worked twelve hours a day, and activists who received death threats, it was clear to me that the survey was not a good instrument. I could not reduce the complex issues that activists faced to a numerical scale.

Thus I developed a questionnaire structured around questions on attitudes and the experience of participation, but that allowed sufficient flexibility for participants to get sidetracked and talk about issues that interested them (on these methodological aspects, see Hecht 1998: 13–14). The questions covered a broad range of topics including social trust, tolerance, system support, relations with government agencies and perception of the state apparatus, views on conflict and common interests in society, personal and group priorities, willingness to compromise, and embeddedness in social networks. Interviews were codified, independently, by me and another analyst. Data analysis was focused on identifying concepts that expressed social trust, tolerance, predispositions toward dialogue and cooperation, and attitudes toward institutions and other groups of civil society. When coding the raw data, I considered both what the evidence said (for example, a statement made by a respondent in an interview) and how a particular piece of evidence related to a general framework (such as the entire conversation with the interviewee). In evaluating each organization, I sought to make a comprehensive judgment about group attributes. For example, I triangulated data from various sources to determine if the association had a single "comprehensive *Weltanschauung*" (a conceptual scheme from which its actions derive) or if there were competing internal views that influenced the behavior of the group (see Putnam 1973: 241–44). Given the nonrepresentative nature of the sample of civic participants, the results do not apply to the broader society; however, when possible, I employed survey data to examine the correspondence between attitudes found in the ethnographic study (e.g., social trust) and in the overall society.

37. In choosing this subset of interviewees, I considered socioeconomic factors in order to balance the composition. The original wave of interviews asked for perceptions at the time of joining the organization in order to establish a baseline for evaluating the relationship between civic engagement and attitudinal change. The 2000 interviews allowed me to establish some trends over time for a smaller sample within the original set of participants.

38. In the case of CORREPI, there was a wide division between professionals and relatives of victims, which convinced me to treat the organization as two different groups for the purpose of the analysis.

39. Since its creation, COFAVI has been led by relatives of victims. This organization was initially called Committee of Relatives of Innocent Victims of Police, Judicial, and Institutional Violence (Comisión de Familiares de Víctimas Inocentes de la Violencia Policial, Judicial e Institucional). In COFAVI, the relatives were in charge of managing the internal affairs of the organization, while lawyers and other volunteers had technical and support roles. This was not true of CORREPI, which had a core leadership of lawyers with a background of political activism.

40. In fact, civic organizations engaged in advocacy or watchdog activities sometimes faced many obstacles in the process of obtaining legal recognition as civil associations. This was true of COFAVI, for example.

CHAPTER 4

1. To guarantee the anonymity of my respondents, I do not identify them when reporting my findings. Also, I have tried to avoid revealing which group produced which discourse or behavior. I believe that this kind of information may have a negative impact on the already strained links within this segment of civil society.

2. The direct impact of civic engagement on state practices is a problem that was amply discussed in the social movement literature during the late 1990s, when the emphasis on the importance of social movements as devices to shape collective identities gave way to a concern with the political role of these movements in the legal and institutional spheres of new democratic regimes. As some scholars have argued, a concern with the production of power understood "as the creation of space for dissent" must be complemented by tangible evidence that civil society can influence formal structures of government and institutional processes (Roberts 1997: 142, 145). See also Haber 1996; Pratchett 1999; Lomax 1997.

3. Consider, for example, the serious problem of police violence in Argentina.

4. This same interviewee had told me in 1996, before joining the group, "I felt I deserved to be mistreated or discriminated against, particularly because I was the mother of a person killed by the police."

5. As shown by a Gallup Argentina poll conducted in 1994, which asked about the rights of victims, suspects, and criminals.

6. Here the use of the term "black" does not correspond to its use in the United States. In Argentina, "black" refers to individuals who have some indigenous heritage, *mestizos*.

7. I found that, for most of the organizations, the problem of race / ethnicity was very difficult to deal with. Even though the kind of open remark such as the one cited was unusual, groups and individual participants did not show racial tolerance; they often chose to ignore the question of racial discrimination. Racism and xenophobia were often present in the discourse of public officials. For example, some officials publicly accused immigrants of being disproportionately involved in criminal activities, when actual police reports showed the opposite trend. On occasion, some civil society activists repeated this kind of xenophobic argument.

8. On particularized trust, see Williams 1988: 12; Newton 1997: 578; Uslaner 1999: 124. See also Yamagishi and Yamagishi 1994. I discuss the difference between generalized and particularized trust in Chapter 1.

9. I divided participants into three categories: upper-middle, middle, and lower-middle class, based on income, occupation, and educational level.

10. As explained earlier in the book, civic participation is mediated by the specific conditions in which organizational activity takes place (Foley and Edwards 1997b: 670–71). For instance, neo-Tocquevilleans (e.g., Putnam) do not take into account the fact that context can raise the costs of cooperation, thus

stimulating defection among those who are in a vulnerable position (Williams 1988: 8).

11. Trust in others is necessary to motivate people to cooperate. Said Williams (1988): "Cooperation requires trust in the sense that dependent parties need some degree of assurance that non-dependent parties will not defect" (p. 8).

12. The World Values Surveys asked respondents whether they trusted others. Respondents were asked: "Generally speaking, would you say that most people can be trusted or that you can't be too careful in dealing with people?" This trust variable is one of the classic social trust measures (see Rosenberg 1956). It was coded as a dichotomous variable. Those who answered that "most people can be trusted" were coded 1. Those who responded that one "can't be too careful" were coded 0. For details on the group membership variable, see Chapter 3.

13. If we observe the nature of the relationship between levels of civic engagement (the number of different groups to which individuals belong) and social trust, we find a decline in trust among those individuals who participate in three or more types of groups (see Chapter 3). Even though this segment represents only 11.5 percent of all group members, this downward trend in trust among those who might be seen as "intense" activists is puzzling.

14. The sex of respondents was coded 1 for males and 2 for females. The education item asked the respondent the following question: "At what age did you or will you complete your full-time education, either at school, or at an institution of higher education?" The resulting ten-point scale ranged from "completed formal education at 12 years of age or earlier" (coded 1) to "completed education at 21 years of age or older" (coded 10). The respondent's household income level was measured as a ten-point scale ranging from "lowest" (coded 1) to "highest" (coded 10).

15. Though income is not statistically significant, it is the most important predictor of trust in the equation. This concurs with the cross-national findings presented in Chapter 5.

16. These interactions are influenced, among other factors, by the various, changing, and competing strategies that dominate state action at different levels, such as the willingness to employ co-optation or coercive mechanisms to reduce the level of civil society criticism toward the government or to control its repertoire of activities.

17. This is "a conflict of interest such that what one side gains the others involved necessarily must lose" (Putnam 1973: 258).

18. Relatives of those killed in the 1994 bombing of the AMIA headquarters created a civic organization called Active Memory (Memoria Activa). Since the creation of the group, members have been harassed by the police and received death threats. As a result of internal disagreements, the original organization broke into three groups. On July 18, 2002, for example, there were three commemorative events, each organized by a different group, on the anniversary of the terrorist attack.

19. Festivals and mass rallies to protest police abuse attracted thousands after 1995. In a context of heightened social tensions, the type of violent message cited in the text could lead to violence. This is what happened in April 1996 when violence broke out at a festival in the city of Buenos Aires to protest police brutality (thousands of people attended the event). A dispute between rival gangs developed into major clashes between participants, rampage, theft, and violent attacks on property. A young man died after being savagely beaten by members of the audience, and more than thirty people were seriously injured. The festival, which had received the endorsement of some thirty human rights organizations, turned into chaos. Following the festival, which was widely covered in the media, the mayor of Buenos Aires banned the organizer (a civic group) from planning any other public event in the city. Most of the media stressed that the police should control young people with a strong hand to prevent similar events. The police, at least for a while, regained legitimacy before the citizens of Buenos Aires for choosing not to intervene, whereas the overall legitimacy of human and civil rights groups was seriously eroded in the eyes of government officials, other segments of civil society, and public opinion.

20. In the 1990s, another government agency, the National Center for Community Organizations (CENOC), launched a series of programs—including a voluntary census of civic organizations in Argentina—oriented toward developing a closer interaction with civil society. Even though the agency sought to serve as a nucleus to promote relationships among civic groups, it lacked the expertise to do so. For instance, the census questionnaire was insufficient for mapping the sphere of civic organizations in Argentina—a problem that could have been solved with the expertise of some NGOs. Also, the agency often adopted a paternalistic approach to organizations by seeking to impose, for example, its own model of state–civil society interaction on civic groups—a behavior that alienated important segments of civil society (such as the human and civil rights sector).

21. Inequality, social exclusion, and social degradation conform to what some authors refer to as structural violence. See Uvin 1998: 103–8; Leeds 1996: 49.

22. For each item, I used a five-point scale to measure, horizontally, coalescence within civil society (from conflict to consensus), the decision to prioritize civil society contacts (from never to always), and embeddedness in social networks (from no interaction to multiple interactions); and vertically, collaboration with the government (from never to frequently), the decision to prioritize government contacts (from never to always), and perception of the state apparatus (from monolithic to diverse).

23. See the analysis in Putnam's (1973) study of politicians in Great Britain and Italy, pp. 242, 281–83, 285.

24. According to Warren (2001), "the availability of alternatives makes exit less costly for members while at the same time offering greater chances that individuals can find comfortably homogeneous attachments" (p. 105).

25. Organizations were placed in the chart according to their score in each of

the two dimensions. The following are the values obtained for the vertical and horizontal dimensions, respectively: Asociación por los Derechos Civiles (4.5, 2.5); Asociación Travestis Argentinos (1.5, 1.5); CAVIB (1.5, 2.25); CELS (2.75, 3.5); COFAVI (1, 1.25); Conciencia (5, 2.5); CORREPI (1.25, 3); CORREPI-Familiares (1.25, 1.5); FAVIM (4.25, 3.5); Foro del Sector Social (4.5, 2.5); Gays por los Derechos Civiles (2, 2); HIJOS (1, 3); Memoria Activa (2.75, 2.75); Movimiento contra la Discriminación (2.25, 2.5); and Poder Ciudadano (4.25, 4).

26. The terms "commanding heights" and "trenches" as applied to the state are from Migdal 1994: 16–17.

27. On the role that international actors can play in new democracies, see Brysk 2000b. See Edelman 1998 for an insightful analysis of transnational links among associations.

28. Over the years, CELS has received funding from several U.S.-based foundations (e.g., Ford, Tinker, Kellogg) and European organizations based in France, Sweden, Finland, and Belgium, among others.

29. At the same time, some groups working on similar issues were very critical of CELS and other organizations receiving funding from abroad, especially from U.S.-based sources.

30. CELS, in turn, had established programs to provide legal assistance to the poor, but this type of direct involvement diminished significantly throughout the 1990s.

31. See the ruling from the Supreme Court of Justice, "Comunidad Homosexual Argentina c/ Inspección General de Justicia s/ Personería Jurídica," November 22, 1991.

32. Yet CHA's work paved the way for the emergence of new gay organizations. Furthermore, the gay movement obtained an important victory in the struggle for legal recognition when the legislature of the city of Buenos Aires, in December 2002, sanctioned a law that gave marital rights and responsibilities to gay and lesbian couples.

33. I do not examine the link to the armed forces, which had a secondary relevance in the Argentina of the 1990s.

34. Even though there is no systematic data on the socioeconomic status of victims of police violence, a review of hundreds of cases—and interviews with human rights lawyers—suggest that a majority of the victims belonged to the lower middle class and the working class. Most victims were young. According to one organization (CORREPI), the average age was 17. See http://www.derechos.org/correpi/muertes.html.

35. Other organizations (e.g., COFAVI) compiled similar data, but with questionable methodological standards. Their data, however, have been useful as a measure of comparison and for the purpose of triangulation.

36. This figure (33.7 percent) results from adding up the cases set aside, cases not pursued, acquittals or cases dismissed, and cases with lesser charges or in which the wrong person was indicted.

37. There is abundant evidence collected by human and civil rights organizations (such as the annual reports on human rights in Argentina produced

by CELS) on the level of police violence in Argentina and the acute state of crisis of the country's law enforcement system (CELS / Human Rights Watch 1998: 12).

38. These are data collected by CELS on the basis of news reports (see note 46). The criteria for classifying a death as "arbitrary" (i.e., as part of a pattern of police violence) entailed the indication that "there was a violation of a person's right to life and his / her individual integrity" and that "the police and security forces employed excessive and arbitrary firepower" (CELS 1998: 113, my translation). The CELS data start in 1986 while the cases included in the CORREPI inventory date back to 1983. As noted earlier, greater Buenos Aires refers to the suburban counties around the city of Buenos Aires.

39. This was a bill to reform Law 21,965. It was presented in the Chamber of Deputies by Marcelo Vesentini (Frente Grande), who was the leading promoter of the bill, and cosponsored by Carlos Raimundi, Rodolfo Rodil, Alfredo Bravo, Nilda Garré, and Horacio Viqueira.

40. The bill emphasized the need to create a police force committed to protecting the rule of law, democratic values, and constitutional rights. It also introduced the requirement for police officers to have earned a high school diploma before joining the force.

41. The Garrido, Baigorria, and Guardati cases were among those that brought police brutality in Mendoza to national attention (CELS / Human Rights Watch 1998: 34, 159).

42. The "democratic quality" scale was as follows: strongly democratic, democratic, somewhat democratic, neutral, somewhat undemocratic, undemocratic, strongly undemocratic. As with the interviews, coding was done by me and, independently, by another researcher.

43. These criteria are drawn from the analysis developed in CELS / Human Rights Watch 1998: 20–29.

44. Walter Bulacio, 17 years old, was killed by the police in 1991, after being arrested, along with dozens of young people, outside a rock concert in Buenos Aires. The autopsy showed that he had been seriously beaten in the police precinct.

45. Among the organizations mentioned in the bills were CELS, the Buenos Aires Lawyers Association (AABA), the Center for Studies on the National Project, and the Argentine Soccer Association (AFA).

46. Researchers on police issues in Argentina concurred with this approach. The data on police violence (in the federal capital and greater Buenos Aires) was collected by CELS from the newspapers with the largest circulation in Argentina: *Clarín, La Nación, Página/12*, and *Crónica*. As CELS researchers have acknowledged, these data are subject to a number of biases inherent to the dynamics of journalism—such as the preeminence given to cases with the potential to attract the interest of the public or space constraints in the crime section of a newspaper. These are, unfortunately, the only systematic data available on police violence in Argentina (the police institution does not make this information available to the public, and it is logistically impossible to collect

these data from the courts, given the lack of centralized databases). See CELS 1998: 112–13.

47. Of the ninety-six bills that originated in the Chamber of Deputies, seventy-seven were classified as democratic; of sixteen bills that originated in the Senate, thirteen were democratic; and of eight bills that originated in the executive, five were classified as democratic. There was no input from civil society in the bills that originated in the executive, and there were references to civil society in only three of all the undemocratic bills.

48. A majority of the democratic bills with a reference to civil society fell in the top two categories on the "democratic quality" scale: 46.2 percent in the strongly democratic category and 42.3 percent in the democratic one.

49. I did not include 1983 in the calculation because Congress was in session only during the month of December.

50. Of the two bills with a reference to civil society that were enacted in the 1990s, one eliminated the power of the police to make arrests with the sole purpose of "identifying" suspects, and the other regulated the role of domestic security agencies with an emphasis on the protection of citizens' constitutional rights. The first law originated in a Senate bill cosponsored by Simón Lázara and Dante Caputo (Ley 23,950, "Derogación del inciso 1° del artículo 5° de la Ley Orgánica de la Policía Federal"). The bill said that the power of the police to detain an individual for twenty-four hours with the sole purpose of investigating his/her background is unconstitutional and not acceptable under a democratic system of government. The second law also originated in the Senate, cosponsored by Victorio Biscotti and Miguel A. Toma (Ley 24,059, "Ley de Seguridad Interior"). This law established a coordinated (interagency) system of internal security committed to respecting constitutional guarantees and the individual rights of citizens.

51. Half of the approved democratic bills had been submitted by the executive.

52. It is important to note that, in the years before this decision, many civilian deaths occurred inside police stations, while the victim was under arrest for violating an edict.

53. In May 2002, Congress passed a bill (proposed by the executive) that introduced an important modification into the penal process code: the murder of a member of the security forces (police and penitentiary forces, as well as Prefectura and Gendarmería) carries an automatic life sentence. This law was widely criticized by scholars, lawyers, and human and civil rights groups (*Clarín.com* 2002b; Baigún 2002).

54. In her study of the human rights movement of the 1970s and 1980s, Brysk (1994) also found that this movement had a limited impact on institutions. She argued that probably the most permanent legacy of the old-line human rights movement was "outside the state, in the creation of citizens" (pp. 121–22, 136, 138, 152, 161–62).

55. Conceptually, this analysis draws from Rutherford 1993.

56. Indeed, the protest movement that emerged in Argentina in the early

2000s was fueled by anger and frustration, showing a negativity toward a perceived common enemy—the political class—and in a broader sense, the "ruling class," including union bosses, business leaders, and other groups seen as responsible for the crisis. The political parties, and particularly the politicians, were the central target of people's ire.

CHAPTER 5

1. Drawing from Knack and Keefer (1997), my sample includes the following countries: (1) "first- and second-wave" democracies: Australia, Austria, Belgium, Great Britain, Canada, Denmark, Finland, France, Germany, Iceland, Ireland, Italy, Japan, Netherlands, Norway, Sweden, Switzerland, and the United States; (2) "third-wave" democracies: Argentina, Brazil, Chile, India, Mexico, Portugal, South Korea, South Africa, Spain, and Turkey. I have dropped Nigeria from Knack and Keefer's original sample. For an explanation of why India is classified as a "third-wave" democracy, see Huntington 1991: 23.

2. The following are the twelve indicators used by Putnam (1993) in his index of institutional performance: 1. cabinet stability; 2. budget promptness; 3. statistical and information services; 4. reform legislation; 5. legislative innovation; 6. day care centers; 7. family clinics; 8. industrial policy instruments; 9. agricultural spending capacity; 10. local health unit expenditures; 11. housing and urban development; 12. bureaucratic responsiveness (pp. 65–73).

3. For a detailed description of sources, see Kaufmann, Kraay, and Zoido-Lobatón 1999b: appendix 1.

4. Data were drawn from the following sources: Business Environment Risk Intelligence; Economist Intelligence Unit; European Bank for Reconstruction and Development; Freedom House; Gallup International; Institute for Management Development; Political Economic Risk Consultancy; Political Risk Services; Standard and Poor's DRI/McGraw-Hill; Wall Street Journal; World Bank; and World Economic Forum. For an explanation of the methodology utilized to construct these indices, see Kaufmann, Kraay, and Zoido-Lobatón 1999a. For an example of a study employing these measures of institutional quality, see Inter-American Development Bank 2000: 23–26. Following Knack and Keefer (1997), the measures of institutional quality are made subsequent to my measures of trust (pp. 1259–60, 1267).

5. The "rule of law" indicator developed by Kaufmann and colleagues (1999a; 1999b) is focused on the institutional level and measures only some aspects of horizontal accountability. Still, it offers a useful indicator to account for this fundamental dimension of democracy.

6. See, for instance, the criticisms raised by Cohen 1999; Newton 1997; Foley and Edwards 1997a; 1997b.

7. These data are drawn from the World Values Surveys (WVS). See Inglehart 1990; 1997; Knack and Keefer 1997; Inglehart, Basáñez, and Moreno 1998. Data collection in the WVS was designed to enable cross-national comparisons. See Inglehart 1997: 348–50; Inglehart and Carballo 1997: 34–46.

8. WVS data. The indicator's mean value for my sample is .694 and the standard deviation is .202 ($N = 27$, no data for Switzerland).

9. WVS data. This is one of the traditional interpersonal trust measures. The indicator of social trust is the percentage of respondents in each country answering that "most people can be trusted."

10. See Deininger and Squire 1996 for a description of the data and sources for individual countries.

11. Social polarization (along class and ethnic lines) has been linked to poor macroeconomic performance (such as inflation) and ambivalent property rights (Knack and Keefer 1997: 1266–67). See Keefer and Knack 1995. As for its political impact, social polarization has been associated, for instance, with strain and hostility (in societies segmented along ethnic lines) and low levels of citizen autonomy and efficacy (in highly unequal societies) (Lijphart 1977: 88; Vilas 1997: 58).

12. Like Knack and Keefer 1997, I followed Barro 1991 in the selection and measurement of the variables that control for education, namely, the percentage of eligible students over 15 years old who completed primary school in 1970 and the percentage of eligible students over 15 years old who completed secondary school in 1980 (Barro and Lee, dataset on educational attainment, 1960–90). My other control variable—GDP per capita—was measured for the same period as the institutional quality indicators (1997–98) (Euromonitor International, World Economic Factbook 1999–2000).

13. India and Turkey are missing data on group membership.

14. "Olsonian" groups include trade unions, political parties or groups, and professional associations. "Putnamesque" groups include religious or church organizations, education / cultural groups, and youth organizations. As Foley and Edwards (1999) acknowledge in a survey of forty-five recent studies on social capital, the idea to investigate the differences between "Olsonian" and "Putnamesque" groups is an original attempt "to test the conflicting claims that associational participation promotes trust and cooperative habits (Putnam) or harmful rent-seeking behavior (Olson)" (p. 169 n. 1).

15. As equations 7 and 8 show, the impact of GDP per capita shows a positive and significant association between national wealth and institutions that sustain the rule of law.

16. There is a positive relationship between social trust and the measures of institutional quality in the cross-national sample. The simple and partial (controlling for GDP per capita) correlations between social trust and the institutional quality variables are the following: voice (.72; .43); government effectiveness (.71; .40); control of corruption (.73; .44); and rule of law (.75; .45). Patricia Bayer Richard and John Booth (2000) have argued that political institutions "construct and constrain" the production of social capital, leading to a pattern of interaction in which institutions and attitudes / norms shape each other over time. Rothstein (1998a) advanced the idea that "institutions give rise to certain interests and norms, which in turn reinforce or undermine the original institutions" (p. 135). Since the data on institutional quality are measured subsequent

to the measures of trust, I cannot test the cross-national impact of institutional quality on social trust. As data become available, this will be an interesting question for future research.

17. Social trust is not a predictor of civic engagement either (measuring civic engagement both as group membership and as political engagement). For an interesting analysis of the relationship between social trust and civic engagement (focused on the United States), see Uslaner 2000–2001: 575–79.

18. OLS regression analysis. Iceland is missing data on income inequality (Gini coefficient).

19. There are strong reasons to believe that there are measurement problems that impair the effectiveness of this indicator. One possibility is that the measure fails to capture ingrained patterns of discrimination in some nations, which are not easily uncovered by this type of measure. Evidence of this problem could be found in the case of Argentina, whose high score—91 out of a maximum of 100—suggests that the index does not capture widespread patterns of discrimination documented by ethnographic studies (see the discussion of discrimination in Argentina in Chapter 3).

20. The figures on income distribution and social trust in Scandinavia are as follows. Income distribution: for the lowest 20 percent of the population, 9.6 percent in Denmark and Sweden, and 10 percent in Norway and Finland; for the highest 20 percent, 34.5 in Denmark and Sweden, 35.3 in Norway, and 35.8 in Finland (World Bank 2000a). Average social trust scores: Finland: 46.9; Sweden: 56.6; Denmark: 57.7 (WVS). Data for Brazil are from World Bank 1997 and WVS.

21. Data are drawn from WVS 1990–93, as reported in Inglehart, Basañez, and Moreno 1998.

22. It is interesting to observe that the percentage differences are larger in first- and second-wave democracies than in third-wave democracies. In more egalitarian nations, those at the bottom of the socioeconomic scale seem to feel more dissociated from the rest of society.

23. Employing WVS data, I found patterns similar to those shown in Table 5.5 when examining people's sense of political efficacy across socioeconomic cleavages. Less-educated and lower-income respondents were more likely to feel helpless if the government passed an unjust law than those with higher levels of education and income.

24. They define democracy in a procedural way as "a regime in which governmental offices are filled as a consequence of contested elections" (Przeworski et al. 1997: 305–6). See also Przeworski et al. 2000: esp. 117–22; Welzel and Inglehart 1999.

25. Other surveys in the 1990s (e.g., in Rio de Janeiro) showed that only a small proportion of the population believed that all citizens are equal before the law in Brazil (Fry 1999: 188).

26. I have modeled the rule-of-law index with income inequality (Gini), GDP per capita, and the education variables as predictors. The results show that income inequality is a strong predictor of the rule of law. The results of the OLS

*Notes to Chapter 6*

regression analysis are the following (standardized beta coefficients): income inequality = -.424 ($p \leq .01$); GDP per capita = .591 ($p \leq .001$); primary school = -.142 (not statistically significant); secondary school = .053 (not significant). $R^2$ is .801. For sources, see Figure 5.1.

27. In addition, as shown earlier (Table 5.1), national wealth (GDP per capita) is a strong predictor of an effective rule of law at the level of institutions.

28. The outlier on the top right side of the graph is Chile. This country stands apart as a case of high institutional quality in the rule-of-law dimension relative to a high level of economic inequality. It is likely that a legalistic tradition and a political leadership committed to respecting the law have contributed to strengthening the rule-of-law dimension of Chile's new democracy. See Schamis 2002: chap. 4.

CHAPTER 6

1. The Catholic Church was an important actor in this setting (de Waal 2000: 52).

2. The case of Kenya is especially relevant for understanding regime change in which elites dominate the political arena by force—for instance, by using the military as proxy—or by altering the rules of the game in their favor when the political system gradually opens up to political competition.

3. See Sparrow 1992 for the theoretical implications of this analysis.

4. For a definition of the term "participatory publics," see Avritzer 2002a: 136.

5. The Workers' Party (PT) in Brazil and, primarily, the Democratic Revolutionary Party (PRD) in Mexico.

6. It is important to mention that, in the case of housing, the market—that is, high real estate prices—played a vital role in ensuring the survival of racial segregation after legal devices were dismantled. The phenomenon of gated communities discussed in Chapter 2 is relevant in this respect.

7. Formal mechanisms to prevent abuse by state agents (and to seek redress for arbitrary actions) can facilitate associational strength, social capital formation, and the development of norms and behaviors that enhance democratic practices (Richard and Booth 2000: 237). For a discussion of strategies of state involvement in the promotion of a democratic civil society—from economic stimuli to regulatory mechanisms and collective bargaining—see Warren 2001: 216–20.

8. Decentralization of authority, power, and resources should be complemented with institutional building in the sphere of the rule of law at the local and regional levels for decentralization to result in a generally more responsive, accountable, and transparent state. See Selee 2003.

9. While these trends reflect the influence of the state in the Norwegian voluntary sector, changes within the organizations have helped to shape their relationship with the state. As neoliberal ideas gained more acceptance, the voluntary sector has started to pay more attention to the private sector and to the

possibility of hybrid-organizations involving semiprofessional volunteerism (voluntary and paid positions) to offer services to its members or the state (Selle 1999: 152–54, 157).

10. According to figures from the Pan American Health Organization. For homicide rates in Latin America, see http://www.paho.org/English/HCP/HCN/VIO/violence-graphs.htm.

11. On the emergence of the Palestinian Islamist "arsenal of believers," see Hassan 2001. A suicide operation promotes a wealth of activity that strengthens social ties in the community. The "martyr" is honored in festivities, sermons, posters, videos, songs, graffiti, reenactments, and other activities that bring people together and reinforce their shared beliefs.

12. On global activism in areas such as human rights, violence against women, and the environment, see Keck and Sikkink 1998.

13. The differential access to rights is expressed, for instance, in disproportionate exposure to health risks (as a result of environmental deprivation in certain areas), extremely weak judicial guarantees, or systematic exposure to arbitrary police violence for some sectors of the population in democratic systems that sustain fairly effective political rights for all citizens (the right to vote, for example).

14. Let me clarify three points. First, my definition of "relational settings" is slightly different from that of Somers (1993: 595). Second, the operationalization of the concept of fields of citizenship is likely to yield, within a country, different spatial zones expressing degrees of effectiveness in the rights of social groups. It is interesting to note that O'Donnell (1993) has outlined the idea of mapping the geographical variation of the rule of law (actually, only the presence of the state-as-law) across the national territory. Finally, I have mentioned factors at the level of the nation-state, but international and transnational forces are also critical for the constitution of citizenship rights. The formation of fields of citizenship is shaped by the various ways in which "components of globalization are embedded in particular locations within national territories" (Sassen 1999: 186).

# References

Abers, Rebecca Neaera. 2000. *Inventing Local Democracy: Grassroots Politics in Brazil*. Boulder, Colo.: Lynne Rienner.

Abraham, David. 1981. *The Collapse of the Weimar Republic: Political Economy and Crisis*. Princeton, N.J.: Princeton University Press.

Abrams, Charles. 1955. *Forbidden Neighbors*. New York: Harper and Brothers.

Acosta, Mariclaire. 1999. "Overcoming the Discrimination against Women in Mexico: A Task for Sisyphus." In Méndez, O'Donnell, and Pinheiro 1999.

Allen, William S. 1984. *The Nazi Seizure of Power: The Experience of a Single German Town 1922–1945*. Rev. ed. New York: Franklin Watts.

Almond, Gabriel A., and Sidney Verba. 1963. *The Civic Culture: Political Attitudes and Democracy in Five Nations*. Princeton, N.J.: Princeton University Press.

Alvarez, Sonia E., Evelina Dagnino, and Arturo Escobar. 1998. "Introduction: The Cultural and the Political in Latin American Social Movements." In Sonia E. Alvarez, Evelina Dagnino, and Arturo Escobar, eds., *Cultures of Politics, Politics of Cultures: Re-visioning Latin American Social Movements*. Boulder, Colo.: Westview.

Anderson, Benedict. 1994. "Exodus." *Critical Inquiry* 20, no. 2 (Winter): 314–27.

Arendt, Hannah. 1966. *The Origins of Totalitarianism*. New York: Harcourt, Brace.

Armony, Víctor. 2001. "National Identity and State Ideology in Argentina." In Mercedes F. Durán-Cogan and Antonio Gómez-Moriana, eds., *National Identities and Sociopolitical Changes in Latin America*. New York: Routledge.

Arnesen, Eric. 1998. "History First: Putting Urban Poverty in Perspective" (Symposium on Thomas Sugrue's *The Origins of the Urban Crisis*). *Labor History* 39, no. 1 (February): 43–47.

Arneson, Richard. 2000. "Economic Analysis Meets Distributive Justice." *Social Theory and Practice* 26, no. 2 (Summer): 328–45.

Asamblea Permanente por los Derechos Humanos (APDH). 1995. Encuesta Programa PREVENIR.

Associated Press. 1999. "'You Have to Spill Blood to Get In': Inmate: Killing Was Initiation Rite." *Newsday*, February 19, p. A22.

Auyero, Javier. 2000. "The Logic of Clientelism in Argentina: An Ethnographic Account." *Latin American Research Review* 35, no. 3: 55–81.

———. 2001. *Poor People's Politics: Peronist Survival Networks and the Legacy of Evita*. Durham, N.C.: Duke University Press.

Avritzer, Leonardo. 2002a. *Democracy and the Public Space in Latin America*. Princeton, N.J.: Princeton University Press.

———. 2002b. "Modelos de formación de estado y sociedad y su impacto en la accountability: comentarios sobre el caso brasileño." In Enrique Peruzzotti and Catalina Smulovitz, eds., *Controlando la política: ciudadanos y medios en las nuevas democracias latinoamericanas*. Buenos Aires: Temas.

Baigún, David. 2002. "Política demagógica." *Clarín.com*, May 24. Available at http://old.clarin.com/diario/2002/05/24/s-03107.htm.

Barber, Benjamin R. 1998. *A Place for Us: How to Make Society Civil and Democracy Strong*. New York: Hill and Wang.

Barcelona, Eduardo. 1994. "Menem quiso ganar de mano con lo de la conscripción." *La Nación*, June 11. Quoted in Waisbord 2000.

Barnett, Michael. 2002. *Eyewitness to a Genocide: The United Nations and Rwanda*. Ithaca, N.Y.: Cornell University Press.

Barro, Robert. 1991. "Economic Growth in a Cross-Section of Countries." *Quarterly Journal of Economics* 106, no. 2 (May): 407–44.

Bartley, Numan V. 1969. *The Rise of Massive Resistance: Race and Politics in the South during the 1950's*. Baton Rouge: Louisiana State University Press.

———. 1995. *The New South 1945–1980*. Baton Rouge: Louisiana State University Press.

Bayer, Osvaldo. 2001. "Pequeño recordatorio para un país sin memoria." *Página/12 Web*, March 22. Available at http://www.pagina12.com.ar/2001/01-03/01-03-22/htm.

Becker, David G. 1997. "The Rule of Law in Latin America: A Framework for Analysis." Paper presented at the Ninety-Third Annual Meeting of the American Political Science Association, Washington, D.C.

Belvedere, Carlos. 1999. "La discriminación social en Buenos Aires: una aproximación cuantitativa." In Margulis et al. 1999.

Bendix, Reinhard. 1977. *Nation-Building and Citizenship: Studies of Our Changing Social Order*. Berkeley: University of California Press.

Berman, Sheri. 1997a. "Civil Society and the Collapse of the Weimar Republic." *World Politics* 49, no. 3 (April): 401–29.

———. 1997b. "Civil Society and Political Institutionalization." *American Behavioral Scientist* 40, no. 5 (March/April): 562–74.

Bermeo, Nancy. 2000. "Civil Society after Democracy: Some Conclusions." In Bermeo and Nord 2000.

Bermeo, Nancy, and Philip Nord, eds. 2000. *Civil Society before Democracy: Lessons from Nineteenth-Century Europe*. Lanham, Md.: Rowman and Littlefield.

Berryhill, Michael. 1999. "Prisoner's Dilemma." *The New Republic*, December 27, pp. 18–23.

Blakely, Edward J., and Mary Gail Snyder. 1997. *Fortress America*. Washington, D.C.: Brookings Institution Press.

Blair, Harry. 1994. *A Strategic Assessment of Legal Systems' Development in Uruguay and Argentina*. Washington, D.C.: U.S. Agency for International Development. Quoted in Ungar 2002.

Bobbio, Norberto. 1987. *The Future of Democracy: A Defense of the Rules of the Game*. Minneapolis: University of Minnesota Press.

Booth, John A., and Patricia Bayer Richard. 1998. "Civil Society and Political Context in Central America." *American Behavioral Scientist* 42, no. 1 (September): 33–47.

Bourdieu, Pierre. 1986. "The Forms of Capital." In John G. Richardson, ed., *Handbook of Theory and Research for the Sociology of Education*. New York: Greenwood Press.

———. 1990. *The Logic of Practice*. Translated by Richard Nice. Oxford, U.K.: Polity Press.

Brady, Henry E., David Collier, and Jason Seawright. 2002. "Refocusing the Discussion of Methodology." In Henry E. Brady and David Collier, eds., *Rethinking Social Inquiry: Diverse Tools, Shared Standards*. Lanham, Md.: Rowman and Littlefield.

Brehm, John, and Wendy Rahn. 1997. "Individual-Level Evidence for the Causes and Consequences of Social Capital." *American Journal of Political Science* 41, no. 3 (July): 999–1023.

Bresciani-Turroni, Costantino. 1953. *The Economics of Inflation*. 2d ed. London: George Allen and Unwin.

Brinks, Daniel M. 2002. "Legal Tolls and Illusory Rights: The Courts and State Killings in Uruguay, Argentina, and Brazil." Paper presented at the Ninety-Eighth Annual Meeting of the American Political Science Association, Boston.

Brysk, Alison. 1994. *The Politics of Human Rights in Argentina: Protest, Change, and Democratization*. Stanford, Calif.: Stanford University Press.

———. 2000a. *From Tribal Village to Global Village: Indian Rights and International Relations in Latin America*. Stanford, Calif.: Stanford University Press.

———. 2000b. "Democratizing Civil Society in Latin America." *Journal of Democracy* 11, no. 3 (July): 151–65.

Buell, Emmett H., Jr. (with Richard A. Brisbin Jr.). 1982. *School Desegregation and Defended Neighborhoods: The Boston Controversy*. Lexington, Mass.: Lexington Books.

Bulat, Tomás, and Hernán López. 1999. "Seguridad y justicia en la Provincia de Buenos Aires: acerca de la eficiencia del gasto en la disuación del delito." Working paper. Quoted in Palmieri, Filippini, and Thomas 2001.

Button, James W. 1989. *Blacks and Social Change: Impact of the Civil Rights Movement in Southern Communities*. Princeton, N.J.: Princeton University Press.

Caldeira, Teresa P. R. 1996. "Crime and Individual Rights: Reframing the Question of Violence in Latin America." In Elizabeth Jelin and Eric Hershberg, eds., *Constructing Democracy: Human Rights, Citizenship, and Society in Latin America*. Boulder, Colo.: Westview.

———. 2000. *City of Walls: Crime, Segregation, and Citizenship in São Paulo*. Berkeley: University of California Press.

Caldeira, Teresa P. R., and James Holston. 1999. "Democracy and Violence in Brazil." *Comparative Studies in Society and History* 41, no. 4 (October): 691–729.

Campetella, Andrea, Inés González Bombal, and Mario Roitter. 1998. "Defining the Nonprofit Sector: Argentina." Working Paper no. 33. Comparative Nonprofit Sector Project, Institute for Policy Studies, Johns Hopkins University.

Carbonetto, Sergio, and Dévora Brites. 2001. "Sector informal urbano y exclusión técnico-ocupacional." In Instituto para el Proyecto Nacional (IPRON) and Centro de Estudios Socioeconómicos y Sindicales (CESS), *Programa de emergencia económico social*. Buenos Aires: Polo Social.

Carothers, Thomas. 1999–2000. "Think Again: Civil Society." *Foreign Policy* 117 (Winter): 18–29.

Carter, Hodding. 1959. *The South Strikes Back*. Garden City, N.Y.: Doubleday.

Case, Anne C., and Lawrence F. Katz. 1991. "The Company You Keep: The Effects of Family and Neighborhood on Disadvantaged Youths." Working Paper no. 3705. National Bureau of Economic Research, Cambridge, Mass.

Centro de Estudios Judiciales de la República Argentina (CEJURA). 1994. "Estudio de opinión acerca de la administración de justicia," conducted by Gallup Argentina. Buenos Aires.

Centro de Estudios Legales y Sociales (CELS). 1996. *Informe anual sobre la situación de los derechos humanos en la Argentina 1995*. Buenos Aires: CELS.

———. 1997. *Informe anual sobre la situación de los derechos humanos en la Argentina 1996*. Buenos Aires: CELS.

———. 1998. *Informe sobre la situación de los derechos humanos en Argentina 1997*. Buenos Aires: CELS and Eudeba.

———1999. *Derechos humanos en la Argentina: informe anual enero-diciembre 1998*. Buenos Aires: CELS and Eudeba.

———. 2000. *Derechos humanos en Argentina: informe anual 1999*. Buenos Aires: CELS and Eudeba.

———. 2001. *Informe sobre la situación de los derechos humanos en Argentina: enero-diciembre 2000*. Buenos Aires: CELS, Catálogos, and Siglo Veintiuno.

Centro de Estudios Legales y Sociales (CELS) and Human Rights Watch (HRW). 1998. *La inseguridad policial: violencia de las fuerzas de seguridad en la Argentina*. Buenos Aires: Eudeba.

Centro de Implementación de Políticas Públicas para la Equidad y el Crecimiento (CIPPEC). 2001. "Sistemas nacionales de integridad: informe sobre Argentina para Transparency International." Buenos Aires. Available at http://www.cippec.org/ES/pdf/Transparency_Internacional.pdf.

Chalmers, Douglas A. 1997. "What Is It about Associations in Civil Society That

Promotes Democracy?" Working paper, Department of Political Science, Columbia University. Available at http://www.columbia.edu/cu/ilas/publications/htm/papers/chalmers48.

Chalmers, Douglas A., Scott B. Martin, and Kerianne Piester. 1997. "Associative Networks: New Structures of Representation for the Popular Sectors?" In Douglas A. Chalmers, Carlos M. Vilas, Katherine Hite, Scott B. Martin, Kerianne Piester, and Monique Segarra, eds., *The New Politics of Inequality in Latin America: Rethinking Participation and Representation.* New York: Oxford University Press.

Chandhoke, Neera. 1995. *State and Civil Society: Explorations in Political Theory.* Thousand Oaks, Calif.: Sage.

Chazan, Naomi. 1992. "Africa's Democratic Challenge." *World Policy Journal* 9, no. 2 (Spring): 279–307.

——. 1994. "Engaging the State: Associational Life in Sub-Saharan Africa." In Migdal, Kohli, and Shue 1994.

Chevigny, Paul. 1995. *Edge of the Knife: Police Violence in the Americas.* New York: New Press.

——. 1999. "Defining the Role of the Police in Latin America." In Méndez, O'Donnell, and Pinheiro 1999.

Childers, Thomas. 1983. *The Nazi Voter: The Social Foundations of Fascism in Germany, 1919–1933.* Chapel Hill: University of North Carolina Press.

——. 1986. "The Limits of National Socialist Mobilization: The Elections of 6 November 1932 and the Fragmentation of the Nazi Constituency." In Thomas Childers, ed., *The Formation of the Nazi Constituency, 1919–1933.* Totowa, N.J.: Barnes and Noble Books.

CIVICUS. 1997. *The New Civic Atlas: Profiles of Civil Society in 60 Countries.* Washington, D.C.: CIVICUS.

*Clarín.com.* 2001. "Sancionaron una ley que le da más facultades a la Federal," June 14. Available at http://old.clarin.com/diario/2001/06/14/s-04001.htm.

——. 2002a. "Los más ricos ganan 28 veces más que los más pobres," March 31. Available at http://old.clarin.com/diario/2002/03/31/e-01001.htm.

——. 2002b. "Prisión perpetua para los que asesinen a policías," May 24. Available at http://old.clarin.com/diario/2002/05/24/s-03106.htm.

——. 2003. "El patrón y la 'rameada,'" February 16. Available at http://old.clarin.com/diario/2003/02/16/s-03815.htm.

Clemens, Elisabeth S. 2001. "Securing Political Returns to Social Capital: Women's Associations in the United States, 1880s–1920s." In Robert I. Rotberg, ed., *Patterns of Social Capital: Stability and Change in Historical Perspective.* Cambridge, U.K.: Cambridge University Press.

Cohen, Jean L. 1999. "American Civil Society Talk." In Robert K. Fullinwider, ed., *Civil Society, Democracy, and Civic Renewal.* Lanham, Md.: Rowman and Littlefield.

Cohen, Jean L., and Andrew Arato. 1992. *Civil Society and Political Theory.* Cambridge, Mass.: MIT Press.

Cohen, Joshua, and Joel Rogers. 1995. "Secondary Associations and Democratic

Institutions." In Erik Olin Wright, ed., *Associations and Democracy*. London: Verso.

Coleman, James S. 1988. "Social Capital in the Creation of Human Capital." Supplement to *American Journal of Sociology* 94 (July): 95–120.

———. 1990. *Foundations of Social Theory*. Cambridge, Mass.: Harvard University Press.

Cook, James G. 1962. *The Segregationists*. New York: Appleton-Century-Crofts.

Crahan, Margaret E. 1982. "The State and the Individual in Latin America: A Historical Overview." In Margaret E. Crahan, ed., *Human Rights and Basic Needs in the Americas*. Washington, D.C.: Georgetown University Press.

da Matta, Roberto. 1987. "The Quest for Citizenship in a Relational Universe." In John D. Wirth, Edson de Oliveira Nunes, and Thomas E. Bogenschild, eds., *State and Society in Brazil: Continuity and Change*. Boulder, Colo.: Westview.

———. 1991. *Carnivals, Rogues, and Heroes: An Interpretation of the Brazilian Dilemma*. Notre Dame, Ind.: University of Notre Dame Press.

Dahl, Robert A. 1989. *Democracy and Its Critics*. New Haven, Conn.: Yale University Press.

*Daily News* (New York). 1998. "A Modern-Day Lynching," June 11, p. 42.

Dandler, Jorge. 1999. "Indigenous Peoples and the Rule of Law in Latin America: Do They Have a Chance?" In Méndez, O'Donnell, and Pinheiro 1999.

Davis, Mike. 1990. *City of Quartz: Excavating the Future in Los Angeles*. London: Verso.

de Almeida, Alfredo Wagner Berno. 1996. "Amazonia: Rite of Passage from Massacre to Genocide." Paper presented at the conference "The Rule of Law and the Underprivileged in Latin America," Kellogg Institute, University of Notre Dame.

de Brito, Alexandra Barahona. 1997. *Human Rights and Democratization in Latin America: Uruguay and Chile*. New York: Oxford University Press.

Deininger, Klaus, and Lyn Squire. 1996. "A New Data Set Measuring Income Inequality." *The World Bank Economic Review* 10, no. 3 (September): 565–91.

del Cid Avalos, Silvia L. 2001. "Building Citizenship and Ethnicity in Guatemala." Paper presented at the Twenty-Third International Congress of the Latin American Studies Association, Washington, D.C.

de Waal, Alex, ed. 2000. *Who Fights? Who Cares? War and Humanitarian Action in Africa*. Trenton, N.J.: Africa World Press.

Diamond, Larry. 1994. "Toward Democratic Consolidation." *Journal of Democracy* 5, no. 3 (July): 4–17.

———. 1999. *Developing Democracy: Toward Consolidation*. Baltimore: Johns Hopkins University Press.

Dryzek, John S. 1996. "Political Inclusion and the Dynamics of Democratization." *American Political Science Review* 90, no. 1 (September): 475–87.

Dryzek, John S., Hans-Kristian Hernes, and David Schlosberg. 2001. "States and Social Movements: Environmentalism in Four Countries." Paper presented at the Ninety-Seventh Annual Meeting of the American Political Science Association, San Francisco.

Eastis, Carla. 1998. "Organizational Diversity and the Production of Social Capital: One of These Groups Is Not Like the Other." *American Behavioral Scientist* 42, no. 1 (September): 66–77.

Eckstein, Harry. 1975. "Case Study and Theory in Political Science." In Fred I. Greenstein and Nelson W. Polsby, eds., *Strategies of Inquiry*. Reading, Mass.: Addison-Wesley.

*Economist*. 1999. "Cops and Robbers in Argentina," May 1, pp. 33–34.

Edelman, Marc. 1998. "Transnational Peasant Politics in Central America." *Latin American Research Review* 33, no. 3: 49–86.

Edwards, Bob, and Michael E. Foley. 2001. "Much Ado about Social Capital" (Symposium on Robert Putnam's *Bowling Alone*). *Contemporary Sociology* 30, no. 3 (June): 227–30.

El Nasser, Haya. 2002. "Gated Communities Are Not Just for the Wealthy." *USA Today*, December 16, p. A1.

Eley, Geoff. 1992. "Nations, Publics, and Political Cultures: Placing Habermas in the Nineteenth Century." In Craig Calhoun, ed., *Habermas and the Public Sphere*. Cambridge, Mass.: MIT Press.

Esman, Milton J., and Norman T. Uphoff. 1984. *Local Organizations: Intermediaries in Rural Development*. Ithaca, N.Y.: Cornell University Press.

Etzioni, Amitai. 1996. *The New Golden Rule: Community and Morality in a Democratic Society*. New York: Basic Books.

Fainstein, Norman, and Susan Fainstein. 1996. "Urban Regimes and Black Citizens: The Economic and Social Impacts of Black Political Incorporation in U.S. Cities." *International Journal of Urban and Regional Research* 20, no. 1: 22–37.

Falter, Jurgen W., and Reinhard Zintl. 1998. "The Economic Crisis of the 1930s and the Nazi Vote." *Journal of Interdisciplinary History* 19, no. 1 (Summer): 55–85.

Feldman, Gerald D. 1993. *The Great Disorder: Politics, Economics, and Society in the German Inflation, 1914–1924*. New York: Oxford University Press.

Fernández, Daniel R., and Luis D'Angelo. 1999. "Estudios criminológicos para la prevención del delito (I and II)." Working paper, Dirección Nacional de Política Criminal del Ministerio de Justicia de la Nación, Buenos Aires.

Finnis, John. 1980. *Natural Law and Natural Rights*. Oxford, U.K.: Clarendon Press. Quoted in O'Donnell 1999b.

Fiorina, Morris P. 1999. "Extreme Voices: A Dark Side of Civic Engagement." In Skocpol and Fiorina 1999a.

Fish, M. Steven. 1994. "Russia's Fourth Transition." *Journal of Democracy* 5, no. 3 (July): 31–42.

Fisher, Julie. 1992. "Local Governments and the Independent Sector in the Third World." In Kathleen D. McCarthy, Russy D. Sumariwalla, and Virginia A. Hodgkinson, eds., *The Nonprofit Sector in the Global Community*. San Francisco: Jossey-Bass.

———. 1993. *The Road from Rio: Sustainable Development and the Nongovernmental Movement in the Third World*. Westport, Conn.: Praeger.

Foley, Michael W. 1996. "Laying the Groundwork: The Struggle for Civil Society in El Salvador." *Journal of Interamerican Studies and World Affairs* 38, no. 1 (Spring): 67–104.

Foley, Michael W., and Bob Edwards. 1996. "The Paradox of Civil Society." *Journal of Democracy* 7, no. 3 (July): 38–52.

———. 1997a. "Escape from Politics? Social Theory and the Social Capital Debate." *American Behavioral Scientist* 40, no. 5 (March / April): 550–61.

———. 1997b. "Social Capital and the Political Economy of Our Discontent." *American Behavioral Scientist* 40, no. 5 (March / April): 669–78.

———. 1999. "Is It Time to Disinvest in Social Capital?" *Journal of Public Policy* 19, no. 2 (May–August): 141–73.

Formisano, Ronald P. 1991. *Boston against Busing: Race, Class, and Ethnicity in the 1960s and 1970s*. Chapel Hill: University of North Carolina Press.

Foweraker, Joe, and Todd Landman. 1997. *Citizenship Rights and Social Movements: A Comparative and Statistical Analysis*. New York: Oxford University Press.

Fraser, Nancy. 1993. "Rethinking the Public Sphere: A Contribution to the Critique of Actually Existing Democracy." In Bruce Robbins, ed., *The Phantom Public Sphere*. Minneapolis: University of Minnesota Press.

Friedan, Betty. 1963. *The Feminine Mystique*. New York: Norton.

Fritzsche, Peter. 1990. *Rehearsals for Fascism: Populism and Political Mobilization in Weimar Germany*. New York: Oxford University Press.

Fry, Peter. 1999. "Color and the Rule of Law in Brazil." In Méndez, O'Donnell, and Pinheiro 1999.

Fukuyama, Francis. 1995. *Trust: The Social Virtues and the Creation of Prosperity*. New York: Free Press.

———. 1999. "Social Capital and Civil Society." Paper presented at the International Monetary Fund (IMF) Conference on Second Generation Reforms, Washington, D.C. Available at http://www.imf.org/external/pubs/ft/seminar/1999/reforms/fukuyama.htm.

Gallin, Alice. 1986. *Midwives to Nazism: University Professors in Weimar Germany, 1925–1933*. Macon, Ga.: Mercer University Press.

Gambetta, Diego. 1988. "Mafia: The Price of Distrust." In Diego Gambetta, ed., *Trust: Making and Breaking Cooperative Relations*. Oxford, U.K.: Basil Blackwell.

Gamm, Gerald, and Robert D. Putnam. 2001. "The Growth of Voluntary Associations in America, 1840–1940." In Robert I. Rotberg, ed., *Patterns of Social Capital: Stability and Change in Historical Perspective*. Cambridge, U.K.: Cambridge University Press.

Garro, Alejandro M. 1999. "Access to Justice for the Poor in Latin America." In Méndez, O'Donnell, and Pinheiro 1999.

Gerstle, Gary. 1995. "Race and the Myth of the Liberal Consensus." *Journal of American History* 83, no. 2 (September): 579–86.

Glaeser, Edward L., Bruce Sacerdote, and José A. Scheinkman. 1996. "Crime and Social Interactions." *Quarterly Journal of Economics* 111, no. 2 (May): 507–48.

Goldhagen, Daniel. 1996. *Hitler's Willing Executioners: Ordinary Germans and the Holocaust*. New York: Knopf.

González Bombal, Inés. 1995. "¿Entre el estado y el mercado? ONGs y sociedad civil en la Argentina." In Andrés Thompson, ed., *Público y privado: las organizaciones sin fines de lucro en la Argentina*. Buenos Aires: UNICEF / Losada.

Gotham, Kevin F. 2000. "Racialization and the State: The Housing Act of 1934 and the Creation of the Federal Housing Administration." *Sociological Perspectives* 43, no. 2 (Summer): 291–317.

Governance Research Indicators. 1997–98. Dataset compiled by Daniel Kaufmann, Aart Kraay, and Pablo Zoido-Lobatón. Policy Research Department, World Bank, Washington, D.C. Available at http://www.worldbank.org/wbi/governance/datasets.htm.

Greene, Jack P. 2001. "Social and Cultural Capital in Colonial British America: A Case Study." In Robert I. Rotberg, ed., *Patterns of Social Capital: Stability and Change in Historical Perspective*. Cambridge, U.K.: Cambridge University Press.

Haber, Paul Lawrence. 1996. "Identity and Political Process: Recent Trends in the Study of Latin American Social Movements." *Latin American Research Review* 31, no. 1: 171–88.

Habermas, Jürgen. 1989. *The Structural Transformation of the Public Sphere: An Inquiry into a Category of Bourgeois Society*. Cambridge, Mass.: MIT Press.

———. 1995. *Between Facts and Norms*. Cambridge, Mass.: MIT Press.

Hadenius, Axel. 2001. *Institutions and Democratic Citizenship*. New York: Oxford University Press.

Hadenius, Axel, and Fredrik Uggla. 1996. "Making Civil Society Work, Promoting Democratic Development: What Can States and Donors Do?" *World Development* 24, no. 10 (October): 1621–39.

Hagopian, Frances. 2000. "Political Development, Revisited." *Comparative Political Studies* 33, nos. 6/7 (August/September): 880–911.

Hagtvet, Bernt. 1980. "The Theory of Mass Society and the Collapse of the Weimar Republic: A Re-Examination." In Stein Ugelvik Larsen, Bernt Hagtvet, and Jan Petter Myklebust, eds., *Who Were the Fascists: Social Roots of European Fascism*. Bergen: Universitetsforlaget.

Hardin, Russell. 1982. *Collective Action*. Baltimore: Resources for the Future. Quoted in Knack and Keefer 1997.

Hassan, Nasra. 2001. "An Arsenal of Believers: Islamic Suicide Bombers." *New Yorker* 77, November 19, pp. 36–41.

Hasson, Shlomo, and David Ley. 1997. "Neighborhood Organizations, the Welfare State, and Citizenship Rights." *Urban Affairs Review* 33, no. 1 (September): 28–59.

Hecht, Tobias. 1998. *At Home in the Street: Street Children of Northeast Brazil*. Cambridge, U.K.: Cambridge University Press.

Heller, Patrick. 2001. "Moving the State: The Politics of Democratic Decentralization in Kerala, South Africa, and Porto Alegre." *Politics and Society* 29, no.
1 (March): 131–63.

Heredia, Blanca. 1997. "Clientelism in Flux: Democratization and Interest Intermediation in Contemporary Mexico." Paper presented at the Twentieth International Congress of the Latin American Studies Association, Guadala-
jara, Mexico.

Hershberg, Eric. 2000. "Democracy and Its Discontents: Constraints on Political
Citizenship in Latin America." In Howard Handelman and Mark A. Tessler,
eds., *Democracy and Its Limits: Lessons for Asia, Latin America, and the Middle
East*. Notre Dame, Ind.: University of Notre Dame Press.

Hirsch, Arnold R. 1983. *Making the Second Ghetto: Race and Housing in Chicago,
1940–1960*. Cambridge, U.K.: Cambridge University Press.

———. 1995. "Massive Resistance in the Urban North: Trumbull Park, Chicago,
1953–1966." *Journal of American History* 82, no. 2 (September): 522–50.

Holston, James, and Arjun Appadurai. 1999. "Cities and Citizenship." In James
Holston, ed., *Cities and Citizenship*. Durham, N.C.: Duke University Press.

Holston, James, and Teresa P. R. Caldeira. 1998. "Democracy, Law, and Vio-
lence: Disjunctions of Brazilian Citizenship." In Felipe Agüero and Jeffrey
Stark, eds., *Fault Lines of Democracy in Post-Transition Latin America*. Miami:
North-South Center Press.

Holtfrerich, Carl-Ludwig. 1990. "Economic Policy Options and the End of the
Weimar Republic." In Ian Kershaw, ed., *Weimar: Why Did German Democracy
Fail?* New York: St. Martin's.

Howard, Mark Morjé. 2002. "The Weakness of Postcommunist Civil Society."
*Journal of Democracy* 13, no. 1 (January): 157–69.

Hughes, Michael. 1982. "Economic Interest, Social Attitudes, and Creditor Ideology: Popular Responses to Inflation." In Gerald D. Feldman, Carl-Ludwig
Holtfrerich, Gerhard A. Ritter, and Peter-Christian Witt, eds., *The German Inflation Reconsidered: A Preliminary Balance*. Berlin: de Gruyter.

Human Rights Watch. 1998. *Shielded from Justice: Police Brutality and Accountability in the United States*. New York: Human Rights Watch.

Huntington, Samuel P. 1968. *Political Order in Changing Societies*. New Haven,
Conn.: Yale University Press.

———. 1991. *The Third Wave: Democratization in the Late Twentieth Century*. Norman: University of Oklahoma Press.

Inglehart, Ronald. 1990. *Culture Shift in Advanced Industrial Society*. Princeton,
N.J.: Princeton University Press.

———. 1997. *Modernization and Postmodernization: Cultural, Economic, and Political Change in 43 Societies*. Princeton, N.J.: Princeton University Press.

———. 1999. "Trust, Well-Being and Democracy." In Warren 1999.

Inglehart, Ronald, and Marita Carballo. 1997. "Does Latin America Exist? (And
Is There a Confucian Culture?): A Global Analysis of Cross-Cultural Differences." *PS: Political Science and Politics* 30, no. 1 (March): 34–46.

Inglehart, Ronald, Miguel Basañez, and Alejandro Moreno. 1998. *Human Values and Beliefs: A Cross-Cultural Sourcebook.* Ann Arbor: University of Michigan Press.

Inter-American Development Bank (IDB). 2000. *Development beyond Economics: Economic and Social Progress in Latin America.* Washington, D.C.: Inter-American Development Bank and Johns Hopkins University Press.

———, Consejo Asesor de la Sociedad Civil. 1998. *Conjuntos: sociedad civil en Argentina.* Buenos Aires: Edilab.

International Labour Organization (ILO) / United Nations Development Program (UNDP). 1996. *Overcoming Social Exclusion: A Contribution to the World Summit for Social Development.* Geneva: ILO. Quoted in Uvin 1999.

Isuani, Ernesto Aldo. 1999. "Anomia social y anemia estatal: sobre integración social en la Argentina." In Daniel Filmus, ed., *Los noventa: política, sociedad y cultura en América Latina y Argentina de fin de siglo.* Buenos Aires: Facultad Latinoamericana de Ciencias Sociales (FLACSO).

James, Harold. 1986. *The German Slump.* New York: Oxford University Press.

Janoski, Thomas. 1998. *Citizenship and Civil Society: A Framework of Rights and Obligations in Liberal, Traditional, and Social Democratic Regimes.* Cambridge, U.K.: Cambridge University Press.

Jelin, Elizabeth. 1996. "Citizenship Revisited: Solidarity, Responsibility, and Rights." In Elizabeth Jelin and Eric Hershberg, eds., *Constructing Democracy: Human Rights, Citizenship, and Society in Latin America.* Boulder, Colo.: Westview.

Jenkins, J. Craig. 1983. "Resource Mobilization Theory and the Study of Social Movements." *Annual Review of Sociology* 9: 527–53.

Jones, Larry Eugene. 1979. "Inflation, Revaluation, and the Crisis of Middle-Class Politics: A Study in the Dissolution of the German Party System, 1923–28." *Central European History* 12, no. 2 (June): 143–68.

Jones-Correa, Michael. 2000–2001. "The Origins and Diffusion of Racial Restrictive Covenants." *Political Science Quarterly* 115, no. 4 (Winter): 541–68.

Kane, Gregory. 1998. "Prisons Are Hotbeds of Racism, Hatred." *Baltimore Sun,* June 17, p. 1C.

Kaplan, Marion. 1984. "Sisterhood under Siege: Feminism and Anti-Semitism in Germany, 1904–1938." In Renate Bridenthal, Atina Grossmann, and Marion Kaplan, eds., *When Biology Became Destiny: Women in Weimar and Nazi Germany.* New York: Monthly Review Press.

Karl, Terry. 1986. "Imposing Consent? Electoralism vs. Democratization in El Salvador." In Paul W. Drake and Eduardo Silva, eds., *Elections and Democratization in Latin America, 1980–1985.* San Diego: Center for Iberian and Latin American Studies, University of California, San Diego.

Kater, Michael H. 1986. "The Nazi Physicians' League of 1929: Causes and Consequences." In Thomas Childers, ed., *The Formation of the Nazi Constituency, 1919–1933.* Totowa, N.J.: Barnes and Noble Books.

Kaufmann, Daniel, Aart Kraay, and Pablo Zoido-Lobatón. 1999a. "Aggregating Governance Indicators." Working Paper no. 2195. Policy Research Department, World Bank, Washington, D.C.

————. 1999b. "Governance Matters." Working Paper no. 2196. Policy Research Department, World Bank, Washington, D.C.

Keane, John. 1998. *Civil Society: Old Images, New Visions*. Stanford, Calif.: Stanford University Press.

Keck, Margaret E., and Kathryn Sikkink. 1998. *Activists beyond Borders: Advocacy Networks in International Politics*. Ithaca, N.Y.: Cornell University Press.

Keefer, Philip, and Stephen Knack. 1995. "Polarization, Property Rights and the Links between Inequality and Growth." Working Paper no. 153. IRIS Center, University of Maryland, College Park.

Kennedy, David J. 1995. "Residential Associations as State Actors: Regulating the Impact of Gated Communities on Non-Members." *Yale Law Journal* 105, no. 3 (December): 761–93.

King, Gary, Robert O. Keohane, and Sidney Verba. 1994. *Designing Social Inquiry: Scientific Inference in Qualitative Research*. Princeton, N.J.: Princeton University Press.

————. 1995. "The Importance of Research Design in Political Science." *American Political Science Review* 89, no. 2 (June): 475–81.

Kirkpatrick, Jeane J. 1971. *Leader and Vanguard in Mass Society: A Study of Peronist Argentina*. Cambridge, Mass.: MIT Press.

Knack, Stephen, and Philip Keefer. 1997. "Does Social Capital Have an Economic Payoff? A Cross-Country Investigation." *Quarterly Journal of Economics* 112, no. 4 (November): 1251–88.

Kohli, Atul. 1994. "Centralization and Powerlessness: India's Democracy in a Comparative Perspective." In Joel S. Migdal, Atul Kohli, and Vivienne Shue, eds., *State Power and Social Forces: Domination and Transformation in the Third World*. Cambridge, U.K.: Cambridge University Press.

Kolb, Eberhard. 1988. *The Weimar Republic*. London: Unwin Hyman.

Kornblit, Ana Lía, Mario Pecheny, and Jorge Vujosevich. 1998. *Gays y lesbianas: formación de la identidad y derechos humanos*. Buenos Aires: La Colmena.

Kornhauser, William. 1959. *The Politics of Mass Society*. Glencoe, Ill.: Free Press.

Koshar, Rudy. 1986a. *Social Life, Local Politics, and Nazism: Marburg, 1880–1935*. Chapel Hill: University of North Carolina Press.

————. 1986b. "Contentious Citadel: Bourgeois Crisis and Nazism in Marburg/Lahn, 1880–1933." In Thomas Childers, ed., *The Formation of the Nazi Constituency, 1919–1933*. Totowa, N.J.: Barnes and Noble Books.

Krygier, Martin. 1997. "Virtuous Circles: Antipodean Reflections on Power, Institutions, and Civil Society." *East European Politics and Societies* 11, no. 1 (Winter): 36–88.

Kuperman, Alan. 2001. *The Limits of Humanitarian Intervention: Genocide in Rwanda*. Washington, D.C.: Brookings Institution Press.

Lagos, Marta. 1997. "Latin America's Smiling Mask." *Journal of Democracy* 8, no. 3 (July): 125–38.

————. 2001. "Between Stability and Crisis in Latin America." *Journal of Democracy* 12, no. 1 (January): 137–45.

Landi, Oscar, and Inés González Bombal. 1995. "Los derechos en la cultura política." In Carlos H. Acuña et al., *Juicio, castigos y memorias: derechos humanos y justicia en la política argentina*. Buenos Aires: Nueva Visión.

Landim, Leilah. 1997. "Brazil." In Salamon and Anheier 1997.

Lane, Jan-Erik. 1996. *Constitutions and Political Theory*. Manchester, U.K.: Manchester University Press.

Larkins, Christopher. 1998. "The Judiciary and Delegative Democracy in Argentina." *Comparative Politics* 30, no. 4 (July): 423–42.

Laumann, Edward O., and David Knoke. 1987. *The Organizational State: Social Choice in National Policy Domains*. Madison: University of Wisconsin Press.

Leeds, Elizabeth. 1996. "Cocaine and Parallel Polities in the Brazilian Urban Periphery: Constraints on Local-Level Democratization." *Latin American Research Review* 31, no. 3 (Summer): 47–83.

Lepsius, M. Rainer. 1978. "From Fragmented Party Democracy to Government by Emergency Decree and National Socialist Takeover: Germany." In Juan J. Linz and Alfred Stepan, eds., *The Breakdown of Democratic Regimes*. Baltimore: Johns Hopkins University Press.

Levi, Margaret. 1996. "Social and Unsocial Capital: A Review Essay of Robert Putnam's *Making Democracy Work*." *Politics and Society* 24, no. 1 (March): 45–55.

———. 1999. "Trust, Trade and the Role of Government." *APSA-CP Newsletter* 10, no. 1 (Winter): 18–20.

Levy, Daniel C. 1996. *Building the Third Sector: Latin America's Private Research Centers and Nonprofit Development*. Pittsburgh: University of Pittsburgh Press.

Lieberman, Ben. 1998. "The Meanings and Function of Anti-System Ideology in the Weimar Republic." *Journal of the History of Ideas* 59, no. 2 (April): 355–75.

Lijphart, Arend. 1977. *Democracy in Plural Societies: A Comparative Exploration*. New Haven, Conn.: Yale University Press.

Linz, Juan J., and Alfred Stepan. 1996. *Problems of Democratic Transition and Consolidation: Southern Europe, South America, and Post-Communist Europe*. Baltimore: Johns Hopkins University Press.

Lomax, Bill. 1997. "The Strange Death of 'Civil Society' in Post-Communist Hungary." *Journal of Communist Studies and Transition Politics* 13, no. 1 (March): 41–63.

Loury, Glenn C. 2002. *The Anatomy of Racial Inequality*. Cambridge, Mass.: Harvard University Press.

Low, Setha M. 2001. "The Edge and the Center: Gated Communities and the Discourses of Urban Fear." *American Anthropologist* 103, no. 1 (March): 45–58.

———. 2003. *Behind the Gates: Life, Security, and the Pursuit of Happiness in Fortress America*. New York: Routledge.

Mainwaring, Scott. 1995. "Democracy in Brazil and the Southern Cone: Achievements and Problems." *Journal of Interamerican Studies and World Affairs* 37, no. 1 (Spring): 113–79.

Malamud-Goti, Jaime. 1996. *Game without End: State Terror and the Politics of Justice*. Norman: University of Oklahoma Press.

270    *References*

Mamdani, Mahmood. 1996. *Citizen and Subject: Contemporary Africa and the Legacy of Late Colonialism.* Princeton, N.J.: Princeton University Press.
———. 2001. *When Victims Become Killers: Colonialism, Nativism, and the Genocide in Rwanda.* Princeton, N.J.: Princeton University Press.
Maraffi, Marco. 1998. "Voluntary Associations, Political Culture, and Social Capital in Italy: A Complex Relationship." *ECPR News* 3. Quoted in Wilson 1999.
Margalit, Avishai. 1996. *The Decent Society.* Cambridge, Mass.: Harvard University Press. Quoted in O'Donnell 1999b.
Margulis, Mario. 1999a. "La 'racialización' de las relaciones de clase." In Margulis et al. 1999.
———. 1999b. "Cultura y discriminación social en la época de la globalización." In Margulis et al. 1999.
Margulis, Mario, Marcelo Urresti, et al. 1999. *La segregación negada: cultura y discriminación social.* Buenos Aires: Biblos.
Marks, Dorrit K., ed. 1993. *Women and Grass Roots Democracy in the Americas.* Miami: North-South Center Press.
———. 1996. *Women and Grass Roots Democracy in the Americas: Sustaining the Initiative.* Miami: North-South Center Press.
Marshall, Thomas H. 1950. *Citizenship and Social Class, and Other Essays.* Cambridge, U.K.: Cambridge University Press.
Martin, John B. 1957. *The Deep South Says "Never."* New York: Ballantine Books.
Massey, Douglas S., and Nancy A. Denton. 1993. *American Apartheid: Segregation and the Making of the Underclass.* Cambridge, Mass.: Harvard University Press.
McAdam, Doug, Sidney Tarrow, and Charles Tilly. 2001. *Dynamics of Contention.* Cambridge, U.K.: Cambridge University Press.
McCarthy, John D., and Mayer N. Zald. 1977. "Resource Mobilization and Social Movements: A Partial Theory." *American Journal of Sociology* 82, no. 6 (May): 1212–41.
McElligott, Anthony. 1993. "The Collapse of Weimar." *History Today* 43, no. 5 (May): 18–24.
McIntosh, Marjorie K. 2001. "The Diversity of Social Capital in English Communities, 1300–1640 (with a Glance at Modern Nigeria)." In Robert I. Rotberg, ed., *Patterns of Social Capital: Stability and Change in Historical Perspective.* Cambridge, U.K.: Cambridge University Press.
McMillen, Neil R. 1994. *The Citizens' Council: Organized Resistance to the Second Reconstruction 1954–64.* Rev. ed. Urbana: University of Illinois Press.
McSherry, Patrice. 1997. "Strategic Alliance: Menem and the Military-Security Forces in Argentina." *Latin American Perspectives* 24, no. 6 (November): 63–92.
Mendelson, Sarah E., and John K. Glenn, eds. 2002. *The Power and Limits of NGOs: A Critical Look at Building Democracy in Eastern Europe and Eurasia.* New York: Columbia University Press.
Méndez, Juan E., Guillermo O'Donnell, and Paulo Sérgio Pinheiro, eds. 1999.

*The (Un)Rule of Law and the Underprivileged in Latin America.* Notre Dame, Ind.: University of Notre Dame Press.

Messi, Virginia. 2000. "Luque tiene una página de Internet, y Tula trabaja y volvió con su ex mujer." *Clarín.com*, September 11. Available at http://old.clarin.com.ar/diario/2000/09/11/s-04601.htm.

Migdal, Joel S. 1994. "The State in Society: An Approach to Struggles for Domination." In Migdal, Kohli, and Shue 1994.

Migdal, Joel S., Atul Kohli, and Vivienne Shue, eds. 1994. *State Power and Social Forces: Domination and Transformation in the Third World.* Cambridge, U.K.: Cambridge University Press.

Minujin, Alberto, ed. 1992. *Cuesta abajo: los nuevos pobres, efectos de la crisis en la sociedad argentina.* Buenos Aires: UNICEF/Losada.

———. 1993. *Desigualdad y exclusión: desafíos para la política social en la Argentina de fin de siglo.* Buenos Aires: UNICEF/Losada.

Mitchell, Michael J., and Charles H. Wood. 1999. "Ironies of Citizenship: Skin Color, Police Brutality, and the Challenge to Democracy in Brazil." *Social Forces* 77, no. 3 (March): 1001–20.

Mitchell, Timothy. 1991. "The Limits of the State: Beyond Statist Approaches and Their Critics." *American Political Science Review* 85, no. 1 (March): 77–96.

Molinelli, N. Guillermo, M. Valeria Palanza, and Gisela Sin. 1999. *Congreso, presidencia y justicia en Argentina.* Buenos Aires: Temas.

Mommsen, Hans. 1991. *From Weimar to Auschwitz.* Princeton, N.J.: Princeton University Press.

Mondragón, Héctor. 2000. "La Oxy invade a los U'wa." Working paper, Oak Institute for the Study of International Human Rights, Colby College.

Morgan, Edmund S. 1975. *American Slavery, American Freedom: The Ordeal of Colonial Virginia.* New York: Norton.

Muller, Edward N., and Mitchell A. Seligson. 1994. "Civic Culture and Democracy: The Question of Causal Relations." *American Political Science Review* 88, no. 3 (September): 635–52.

Murphy, Andrew R. 2001. "In a League of Its Own." Review of *Bowling Alone*, by Robert Putnam. *Review of Politics* 63, no. 2 (Spring): 408–11.

Muse, Benjamin. 1964. *Ten Years of Prelude: The Story of Integration since the Supreme Court's 1954 Decision.* New York: Viking.

Ndegwa, Stephen N. 1996. *The Two Faces of Civil Society: NGOs and Politics in Africa.* West Hartford, Conn.: Kumarian Press.

Negretto, Gabriel, and Mark Ungar. 1996. "Judicial Independence, Rule of Law, and Democratization in Latin America." Working paper, Department of Political Science, Columbia University.

Neilson, James. 1993. "Parque jurásico." *Noticias*, July 18. Quoted in Malamud-Goti 1996.

Nelson, Bruce. 1996. "Class, Race and Democracy in the CIO: The 'New' Labor History Meets the 'Wages of Whiteness.'" *International Review of Social History* 41, no. 3: 351–74.

Newton, Kenneth. 1997. "Social Capital and Democracy." *American Behavioral Scientist* 40, no. 5 (March / April): 575–86.

———. 1999."Social and Political Trust in Established Democracies." In Pippa Norris, ed., *Critical Citizens: Global Support for Democratic Government*. New York: Oxford University Press.

———. 2001. "Trust, Social Capital, Civil Society, and Democracy." *International Political Science Review* 22, no. 2 (April): 201–14.

Nino, Carlos S. 1992. *Un país al margen de la ley*. Buenos Aires: Emecé.

Noakes, Jeremy, and Geoffrey Pridham, eds. 1983. *Nazism, 1919–1945*. Vol. 1, *The Rise to Power, 1919–1934*. Exeter, U.K.: University of Exeter Press.

Nord, Philip. 2000. Introduction to Bermeo and Nord 2000.

Nugent, David. 1999. "State and Shadow in Northern Peru circa 1900: Illegal Political Networks and the Problem of State Boundaries." In Josiah Heyman, ed., *States and Illegal Practices*. Oxford, U.K.: Berg.

O'Donnell, Guillermo. 1973. *Modernization and Bureaucratic-Authoritarianism: Studies in South American Politics*. Berkeley: Institute of International Studies, University of California, Berkeley.

———. 1993. "The Browning of Latin America." *New Perspectives Quarterly* 10, no. 4 (Fall): 50–54.

———. 1996a. "Illusions about Consolidation." *Journal of Democracy* 7, no. 2 (April): 34–51.

———. 1996b. "Illusions and Conceptual Flaws." *Journal of Democracy* 7, no. 4 (October): 160–68.

———. 1998. "Horizontal Accountability in New Democracies." *Journal of Democracy* 9, no. 3 (July): 112–26.

———. 1999a. *Counterpoints: Selected Essays on Authoritarianism and Democratization*. Notre Dame, Ind.: University of Notre Dame Press.

———. 1999b. "Polyarchies and the (Un)Rule of Law in Latin America: A Partial Conclusion." In Méndez, O'Donnell, and Pinheiro 1999.

———. 1999c. "Democratic Theory and Comparative Politics." Working paper, Department of Political Science, University of Notre Dame. Available at http://darkwing.uoregon.edu/ _caguirre/guillermo_o'donnell.htm.

———. 2001. "Hay síntomas de muerte de nuestra democracia." Interview by Nora Veiras. *Página/12 Web*, June 11. Available at http://www.pagina12.com.ar/2001/01-06/01-06-11/pag15.htm.

Offe, Claus. 1996. "Trust and Knowledge, Rules and Decisions: Exploring a Difficult Conceptual Terrain." Paper presented at the "Democracy and Trust" conference, George Washington University. Quoted in Cohen 1999.

Oliveira, Alicia, and Sofía Tiscornia. 1997. "Estructura y prácticas de las policías en la Argentina. Las redes de ilegalidad." Paper presented at the conference "Control democrático de los organismos de seguridad interior en la República Argentina," Centro de Estudios Legales y Sociales (CELS), Buenos Aires.

Oliver, Pamela E., Jorge Cadena-Roa, and Kelley D. Strawn. 2003. "Emerging Trends in the Study of Protest and Social Movements." In Betty A. Dobratz,

Lisa K. Waldner, and Timothy Buzzell, eds., *Theoretical Directions in Political Sociology for the 21st Century*. Boston: JAI.

Ollman, Bertell. 1992. "Going beyond the State?" (Comment). *American Political Science Review* 86, no. 4 (December): 1014–17.

Olson, Mancur. 1982. *The Rise and Decline of Nations*. New Haven, Conn.: Yale University Press.

Olvera Rivera, Alberto. 2002. "Accountability social en México: la experiencia de la Alianza Cívica." In Enrique Peruzzotti and Catalina Smulovitz, eds., *Controlando la política: ciudadanos y medios en las nuevas democracias latinoamericanas*. Buenos Aires: Temas.

Örkény, Antal, and Kim Lane Scheppele. 1999. "Rules of Law: The Complexity of Legality in Hungary." In Martin Krygier and Adam Czarnota, eds., *The Rule of Law after Communism: Problems and Prospects in East-Central Europe*. Aldershot, U.K.: Ashgate.

Osojnik, Andrés. 2000. "Diez años después." *Página/12 Web*, September 3. Available at http://www.pagina12.com.ar/2000/00-09/00-09-03/pag19.htm.

Ospina, Pablo. 1999. "Reflexiones sobre el transformismo: mobilización indígena y régimen político en Ecuador (1990–1998)." Paper presented at the Conference on Democratization and the Role of Indigenous Groups, Facultad Latinoamericana de Ciencias Sociales (FLACSO), Quito, Ecuador.

Oxhorn, Philip. 1999. "The Ambiguous Link: Social Movements and Democracy in Latin America." *Journal of Interamerican Studies and World Affairs* 41, no. 3 (Fall): 129–46.

Palmieri, Gustavo, Leonardo Filippini, and Hernán Thomas. 2001. "La reforma policial en la Provincia de Buenos Aires." Paper presented at the Twenty-Third International Congress of the Latin American Studies Association, Washington, D.C.

Park, David J. 2002. "Media, Democracy, and Human Rights in Argentina." *Journal of Communication Inquiry* 26, no. 3 (July): 237–60.

Pásara, Luis, Nena Delpino, Rocío Valdevellano, and Alonso Zarzar. 1991. *La otra cara de la luna: nuevos actores sociales en el Perú*. Lima: Centro de Estudios de Democracia y Sociedad (CEDYS).

Peel, Mark. 1998. "Trusting Disadvantaged Citizens." In Valerie Braithwaite and Margaret Levi, eds., *Trust and Governance*. New York: Russell Sage Foundation.

Peruzzotti, Enrique. 2002. "Civic Engagement in Argentina: From the Human Rights Movement to the 'Cacerolazos.'" Working paper, Department of Political Science, Universidad Torcuato Di Tella, Buenos Aires.

Pinheiro, Paulo Sérgio. 1996. "Democracies without Citizenship." *NACLA Report on the Americas* 30, no. 2 (September/October): 17–23.

———. 1999. "The Rule of Law and the Underprivileged in Latin America: Introduction." In Méndez, O'Donnell, and Pinheiro 1999.

Poggiese, Héctor, María Elena Redín, and Patricia Alí. 1999. "El papel de las redes de desarrollo local como prácticas asociadas entre el estado y sociedad." In Daniel Filmus, ed., *Los noventa: política, sociedad y cultura en América Latina y Argentina de fin de siglo.* Buenos Aires: Facultad Latinoamericana de Ciencias Sociales (FLACSO).

Portes, Alejandro. 1997. "Globalization from Below: The Rise of Transnational Communities." Working paper, Transnational Communities Programme, Institute of Social and Cultural Anthropology, University of Oxford, U.K. Available at http://www.transcomm.ox.ac.uk/ working%20papers/portes .pdf.

———. 1998. "Social Capital: Its Origins and Applications in Modern Sociology." *Annual Review of Sociology* 24, no. 1: 1–24.

Portes, Alejandro, and Patricia Landolt. 2000. "Social Capital: Promise and Pitfalls of its Role in Development." *Journal of Latin American Studies* 32, no. 2 (May): 529–47.

Pratchett, Lawrence. 1999. "New Fashions in Public Participation: Towards Greater Democracy?" *Parliamentary Affairs* 52, no. 4 (October): 616–33.

Prillaman, William C. 2000. *The Judiciary and Democratic Decay in Latin America: Declining Confidence in the Rule of Law.* Westport, Conn.: Praeger.

Przeworski, Adam, Michael E. Alvarez, José Antonio Cheibub, and Fernando Limongi. 1997. "What Makes Democracy Endure?" In Larry Diamond, Marc F. Plattner, Yun-han Chu, and Hung-mao Tien, eds., *Consolidating the Third Wave Democracies: Themes and Perspectives.* Baltimore: Johns Hopkins University Press.

———. 2000. *Democracy and Development: Political Institutions and Well-Being in the World, 1950–1990.* Cambridge, U.K.: Cambridge University Press.

Putnam, Robert D. 1973. *The Beliefs of Politicians: Ideology, Conflict, and Democracy in Britain and Italy.* New Haven, Conn.: Yale University Press.

———. 1993. *Making Democracy Work: Civic Traditions in Modern Italy.* Princeton, N.J.: Princeton University Press.

———. 1995a. "Bowling Alone: America's Declining Social Capital." *Journal of Democracy* 6, no. 1 (January): 65–78.

———. 1995b. "Tuning In, Tuning Out: The Strange Disappearance of Social Capital in America." *PS: Political Science and Politics* 28, no. 4 (December): 664–83.

———. 2000. *Bowling Alone: The Collapse and Revival of American Community.* New York: Simon and Schuster.

Ragin, Charles C. 2002. "Turning the Tables: How Case-Oriented Research Challenges Variable-Oriented Research." In Henry E. Brady and David Collier, eds., *Rethinking Social Inquiry: Diverse Tools, Shared Standards.* Lanham, Md.: Rowman and Littlefield.

Rao, Vijayendra, and Michael Walton. 2002. "From Equality of Opportunity to Equality of Agency: Grounding a Cultural Lens for Public Policy in an Unequal World." Paper presented at the World Bank Conference on Culture and Public Action, Washington, D.C. Available at http://www.worldbank.org/research/conferences/culture/papers.htm.

Rawls, John. 1971. *A Theory of Justice.* Cambridge, Mass.: Harvard University Press.

Raz, Joseph. 1979. *The Authority of Law: Essays on Law and Morality*. Oxford, U.K.: Clarendon Press.

Reilly, Charles A. 1996. "Social Emergency and Investment Funds (SEFs and SIFs) and NGOs: Who Gets What, When, How?" Paper presented at the conference "La difícil reforma pendiente: rearticulación de las relaciones entre Estado y sociedad civil," Buenos Aires.

Restivo, Néstor. 2002. "La larga caída de la clase media." *Clarín.com*, January 28. Available at http://old.clarin.com/diario/2002/01/28/e-01201.htm.

Richard, Patricia Bayer, and John A. Booth. 2000. "Civil Society and Democratic Transition." In Thomas W. Walker and Ariel C. Armony, eds., *Repression, Resistance, and Democratic Transition in Central America*. Wilmington, Del.: Scholarly Resources.

Roberts, Kenneth M. 1997. "Beyond Romanticism: Social Movements and the Study of Political Change in Latin America." *Latin America Research Review* 32, no. 2 (Spring): 137–51.

Robinson, William I. 1996. *Promoting Polyarchy: Globalization, U.S. Intervention, and Hegemony*. Cambridge, U.K.: Cambridge University Press.

Rockman, Bert A. 1997. "Institutions, Democratic Stability, and Performance." In Metin Heper, Ali Kazancigil, and Bert A. Rockman, eds., *Institutions and Democratic Statecraft*. Boulder, Colo.: Westview.

Rogowski, Ronald. 1995. "The Role of Theory and Anomaly in Social-Scientific Inference." *American Political Science Review* 89, no. 2 (June): 467–70.

Rojas, Patricia. 2000. "La única manera de descansar es morirnos." *Página/12 Web*, July 20. Available at http://www.pagina12.com.ar/2000/suple/no/00-07/00-07-20/nota1.htm.

Romero, Luis Alberto. 1994. *Breve historia contemporánea de Argentina*. Mexico City: Fondo de Cultura Económica.

Rosenberg, Morris. 1956. "Misanthropy and Political Ideology." *American Sociological Review* 21, no. 6 (December): 690–95.

Rosenblum, Nancy L. 1998. *Membership and Morals: The Personal Uses of Pluralism in America*. Princeton, N.J.: Princeton University Press.

Rossetti, Carlo. 1994. "Constitutionalism and Clientelism in Italy." In Luis Roniger and Ayse Günes-Ayata, eds., *Democracy, Clientelism, and Civil Society*. Boulder, Colo.: Lynne Rienner.

Rothchild, Donald, and Letitia Lawson. 1994. "The Interactions between State and Civil Society in Africa: From Deadlock to New Routines." In John W. Harbeson, Donald Rothchild, and Naomi Chazan, eds., *Civil Society and the State in Africa*. Boulder, Colo.: Lynne Rienner.

Rothstein, Bo. 1998a. *Just Institutions Matter: The Moral and Political Logic of the Universal Welfare State*. Cambridge, U.K.: Cambridge University Press.

———. 1998b. "Social Capital in the Social Democratic State: The Swedish Model and Civil Society." Paper presented at the Ninety-Fourth Annual Meeting of the American Political Science Association, Boston.

Rutherford, Bruce K. 1993. "Can an Islamic Group Aid Democratization?" In John W. Chapman and Ian Shapiro, eds., *Democratic Community: NOMOS XXXV*. New York: New York University Press.

Ryan, Mary P. 2001. "Civil Society as Democratic Practice: North American Cities during the Nineteenth Century." In Robert I. Rotberg, ed., *Patterns of Social Capital: Stability and Change in Historical Perspective.* Cambridge, U.K.: Cambridge University Press.

Sabetti, Filippo. 1996. "Path Dependency and Civic Culture: Some Lessons from Italy about Interpreting Social Experiments." *Politics and Society* 24, no. 1 (March): 19–44.

Saidon, Gabriela. 2002. "Los colores del encierro." *Clarín.com,* December 16. Available at http://old.clarin.com/diario/2002/12/16/c-00602.htm.

Salamon, Lester M., and Helmut K. Anheier. 1996. *The Emerging Nonprofit Sector: An Overview.* Manchester, U.K.: Manchester University Press.

——, eds. 1997. *Defining the Nonprofit Sector: A Cross-National Analysis.* Manchester, U.K.: Manchester University Press.

Sassen, Saskia. 1999. "Whose City Is It? Globalization and the Formation of New Claims." In James Holston, ed., *Cities and Citizenship.* Durham, N.C.: Duke University Press.

Schamis, Hector E. 2002. *Re-Forming the State: The Politics of Privatization in Latin America and Europe.* Ann Arbor: University of Michigan Press.

Schedler, Andreas. 1999. "Conceptualizing Accountability." In Andreas Schedler, Larry Diamond, and Marc F. Plattner, eds., *The Self-Restraining State: Power and Accountability in New Democracies.* Boulder, Colo.: Lynne Rienner.

Scheuerman, William E. 1994. *Between the Norm and the Exception: The Frankfurt School and the Rule of Law.* Cambridge, Mass.: MIT Press.

Schlozman, Kay Lehman, Sidney Verba, and Henry E. Brady. 1999. "Civic Participation and the Equality Problem." In Skocpol and Fiorina 1999a.

Schmitter, Philippe C. 1992. "The Consolidation of Democracy and Representation of Social Groups." *American Behavioral Scientist* 35, nos. 4/5 (March/June): 422–49.

——. 1994. "Dangers and Dilemmas of Democracy." *Journal of Democracy* 5, no. 2 (April): 57–74.

Schumpeter, Joseph A. 1942. *Capitalism, Socialism, and Democracy.* New York: Harper.

Seligson, Amber L. 2001. "When Democracies Elect Dictators: Electoral Support for Former Authoritarians in Argentina." Paper presented at the Ninety-Seventh Annual Meeting of the American Political Science Association, San Francisco.

Selee, Andrew. 2003. "Decentralization and Democratic Governance in Latin America." Working paper, Latin American Program, Woodrow Wilson International Center for Scholars, Washington, D.C.

Selle, Per. 1999. "The Transformation of the Voluntary Sector in Norway: A Decline in Social Capital?" In Jan W. van Deth, Marco Maraffi, Kenneth Newton, and Paul F. Whiteley, eds., *Social Capital and European Democracy.* New York: Routledge.

Sen, Amartya K. 1985. *Commodities and Capabilities.* Amsterdam: Elsevier. Quoted in Rao and Walton 2002.

Shapiro, Ian. 1996. *Democracy's Place*. Ithaca, N.Y.: Cornell University Press.

Sharlach, Lisa. 2002. "State Rape: Sexual Violence as Genocide." In Kenton Worcester, Sally Avery Bermanzohn, and Mark Ungar, eds., *Violence and Politics: Globalization's Paradox*. New York: Routledge.

Shklar, Judith N. 1989. "The Liberalism of Fear." In Nancy L. Rosenblum, ed., *Liberalism and the Moral Life*. Cambridge, Mass.: Harvard University Press.

Sidicaro, Ricardo. 1982. "Poder y crisis de la gran burguesía agraria argentina." In Alain Rouquié, ed., *Argentina, Hoy*. Buenos Aires: Siglo Veintiuno.

Skocpol, Theda, and Morris P. Fiorina, eds. 1999a. *Civic Engagement in American Democracy*. Washington, D.C.: Brookings Institution Press.

———. 1999b. "Making Sense of the Civic Engagement Debate." In Skocpol and Fiorina 1999a.

Smith, Robert C. 1965. *They Closed Their Schools: Prince Edward County, Virginia, 1951–1964*. Chapel Hill: University of North Carolina Press.

Smulovitz, Catalina. 2001. "Policiamiento comunitario en Argentina, Brasil y Chile: lecciones de una experiencia incipiente." Paper presented to the Working Group on Citizen Security, Latin American Program, Woodrow Wilson International Center for Scholars, Washington, D.C.

Smulovitz, Catalina, and Enrique Peruzzotti. 2000. "Societal Accountability in Latin America." *Journal of Democracy* 11, no. 4 (October): 147–58.

Somers, Margaret R. 1993. "Citizenship and the Place of the Public Sphere: Law, Community, and Political Culture in the Transition to Democracy." *American Sociological Review* 58, no. 5 (October): 587–620.

Sparrow, Bartholomew H. 1992. "Going beyond the State?" (Comment). *American Political Science Review* 86, no. 4 (December): 1010–14.

Stavenhagen, Rodolfo. 1996. "Indigenous Rights: Some Conceptual Problems." In Elizabeth Jelin and Eric Hershberg, eds., *Constructing Democracy: Human Rights, Citizenship, and Society in Latin America*. Boulder, Colo.: Westview.

Stein, Judith. 1998a. *Running Steel, Running America: Race, Economic Policy, and the Decline of Liberalism*. Chapel Hill: University of North Carolina Press.

———. 1998b. "Opening and Closing Doors" (Symposium on Thomas Sugrue's *The Origins of the Urban Crisis*). *Labor History* 39, no. 1 (February): 52–57.

Stepan, Alfred. 1985. "State Power and the Strength of Civil Society in the Southern Cone of Latin America." In Peter B. Evans, Dietrich Rueschemeyer, and Theda Skocpol, eds., *Bringing the State Back In*. Cambridge, U.K.: Cambridge University Press.

———. 1988. *Rethinking Military Politics: Brazil and the Southern Cone*. Princeton, N.J.: Princeton University Press.

———. 1989. Introduction to *Democratizing Brazil: Problems of Transition and Consolidation*. Edited by Alfred Stepan. New York: Oxford University Press.

Stillwaggon, Eileen. 1998. *Stunted Lives, Stagnant Economies: Poverty, Disease, and Underdevelopment*. New Brunswick, N.J.: Rutgers University Press.

Stolle, Dietlind, and Thomas R. Rochon. 1998. "Are all Associations Alike? Member Diversity, Associational Type, and the Creation of Social Capital." *American Behavioral Scientist* 42, no. 1 (September): 47–65.

Sugrue, Thomas. 1995. "Crabgrass-Roots Politics: Race, Rights, and the Reaction against Liberalism in the Urban North, 1940–1964." *Journal of American History* 82, no. 2 (September): 551–78.

———. 1996. *The Origins of the Urban Crisis: Race and Inequality in Postwar Detroit*. Princeton, N.J.: Princeton University Press.

———. 1998. "Responsibility to the Past, Engagement with the Present" (Symposium on Thomas Sugrue's *The Origins of the Urban Crisis*). *Labor History* 39, no. 1 (February): 60–69.

Svampa, Maristella. 2001. *Los que ganaron: la vida en los countries y barrios privados*. Buenos Aires: Biblos.

Szulik, Dalia, and Enrique Valiente. 1999. "El rechazo a los trabajadores inmigrantes de países vecinos en la Ciudad de Buenos Aires: aproximaciones para su interpretación." In Margulis et al. 1999.

Tarrow, Sidney. 1994. *Power in Movement: Social Movements, Collective Action and Politics*. Cambridge, U.K.: Cambridge University Press.

———. 1996. "Making Social Science Work across Space and Time: A Critical Reflection on Robert Putnam's *Making Democracy Work*." *American Political Science Review* 90, no. 2 (June): 389–97.

Taylor, Steven J. L. 1998. *Desegregation in Boston and Buffalo: The Influence of Local Leaders*. Albany: State University of New York Press.

Tedesco, Laura. 2000. "La ñata contra el vidrio: Urban Violence and Democratic Governability in Argentina." *Bulletin of Latin American Research* 19, no. 4 (October): 527–45.

Thompson, Andrés. 1992. "Democracy and Development: The Role of Nongovernmental Organizations in Argentina, Chile, and Uruguay." In Kathleen D. McCarthy, Russy D. Sumariwalla, and Virginia A. Hodgkinson, eds., *The Nonprofit Sector in the Global Community*. San Francisco: Jossey-Bass.

———. 1994. "'Think tanks' en la Argentina: conocimiento, instrucciones y política," Centro de Estudios de Estado y Sociedad (CEDES), Buenos Aires.

———. 1995a. "El 'tercer sector' en la historia argentina," CEDES, Buenos Aires.

———. 1995b. "¿Qué es el 'tercer sector' en la Argentina? Dimensión, alcance y valor agregado de las organizaciones sin fines de lucro," CEDES, Buenos Aires.

———. 1996. "Night and Day: Cooperation and Conflict between the Third Sector and the State in Argentina." Paper presented at the Second International Conference of the International Society for Third Sector Research, Mexico City.

———, ed. 1995. *Público y privado: las organizaciones sin fines de lucro en la Argentina*. Buenos Aires: UNICEF / Losada.

Tokman, Víctor E., and Guillermo O'Donnell, eds. 1998. *Poverty and Inequality in Latin America: Issues and New Challenges*. Notre Dame, Ind.: University of Notre Dame Press.

Tyler, Tom R. 1998. "Trust and Democratic Governance." In Valerie Braithwaite and Margaret Levi, eds., *Trust and Governance*. New York: Russell Sage Foundation.

Ungar, Mark. 1996. "Prison Mayhem: Venezuela's Explosive Penitentiary Crisis." *NACLA Report on the Americas* 30, no. 2 (September–October): 37–42.

———. 2002. *Elusive Reform: Democracy and the Rule of Law in Latin America.* Boulder, Colo.: Lynne Rienner.

Ungar, Mark, Sally Avery Bermanzohn, and Kenton Worcester. 2002. Introduction to *Violence and Politics: Globalization's Paradox.* Edited by Kenton Worcester, Sally Avery Bermanzohn, and Mark Ungar. New York: Routledge.

United Nations Development Program (UNDP) and Inter-American Development Bank (IDB). 1998. *El capital social: hacia la construcción del índice de desarrollo sociedad civil de Argentina.* Buenos Aires: Edilab.

United States Agency for International Development (USAID). 1992. *Democratic Initiatives and Governance Projects.* Washington, D.C.: USAID. Quoted in Uvin 1998.

Urresti, Marcelo. 1999. "Otredad: las gamas de un contraste." In Margulis et al. 1999.

Uslaner, Eric M. 1997. "Faith, Hope, and Charity: Social Capital, Trust, and Collective Action." Working paper, Department of Government and Politics, University of Maryland, College Park.

———. 1998. "Social Capital, Television, and the 'Mean World': Trust, Optimism, and Civic Participation." *Political Psychology* 19, no. 3 (September): 441–67.

———. 1999. "Democracy and Social Capital." In Warren 1999.

———. 2000–2001. "Producing and Consuming Trust." *Political Science Quarterly* 115, no. 4 (Winter): 569–90.

Uvin, Peter. 1998. *Aiding Violence: The Development Enterprise in Rwanda.* West Hartford, Conn.: Kumarian Press.

———. 1999. "Development Aid and Structural Violence: The Case of Rwanda." *Development* (Society for International Development) 42, no. 3: 49–56.

Vacs, Aldo. 1998. "Between Restructuring and Impasse: Liberal Democracy, Exclusionary Policy Making, and Neoliberal Programs in Argentina and Uruguay." In Kurt von Mettenheim and James M. Malloy, eds., *Deepening Democracy in Latin America.* Pittsburgh: University of Pittsburgh Press.

Varas, Augusto. 1998. "Democratization in Latin America: A Citizen Responsibility." In Felipe Agüero and Jeffrey Stark, eds., *Fault Lines of Democracy in Post-Transition Latin America.* Miami: North-South Center Press.

Verba, Sidney, Kay Lehman Schlozman, and Henry E. Brady. 1995. *Voice and Equality: Civic Voluntarism in American Politics.* Cambridge, Mass.: Harvard University Press.

Verbitsky, Horacio. 1993. *Hacer la corte.* Buenos Aires: Planeta.

Videla, Eduardo. 2001. "La Policía Federal ya consiguió la ley que le da mayores poderes." *Página/12 Web,* June 14. Available at http://www.pagina12.com.ar/2001/01-06/01-06-14/htm.

Vilas, Carlos M. 1996. "Prospects for Democratization in a Post-Revolutionary Setting: Central America." *Journal of Latin American Studies* 28, no. 2 (May): 461–504.

———. 1997. "Participation, Inequality, and the Whereabouts of Democracy." In Douglas A. Chalmers, Carlos M. Vilas, Katherine Hite, Scott B. Martin, Kerianne Piester, and Monique Segarra, eds., *The New Politics of Inequality in Latin America: Rethinking Participation and Representation.* New York: Oxford University Press.

von Mettenheim, Kurt, and James Malloy. 1998a. Introduction to *Deepening Democracy in Latin America.* Edited by Kurt von Mettenheim and James Malloy. Pittsburgh: University of Pittsburgh Press.

———. 1998b. Conclusion to *Deepening Democracy in Latin America.* Edited by Kurt von Mettenheim and James Malloy. Pittsburgh: University of Pittsburgh Press.

Waisbord, Silvio. 2000. *Watchdog Journalism in South America: News, Accountability, and Democracy.* New York: Columbia University Press.

Waldmann, Peter. 1996. *Justicia en la calle: ensayos sobre la policía en América Latina.* Medellín: Konrad Adenauer.

Walker, Jack L. 1966. "A Critique of the Elitist Theory of Democracy." *American Political Science Review* 60, no. 2 (June): 285–95.

Walzer, Michael. 1992. "The Civil Society Argument." In Chantal Mouffe, ed., *Dimensions of Radical Democracy: Pluralism, Citizenship, Community.* London: Verso.

Warren, Mark E. 2001. *Democracy and Association.* Princeton, N.J.: Princeton University Press.

———, ed. 1999. *Democracy and Trust.* Cambridge, U.K.: Cambridge University Press.

Webster, C. J. 2001. "Gated Cities of Tomorrow." *Town Planning Review* 72, no. 2 (April): 149–69.

Weisbrot, Robert. 1990. *Freedom Bound: A History of America's Civil Rights Movement.* New York: Norton.

Wellman, David T. 1993. *Portraits of White Racism.* 2d ed. Cambridge, U.K.: Cambridge University Press. Quoted in Nelson 1996.

Welzel, Christian, and Ronald Inglehart. 1999. "Analyzing Democratic Change and Stability: A Human Development Theory of Democracy." Paper presented at the Fifty-Seventh Annual Meeting of the Midwest Political Science Association, Chicago.

Wilkinson, Harvey, III. 1979. *From Brown to Bakke: The Supreme Court and School Integration, 1954–1978.* New York: Oxford University Press. Quoted in Weisbrot 1990.

Williams, Bernard. 1988. "Formal Structures and Social Reality." In Diego Gambetta, ed., *Trust: Making and Breaking Cooperative Relations.* Oxford, U.K.: Basil Blackwell.

Wilson, David. 1999. "Exploring the Limits of Public Participation in Local Government." *Parliamentary Affairs* 52, no. 2 (April): 246–59.

Wilson, John. 2001. "Dr. Putnam's Social Lubricant" (Symposium on Robert Putnam's *Bowling Alone*). *Contemporary Sociology* 30, no. 3 (June): 225–27.

World Bank. 1987. *Rwanda: The Role of the Communes in Socio-Economic Develop-*

*ment*. Washington, D.C.: South Central and Indian Ocean Department. Quoted in Uvin 1998.

———. 1997. *World Development Report 1997*. Washington, D.C.: World Bank.

———. 2000a. *Entering the 21st Century: World Development Report 1999/2000*. New York: Oxford University Press.

———. 2000b. *Poor People in a Rich Country: A Poverty Report for Argentina*. Vol. 1. Washington, D.C.: World Bank.

World Values Study Group. Various years. *World Values Survey* [Computer File]. ICPSR version. Ann Arbor: Institute for Social Research (producer). Ann Arbor: Inter-University Consortium for Political and Social Research (distributor).

Wuthnow, Robert. 1991a. "The Voluntary Sector: Legacy of the Past, Hope for the Future?" In Robert Wuthnow, ed., *Between States and Markets: The Voluntary Sector in Comparative Perspective*. Princeton, N.J.: Princeton University Press.

———. 1991b. "Tocqueville's Question Reconsidered: Voluntarism and Public Discourse in Advanced Industrial Societies." In Robert Wuthnow, ed., *Between States and Markets: The Voluntary Sector in Comparative Perspective*. Princeton, N.J.: Princeton University Press.

———. 2000. "A Lonely Day in the Neighborhood." Review of *Bowling Alone*, by Robert Putnam. *Christianity Today* 44, no. 7 (July): 91–92.

Yamagishi, Toshio, and Midori Yamagishi. 1994. "Trust and Commitment in the United States and Japan." *Motivation and Emotion* 18, no. 2: 129–66.

Yashar, Deborah J. 1998. "Contesting Citizenship." *Comparative Politics* 31, no. 1 (October): 23–42.

———. 1999. "Democracy, Indigenous Movements, and the Postliberal Challenge in Latin America." *World Politics* 52, no. 1 (October): 76–104.

Young, Iris Marion. 1999. "State, Civil Society, and Social Justice." In Ian Shapiro and Casiano Hacker-Cordón, eds., *Democracy's Value*. Cambridge, U.K.: Cambridge University Press.

Young, Malcolm B., and Mitchell A. Seligson. 1997. *Guatemalan Values and the Prospects for Democratic Development: Third Report*. Arlington, Va.: Development Associates.

Zofka, Zdenek. 1986. "Between Baurenbund and National Socialism: The Political Reorientation of the Peasants in the Final Phase of the Weimar Republic." In Thomas Childers, ed., *The Formation of the Nazi Constituency, 1919–1933*. Totowa, N.J.: Barnes and Noble Books.

# Index

accountability, 43–44, 114, 215; Argentina, 114–18, 130–35, 152, 154–55, 162–74, 215; horizontal, 44, 114, 116*table*, 169, 251n5; police, 48, 118, 162–74; realization of, 133–34; voluntary associations calling for, 32, 130–35, 152

African Americans, 49, 238n62; antidesegregationists and, 61–63, 76–98, 100, 103, 234–38; citizenship rights, 61–63, 76–98, 100, 103, 235n35, 238n62; employment, 209, 232n5, 237n50; housing, 61–62, 63, 85–98, 100, 101; integrationist boycotts, 81, 236n40; murdered, 226n3; poor, 63; relational setting, 221; school integration data, 77; trust, 192; voting rights, 82, 235n35. *See also* racial discrimination, U.S.

age: Argentine groups, 151; and police abuse, 122, 248n34; social cleavages of, 52, 67, 72–74

agency, inequalities of, 217

Allen, William, 65–66, 232–33n12

Almond, Gabriel, 29, 187, 228n18

American Housing Survey, Census Bureau (2001), 94

American Legion, 78, 80, 200

Anheier, Helmut, 30, 228n21

Anti-Corruption Office (OAC), Argentina, 115

antidesegregationists, U.S. *See* racial discrimination, U.S.

antipoliticism: Argentina, 175; Weimar Germany, 67–70, 99, 210–11, 233n14. *See also* antisystem discourse

anti-Semitism: Argentina, 132, 242–43n33, 246n18; U.S. South, 79; Weimar Germany, 60, 74–76

antisystem discourse, 3, 207; antidesegregationist, 90, 236n43; Argentina, 152–53, 157; Weimar Germany, 36, 60, 69, 70, 72, 178, 210. *See also* antipoliticism; rejection patterns

Argentina, 2, 3, 17, 104–76; accountability, 114–18, 130–35, 152, 154–55, 162–74, 215; authoritarianism, 105, 106, 107–9, 113, 143, 152; citizenship rights, 121–22, 127, 136, 172–74, 212, 221–22, 239n2; economic crises, 107, 239n1; economic "miracle," 111, 161; horizontal links within civil society, 53, 107, 139, 141–42, 147–52, 156–58, 158*table*, 174; military, 106, 107–9, 120, 127, 132, 135, 158–59; new democracy / third-wave democracy, 3, 17, 104–40, 159–61, 210; rule of law, 105, 111–26, 133–34, 162–74, 211, 214, 241n17; social movement mobilization, 106, 130–35, 167, 212, 239n1, 250–51n56; socioeconomic equality / inequality, 105, 109–12, 122–23, 145–46, 155, 162, 194, 198, 211, 248n34; trust, 120–25, 141–47, 192, 194, 240n6, 241nn21,22; vertical links between state

busing, for school desegregation, 16, 89, 95–98, 103, 238n58
Byrd, James, 21

Cabezas, José Luis, 131, 132, 133
Caldeira, Teresa, 13
Canada, social trust, 192
Carrasco, Omar, 131, 132
Catamarca, police and judiciary abuses, 131–32, 134–35
Catholics: Argentines vs. gay rights, 161; Boston Irish Americans, 94–98, 102, 103, 238n58; Detroit, 58, 85–86, 101–2
CELS (Center for Legal and Social Studies), 151–53, 158–60, 166, 173–74, 243n35, 248–50
Center for Justice and International Law (CEJIL), 159
Chicago, antidesegregationists, 16, 84, 85, 90–93, 232n4
Childers, Thomas, 70, 233n20
Chile: Argentine human rights groups cooperation, 159; rule of law, 254n28
citizen interaction: mutual trust / distrust, 124–25, 241nn21,22, 246nn12,13; with other citizens, 123–26; with state institutions, 46, 48, 120–23, 241n17. *See also* citizenship; civil society
Citizens' Councils, 76–84, 100, 102, 200, 234–36
citizen-selves, 141
citizenship, 217; field of, 220, 255n14; learning the practices of, 47–48, 141; relational, 50–51, 220–22, 255n14; white homeownership linked with, 89–90. *See also* citizenship rights
citizenship rights, 3, 17, 255n14; African American, 61–63, 76–98, 100, 103, 235n35, 238n62; antidesegregationists vs., 81, 84; Argentina, 121–22, 127, 136, 172–74, 212, 221–22, 239n2; authoritarian relations vs., 199; defined, 39; expansion of, 12, 36–37, 55, 76–77, 103; future research, 220; laws positively and negatively affecting, 45, 132, 135; minorities / underprivileged / marginalized, 43, 47–55, 136, 144, 211; political / civil / social, 55, 121–22, 173–74, 229–30n28, 231n46; rule of law protecting,

41–42; skewed distribution of, 14, 39; state institutions ignoring, 43, 46–49, 82–84, 152; state institutions protecting, 3, 38–40, 46; voting, 76, 82
"civic community," Putnam's, 6
"civic culture," 5, 176, 183
CIVICUS, 127
civic virtue, 5, 6, 23, 61, 141, 226–27n7
Civil Rights Act (1957), 82
civil rights groups: antisystem discourse, 3; Argentina, 127, 136–76, 158*table*, 243–44; Argentine groups against, 242n32; violence, 3, 152–53, 214, 247n19. *See also* African Americans; citizenship rights
civil society, 3, 19–55; analytical perspectives on, 14, 24*table*; approaches to, 10–11, 20–37, 219–23; boom, 5–9; bright side, 80, 204–6; civic virtue, 5, 6, 23, 61, 141, 226–27n7; concept, 9–12; defined broadly, 11, 168; defined restrictively, 9–11, 12; democracy's relation to, 5–7, 13–14, 19–57, 130–223, 238n62; dispositions among participants, 142–47; functions, 19, 23, 32–33, 34, 36, 226n2; indicators of, 19, 23, 180–86, 227n9; institutional effect of, 184–87; Kenya, 204; and market, 11, 229n24; operationalizing, 19, 31–32; participatory budgeting, 204–6; political society's relation to, 11, 34, 37–55, 41*table*, 99, 131–34, 218, 229n27; Rwanda, 201–3; slice of, 136–39, 150; vs. society as a whole, 225n5. *See also* Argentina; context, civil society; formal groups; horizontal links, within civil society; informal networks; mechanisms, civil society; public sphere; racial discrimination, U.S.; undemocratic orientations / dark side; vertical links, civil society-state; voluntary organizations; Weimar Germany
Civitans, 80, 102
class cleavages, 52, 88, 148, 252n11; antidesegregationists and, 63, 89, 101; gated communities and, 93–94; trust and, 179; Weimar Germany, 67, 70–72. *See also* middle class; poor; social stratification; upper class; working class cleavages. *See* social cleavages
Clemens, Elisabeth, 26, 75–76

winners, 103; housing discrimination, 88, 94, 95, 103; trust, 28, 179, 192–94, 197–98 women's movement. *See* feminists working class: antidesegregationists, 61–63, 79, 85–87, 96–98, 100, 200; Argentina, 108, 124, 212, 239n1, 248n34; U.S. black, 92; Weimar Germany, 59–60, 61, 69, 71, 72, 233–34nn20,21. *See also* employment

World Bank, 181, 201–2
World Values Surveys, 128–30, 146, 246n12
World War II, 92

Yomagate, 133

zoning, antidesegregationist, 62, 86, 91, 93, 95, 101